Thomas Dunckerley, his life, labours, and letters, including some masonic and naval memorials of the 18th century

Henry Sadler

Your Affectionate Brother
Thos Dunckerley

THOMAS DUNCKERLEY,

HIS LIFE, LABOURS, AND LETTERS,

INCLUDING SOME

Masonic and Naval Memorials

OF THE 18TH CENTURY,

BY

HENRY SADLER, P.M. & P.Z.,

GRAND TYLER AND SUB-LIBRARIAN OF THE GRAND LODGE OF ENGLAND.

Author of "Masonic Facts and Fictions," &c.

"A wit's a feather, and a chief a rod;
An honest man's the noblest work of God."—POPE.

London:

DIPROSE & BATEMAN, SHEFFIELD STREET, W.C.

SPENCER & Co.,   GEORGE KENNING,
15, GREAT QUEEN STREET, W.C.   16 & 16A, GREAT QUEEN STREET, W.C.

1891.

LONDON
DIPROSE, BATEMAN AND CO., PRINTERS,
LINCOLN'S INN, W.C.

To

The Right Worshipful

Provincial and District Grand Masters,

being

Free and Accepted Masons,

"Wherever dispersed over the Globe,"

These Memorials of a Brother

Whose indefatigable zeal in the cause of Masonry

and earnest devotion

To the Grand Principles of the Order

rendered him pre-eminent among his Fellows,

Are respectfully and fraternally

Dedicated.

London, 1891

PREFACE.

WHETHER it is an idle story or not that Dunckerley at the age of ten years selected the motto, "*Honestas et Fortitudo*" is of little matter. It cannot, however, be denied that his life was ruled by the principles it teaches, and it would be a pity if such man should be forgotten.

That his services to Freemasonry were great is certain, as also that they were fully appreciated by the Masons of his own time. To him Masonry was not a pastime or amusement for idle hours. When, in his letters, he invites to his Lodge any *serious* brother, he evidently expresses his own view of the craft. It is a serious subject, and one with which he might well join his motto "*Honestas et Fortitudo.*" The life of a brother, who devoted his time, thoughts, intellect, and substance to the craft, and literally died in harness, can never be without interest to the thinking Mason. In my opinion, therefore, it was a good thought of Brother Sadler when he had the opportunity of gathering together such a series of Masonic memorials, to place them in our hands in a collected and convenient form.

In reply to the possible, and it is to be feared in many cases probable question, with which he commences his book, Brother Sadler, has with considerable labour arranged in order a large amount of information bearing on the connexion of Dunckerley with Freemasonry. It is true that most of the incidents of his private life have appeared in print before, but other facts and explanations are introduced, now rendering the story more complete. The romantic history of his birth and career are full of interest and will well bear telling again. Whatever may be the opinion as to the truth or falsity of the story of his parentage, it is clear that he himself believed it, and from the fact that he received many advantages, as well as a substantial pension, it seems certain that it was also believed by others, who had the power to help him

His success in early life, marked as it was by his occupying a position which even at that time was only open to men of ability, shows clearly that he rose by his extraordinary perseverance and faithful performance of his duties. This same honesty of purpose, and strength of will was continued in his Masonic career, as may be easily seen from his letters, which now appear in print for the first time.

In following his Masonic career and the history of the many lodges with which his name is connected, Bro. Sadler has been able to collect much that is both new and valuable. I may particularly mention the very early minutes of the Lodge of Friendship held at the Castle, Highgate, which it is to be hoped will ere long be printed in full. Many other notes of interest might be pointed out did space allow, but these must be left to each reader to discover for himself.

I may, however, say a few words with reference to the

heraldic illustrations and seals. The Book-plate, is of considerable interest, and I must not omit to express my thanks to Dr. Jackson Howard who very kindly allowed me the use of the fine example preserved in his splendid collection. It is I believe, as rare as it is curious, possibly because Dunckerley was not a great collector of books. One somewhat defaced copy was shown to me by Bro. Sadler in a copy of Smith's Freemason's Pocket Companion, 1738, in the library of the Grand Lodge, and it is interesting to note that it also contains the impression of a plate, without a name, but bearing a quartered coat (1st and 4th Gules a cross patonce Or, on a chief Azure, three round buckles of the second) which is that borne by the family of Heseltine. I take it to be the plate used by the Grand Secretary of that name, and the book may perhaps have been a present from one to the other.

The plate used by Dunckerley is well engraved upon copper, in what collectors describe as the Chippendale style, and bears upon the lowest centre ornament the name of the engraver, LEVI SCUL, PORTSM. In Lord de Tabley's work entitled "The Study of Bookplates" (p 173), it is entered under the year 1750, a date which judging from the style of ornament, could, I imagine, not be disputed.

Within a shield and border of the period is contained the Royal Arms as borne by George II. when King, the reputed father of Dunckerley, marked with the baton sinister, or badge of illegitimacy. This is surmounted by the royal crest, and below is the motto, "*Falo non merito*," applying very aptly, when thus placed   Below this again are his names, with the addition of the words "Fitz George," *said* to have been also used by Dunckerley in his familiar correspondence.

The date 1750, although it undoubtedly suits the style of the ornaments presents a little difficulty when we glance over the events of Dunckerley's life. He did not become aware of his real parentage until after the death of his mother, which occurred ten years later than the date of the plate, in January, 1760. According to his own statement after he had heard the confession he continued his duties in the Navy and travelled abroad until 1765. In that year he removed his family from Plymouth to Somerset House, and in May, 1767, the first portion of his pension was granted ; in that year also he was first appointed Prov. G.M. It is only natural to suppose that having little or no need for a book plate, Dunckerley would not have ventured to take these arms and the addition of Fitz George before his claim had been allowed, or at least before he left the Naval Service (1764), and settled down permanently. The only explanation I can offer is, that his book plate though engraved probably between 1760 and 1769—or perhaps even later, represents in an imitated form the style of an earlier period, copied, it may be, from some plate which he himself admired.

His armorial seal, given on page 233, is engraved with the same arms, crest, motto, and abatement. It is well executed, and judging from the very floral style of the ornaments, was most probably engraved at a later date than the book-plate. Many examples of it are extant, as it appears to have been the one he most constantly used.   The earliest letter upon which it is found in the collection of the Grand Lodge, is dated 19th January, 1783.   Letters of 1773 and 1776 have a plain seal, bearing simply the initials T. D., of floriated design.

The seal, or paper stamp (p. 133), containing within a circle, various masonic emblems, was ordinarily stamped in printing ink upon his letter paper.   It is printed from a wood block, and was, I imagine, in part, a copy of one of those silver or brass jewels or seals commonly used in the earlier times of Masonry.

Two other seals will be found on pages 261 and 272 They are here inserted, and it is very probable that they were designed by, and executed for, Dunckerley.   The first is that of the Chevalier Kadosh, then worked in Templar Encampments now the thirtieth degree of the Rit Ecossais.   Among a maze of numerals and letters, the latter apparently referring to the pass-words, &c., are three crowns, a ladder and a sword, which are the badges of the degree. At the foot are the numerals 1118, which, I suppose, are intended to refer to the year in which the Order of the Temple was founded, and adopted by the modern Order in the calculation of their A.O., or *Anno Ordinis*.   Thus, on p. 267 the year A.O. 673 would be 1118 added to 673, or A.D. 1791.   As also A.C. or *Anno Caedis*, the year of slaughter or murder, 477, refers to the death of Jaques de Molai, the last Grand Master of the Templars.   It is the difference between the year of his being burned at Paris A.D. 1314 and the year A.D. 1791.   On the dexter side of the

Kadosh Seal the date is given in full, 11 M., *i.e.*, the 11th of March, 1314.

The other seal is that of the Masonic Knights Templar, of which Dunckerley was the first Grand Master in England. It bears several different forms of crosses, masonic emblems, and the date A.L. 5795, or the year A.D. 1791 (see letter, p 266) and is obtained by adding 4004 to that year The Roman Numerals LXXXI. is probably a sacred number, the square of nine.

W. HARRY RYLANDS.

FATO NON MERITO

Thoˢ Dunckerley
Fitz George

Subscribers' Names.

Abbott, G Blizard, No 1385.

Amherst. The Right Hon Earl. Prov. G M Kent.

Amherst, W. A. T. M.P Past J.G. Warden, Eng.

Anderson, Eustace P M Nos 49 & 715.

Anderson. John Eustace, P M. Nos 18 & 255

Archer, Augustus B. W.M. No 1163.

Ashcroft, Lancelot P P.G J.D. Somerset, &c

Atkins, Henry J P P S.G W Norths & Hunts.

Atkinson, J B. P P.J G D. Hants & I W

Atwater, Frank V.. Capitol Lodge, No. 3 Nebraska.

Bailey, B Sykes, J.D. No. 2069.

Bain. George W.. P P G. Reg. Durham. &c.

Baker, Brackstone. Past G. Deacon. Eng

Baker, George J W M No 108

Baker, William, I G No. 2205

Barfield, Asher Past G Treasurer, Eng

Barker, Rev Alfred Gresley P.P G. Chaplain Hants & I W

Barnard G.W G., Prov. G. Sec Norfolk. &c

Barron E. J. P.G D Eng . P M No 2.

Baskett S R . P P G Reg. Dorset.

Bassano, Clement. G. A . P M No 66

Baume, Arthur, P M No 63

Beach William. W.B M P . Prov G Master, Hants & I W.

Beaumont, W. C , P A G D C Eng

Begemann, Dr. W.. Prov. G Master, Mecklenburg

Bell, Seymour P.M & D C No 1626. &c.

Berry, John J , P.M & Treasurer No. 554.

Bethune Alexander M , P M & Sec. No 1397.

Betts. Arthur. P.M No 1351.

Bignell R . No 459 Alipore (2 copies).

Binckes Frederick Past G Swd Bearer, Eng.

Bindley, Col John A , Dep Prov G. Master, Staffordshire

Bishop, Henry, P.M. No 66.

BISHOP, GEORGE, P.M. No 231.

BLANCHARD, M H., I.G. No 309.

BLATCHFORD, PETER, No 704

BLAXLAND, C WILFRED, W.M No 709, Sec No. 125

BODENHAM, JOHN, P A G D.C. Eng.

BOLTON, GEORGE, P.M. Nos. 147, 169, 1155, &c.

BOULTON, JAMES, P.M Nos 28, 1056, 2291, &c

BRACEWELL, WILLIAM, P.G. Steward, East Lancashire, &c

BROADBENT, EDWIN, P M No. 2109

BROOKS, W. E

BROWN, R S, G S E Scotland.

BROWN, WILLIAM P., P.M. No. 90.

BRUTY, W. F., S.D. No. 45.

BULLEN, THOMAS G, P G Std. Bearer, Eng.

BULLING, CHARLES E., No. 1287.

BUSS, H. G, Past A G Sec Eng.

BYWATER, WITHAM M., Past Grand Swd. Bearer, Eng

CAMPBELL, W A., No. 257.

CANNING, C H., W.M. No. 2184, P.M. No. 1472, &c.

CARTER, JAMES G, W.M and P.M. No. 1044.

CARSON, E T, P M Kilwinning Lodge No 356, Cincinnati, U.S.A

CARSON, JOSEPH L, P M St John's Lodge No 891 (I.C.)

CARTERET, Col E C. MALET DE, P.G. Master, Jersey.

CASE, ROBERT, Prov G Sec Dorset

CASSAL, CHARLES E, W M No. 1415 & S W. 1974

CASTELLO, JAMES, P.M. No. 227.

CHADWICK, JOHN, Past G Swd Bearer, Eng Prov G. Sec E Lanc (2 copies)

CHAPMAN, GEORGE B P M Nos 27, 299, &c

CHAPMAN JAMES, P M. No. 191

CLARK, CHARLES L., No. 228

CLARIDGE, J R FITZJAMES, Sec No. 6 Past G Steward

CLERKE, Col SHADWELL H., Grand Secretary, Eng

CLOWES, RICHARD, P P S G W Essex and Sussex

COCHRANE, SAMUEL, P M. No 3, W M. No 2315.

COBHAM, G R., P M No 20 P M No. 1343

COHU, THOMAS, P M No 192

COLLINS, J T, Past G Swd. Bearer, Eng Dep. P G M. Warwickshire

COOK, GEORGE, W.M No 820

COOMBE Masonic Library.

COOPER, EDWARD, P M. No. 73.

COOPER, GEORGE, Past G. Deacon, Eng

CORBY, CHARLES, P M., No. 957.

CORP, JAMES, Steward No. 2148

CORP, JAMES B., J.D. 2309.

COUCH, RICHARD PEARCE, No 121

COUPLAND, C , P P J G.W. Kent P M No 913, &c

COWPER, FRED S , W M. No 2039

COX, CHARLES F., No. 2045.

CREMORNE, LORD, Past S.G.W. Eng.

CRISWICK, G S., P.M No. 1593.

CUBITT, THOMAS, Past G Pursuivant, Eng.

CUMBERLAND, JOHN S , P.P.J G.W N & E Yorks, &c

CUNNINGHAM, J H., G Sec , South Australia

DAIRY, CHARLES. P.M. No 141

DALE, J G., P.M. No. 169.

DANDRIDGE, A C., J W No 871

DANIELS, L E , No 124, Illinois

DARCH, AUGUSTUS, P M and Sec. No. 72.

DARELL, Sir LIONEL E , Bart., Past G Deacon, Eng.

DAVENPORT, GEORGE, King Philip Lodge, Massachusetts

DAVIDSON, J , No 13

DAVIS, Col JOHN, Past D G D.C. Eng

DEEVES, Capt. D.. P D.G.D C. Natal, &c

DE FERRIERES, BARON, Past S.G Deacon, Eng

DEHANE, H. E., P.M. No. 1543. P P S.G.D. Essex   Rep Essex
      Charity Committee

DENING, EDWIN, P P S.G D. Gloucestershire, &c

DEVONSHIRE, ROBERT L., No 4.

DIAMOND, HUGH E., P.P.J.G.W. Derbyshire P M No. 353, W M
      No 1704

DICKESON, WALTER, P M. and Treasurer No 179

DICKEY, HENRY, P M and Secretary No 1744.

DIERPERINK, H W., M D. P P G W. Netherlands, S Africa
      P.M. No. 334 (E.C.), No 86 (S C), &c

DIPROSE, JOHN, P M & Treasurer No 957

DIPROSE, HENRY LANDON, P.M. No. 1853.

DISTRICT GRAND SUPREME CONCLAVE (S M), Eastern Archipelago

DODD, WILLIAM, P P.G D. Middlesex. P.M No 1194

DOVE, EDMUND H W.M No 45

Down, F. J., S.D. No 706.

Drury, C. D. Hill, M.D., P.P.G. Reg. Norfolk. P.M No. 85.

Drysdale, J. W., No 263

Dungarvan, The Rt Hon Viscount, Prov G Master, Somerset

Eastes, James S., Past G Deacon Eng & D.P.G M Kent.

Else, Richard C, P.G. Deacon Eng, Dep. P G M Somerset

Elworthy, Frederick T, P P.G S W Somerset P M No 261 & 1966.

Escott, Albert, P M No 1593, &c

Everett, George, Grand Treasurer, (elect) Eng.

Farnfield, John A., Past A.G.D. Ceremonies, Eng

Farquhar, Alfred, P M No 1629

Felix Gottlieb Conclave (S M.) No 3. Penang.

Fenn, Ambrose, No. 700.

Fenn, Thomas, P G.D. Pres B G. Purposes, Eng (3 copies)

Fenn, W. E, No 4, W.M. No. 1556. P.M. No. 538.

Ferris, Rev. T. B B, P M. No. 2017

Ferry, C. E., P.M. Nos. 65 & 1743.

Few, W Resbury, No. 4.

Filliter, George C., W.M. No. 386

Finnemore, Robert Isaac, J.P., F.R H S., &c &c, District Grand Master, Natal.

Fitzgerald, J. P., P.M. Nos. 1364 and 2168.

Fletcher, W. H., P.M No. 190.

Fox, Walter C., S.D. No. 1260, Sec. No. 2263.

Francis, Charles K., P.M. No. 265. Penna., U S A

Franois, Thomas, P M, P P G D Sussex

Freeman, Vincent P., P.G. Deacon, Eng Prov G Sec. Sussex.

Freeman, Captain Williams, Hon S G W Nat. G. Lodge, Egypt, P.M. No 1068

French, John W., P M. No. 100. P.P G. Reg Norfolk, &c

Friendship, Lodge of, No 6

Fulford, F. H., Nos. 68 and 610.

Gabd, John, P.P J G.W. Bristol, &c.

Gardiner, Thos H., P M. No 657

Garrod, Henry, P M No. 749 Past G Pursuivant, Eng

Gilbert, John, Prov G. Tyler Middlesex

Gilbert, W G P, P M. No. 257

Glover, R.G., Past D G D Ceremonies, Eng.

GOBLE, EDGAR, Past G. Sword Bearer, Eng.

GOLDNEY, F. H., Past G. Deacon, Eng.

GOODACRE, WILLIAM, Past G. Sword Bearer, Eng.

GOTTLIEB, FELIX H , J P Past G Sword Bearer, Eng.
    Past Dep. Dist G. Master, Eastern Archipelago.   (2 copies.)

GOTTLIEB, GEORGE, P.M No. 1555. (2 copies)

GOUGH, COL. FOSTER, Prov G Master, Staffordshire

GRAHAM, JOHN H., Past G. Master, Quebec.

GRAND LODGE LIBRARY (England).

GRAND LODGE, Mark M.M. Library (England).

GRAND LODGE LIBRARY (Massachusetts, U.S A)

GRAND LODGE OF SOUTH AUSTRALIA   (2 copies)

GRANT, CHRISTOPHER, No. 3.

GREAT PRIORY OF ENGLAND AND WALES.

GREEN, ABRAHAM, P P.S.G.W Worcestershire, &c

GREEN, HENRY W., P.M and Sec No 108.

GREEN, J. E., P M., P D G.W. S. Africa, E D.

GREEN, JOHN, P M. No. 27.

GREEN, NEVILLE, P M No. 1962.

GREGORY, WALTER J , P M No. 73

GRETTON, J. H , S.D , No 108.

GREY ROBERT, Past G. Deacon, Prest. B. of Benevolence Eng.

GRIEVE, J. B., P.M., No. 1351.

HADDON, JAMES S., P.M. No. 1966.

HAIGH, JOHN, P M Phœnician Lo. G Reg. Mass U,S.A.

HANHART, NICHOLAS, J.W No 222.

HARDING Col. CHARLES. Past A.G D C. Eng

HARDING, JAMES W , W M No 1585

HARLECH, RIGHT HON LORD, Prov G.M N. Wales.

HARRIS, Sir GEORGE D , Senior G. Deacon, Eng.

HARRIS, WALTER S., J.W. No. 1260. (3 copies)

HARRISON, GEORGE, No 1326.

HARRISON, WILLIAM, P.M No. 265

HAWKINS, JOSEPH, P,M & P Z No. 216

HEDGES, F R W , Past G Swd Bearer, Eng , Sec R M I G.

HICKLIN, WILLIAM, P.M. & W M No 1261

HIGERTY, ALEX. C. A , P.M & Sec. No. 1044 P.P G.O Surrey &c.

HOBBS, HUGH M , P M., P. Prov. J.G.D. Surrey.

HOBSON, E BUSSEY, P M No 700, &c.

HODGES, OLIVER T., Nos 4 & 259

HOELEN, C. L , Treasurer No 2148. (4 copies)

HOGARD, C F , Past G. Std Bearer, Eng.

HOIT, J H , P.M. No 856   P P G S.B. Cornwall

HOLLOWAY, EDWIN B , P.M. & Treasurer No. 108

HOPE PRECEPTORY, No. 4 (K.T.)

HOPEKIRK, WALTER, Past G. Pursuivant, Eng

HORNIMAN, F J., No. 108.

HOVENDEN, R , S.D. No 21

HOWELL, ALEX. No 257   Sec Quatuor Coronati Correspondence
    Circle for Hampshire

HUDSON, ROBERT, Past G Swd. Bearer, Eng   Prov G. Sec
    Durham.

HUGHAN, W. J., Past G Deacon Eng   P P S G.W. Cornwall, &c

HUGHES, J A , P M No 4

HUGHES, ROBERT, Dep. D.G.M. Japan

HUNT, CHARLES, P.M. No 194

HUNT, JOHN E , P M No 1768

HUNTER, WILLIAM S , I G. No. 772 (S C)

HUSEY, E J. V , Past G. Steward, P M. No. 2

HUTCHINSON, THOMAS, No 1900

IMLAY, DAVID G., S W. No 2148.

IRONS, G. B , P.M. & P Z. No. 903

JAQUET, E W , J W No 2323.

JEFFERIS, A. H , P P G D C E Lanc   P.M. Nos 64 & 645

JENNINGS, JAMES, P M No 228.

JOHNSON, W E , Steward, No 1766.

JOHNSTON, REGINALD E , W M No 6

JOHNSTON, W. H , W.M. No 1820   P M No. 1965

JOLLY, CHARLES, P.M & Sec. Nos. 1472 & 2184.

JONES, CHARLES No 1420.

JORDAN, PAUL, Dist. S.G. Warden Hong Kong & S China

JOSEPH, D. DAVIS, No. 237.

JUPE, JOHN, S.W. No. 2,

KELL, C F., late No. 2148

KELLY, WILLIAM, F S A , P P G M. Leicester & Rutland

KEMPSTER, W. H., M D., P M. Nos. 60, 890 & 1420

KENCH, JAMES, P G. Pursuivant Eng.

KENNABY, G. L., P.M. No. 1420, S W. No. 263

KENNEDY, G., P P.G S B Kent. P.M. No. 1536, &c.

KENNING, GEORGE, Past P.G.D. Middlesex. P.M. No. 192 & 1657.

KENNING, GEORGE II.. No. 60. J.W. No 1460

KENTISH, W. G., P.M. Nos. 1293 and 1768.

KER, GEORGE, P P J.G.D Kent. P.M. Nos. 503 & 2046.

KERR, ELLIS, (late of No 241, New York)

KIRBY, W. H., S.W. No. 1965.

KLEIN, SYDNEY T., F.L.S., F.R A.S., &c Nos 404 & 2076.

KUPFERSCHMIDT, C., P.M. No. 238. Steward No. 2076

LAKE, WILLIAM, P.P G. Reg. Cornwall.

LAMB, H. T , No. 1385. (3 copies)

LAMBERT, F S.A., Major GEORGE, Past G.S. Bearer, Eng. W.M.
    No. 198. (3 copies.)

LAMBERT, RICHARD, 32°, P.M. No 59 P G H.P Louisiana, U S A.

LAMB-SMITH, THOS., P.P J G.W. Worcestershire.

LAMONBY, W. F., Past S.G.W. Victoria. P.P.G. Reg. Cumb. &
    Westmoreland.

LANCASTER, G. F., P.P.G. Reg., Assist. G Sec Hants and I.W.

LANE, CHARLES S , P P J G.D. Durham (2 copies)

LANE, JOHN, F C A., P.P.G. Reg Devon. P.M. No 1402, &c

LARDNER, HENRY J , P.P.G A D. Ceremonies, Surrey.

LARKIN, JOHN, P M No 3 J W No. 1657.

LAWRENCE, General SAMUEL C., Past G M. G.L. Massachusetts.

LAWSON, CHARLES H., P.M. No. 913.

LECHMERE, SIR EDMUND A. H., Bart., Prov. G M Worcestershire

LEE, W. H , P P.G.D. & A.G. Sec Middlesex.

LE FEUVRE, J. E., Past G Deacon D P G.M Hants and I W.

LEGG, E., P.M. No. 861. Treasurer No. 1768.

LEMON, D.D , Rev. THOS. W., P.P G.W. Devon, &c.

LETCHWORTH, EDWARD, Past G Deacon, Eng.

LEWIS, HENRY F. W., Sec. No 1296. S D. No 2250

LINCOLN, JOHN F., Magnolia Lodge, No. 20, Ohio.

LININGER, GEORGE W., Past G. Master, Nebraska

LODGE LA TOLERANCE, No. 538.

LODGE OF UNANIMITY & SINCERITY, No. 261.

LONG, PETER DE LANDE, Past G. Deacon, Eng

LUCKING, ALBERT, Past G Purst. Eng Prov G D C. Essex.

LUMLEY, HENRY, P.G. Steward, P M. No. 4

LUNNISS, FRED., No. 1426

*

MACAULAY, FRED. J., P.M. No. 142.

MACBEAN, EDWARD, Gd. Stand. Bearer (R A) Scotland. J D. No. 2076, &c.

MAGEE, Henry, P M , No. 174.

MALLETT, E., P.M. No. 141.

MALTA, DIST GRAND LODGE OF,

MANTEL, L., No. 1897.

MARKHAM, R.N., Capt. A H , (A.D.C.) W.M. No 257.

MARSH, J J., P M. No. 1326 P.P.G. Std. Br. Middlesex.

MARTIN, TEMPLE C., S.D. No. 1768.

MARTYN, Rev C J., Past G Chaplain (4 copies)

MASON, C. LETCH, P.P.G. Treas. W. Yorks, &c

MASON, FREDERICK, No. 2148.

MASON, JOHN, P.P S.G.D Middlesex. (2 copies.)

MASSEY, HENRY, P.M. No 619, &c.

MASTERS, WILLIAM, P.M Nos. 428, 2128, &c.

MATTHEWS, J. H , Past Dep. G D Ceremonies, Eng (2 copies)

McLEOD, J. MORRISON, Prov. S.G.W. Derbyshire. Sec. R. M. I. Boys, &c.

McQUEEN, J. H , P.P.S.G.D. Hants & I. W. P.M. Nos. 11 & 1869.

MEREDITH, T. H., P M., No. 87, Sec. No. 1853, &c

MERCER, DAVID D., Grand Pursuivant, Eng

MEYLER, THOMAS, P P.G. Reg. Somerset. P.M. No 261, &c.

MICKLEY, GEO. M.A., M B , P P S G.W. Herts

MIDDLEMIST, R P., P M & Sec. No. 5. Past G Steward.

MIDDLETON, JAMES, M D , Prov G. Master, Roxburgh & Selkirk

MILLER, FRANCIS H , P.M No. 1593.

MILLINGTON, JAMES, I G. No. 1221.

MITCHELL, FRANCIS H., W M. No. 1953.

MITCHELL, G. W , P.G.D C. Kent. P.M. & Treas No. 615.

MOFFREY, R. W., P.M. No. 957.

MONEY, ERNEST M., G. Steward, P.M. No 28, &c.

MONTEUUIS, EUGENE, Past G. Swd Bearer, Eng. (2 copies.)

MORGAN, W. W., P.M. No. 211. (3 copies)

MOBLEY, R. J., No. 1326

MORRIS, EDWIN, S.W No 1789

MORRIS, SPENCER W , J.D. No. 231

MUKERJI, P. C , Dist. G.J.W. Punjab, P.M. No. 1485, &c.

MURROW, Baron, No. 2189

MURSELL, G. A , P.P S G D. Hants and I. W , W.M. No 35.

MURTON, CHARLES A , Past G. Deacon, Eng.

Neeld, J. G., P.M. and Secretary No. 169.

Nell, Henry T., P.M. and Secretary No 45.

Nevill, Richard, No. 108. P.M. No. 1531

Neville, Henry, J.D., No. 1320.

Newton, James, P.P.S.G.D. E Lanc.

Newton, John, F R.A S., P.M No. 174

Nicholson, T. G., Grand Steward, P.M. No 91.

Noakes, Henry W., No. 108, I.G. No 1982.

Norman, George, P.P.G. Reg. Gloucestershire, &c

Norris, Edward S., P.M. No. 32.

North, C. N. McIntyre, W.M. No. 1275.

Norton, Jacob, Boston, U.S.A.

Nutting, W. J., W.M No. 231.

Ohren, Magnus, Past Assist G.D. Ceremonies, Eng.

Painter, John, P.M. Nos. 749 and 1579.

Pakes, John J., P M. and Sec No 871   (2 copies)

Palmer, Edward, P.M. No 913.

Patchill, E. C., P P.G Treasurer, Notts.

Patchitt, Richard, J D. No. 2017,

Paton, John, M C., S.D. No. 2017.

Patrick, Charles, P M. No. 1227.

Parkhouse, S. H., P.M and Treasurer No 1642.

Parkinson, J C., Past G. Deacon, Eng

Payne, C. F. R., No. 4,

Pearce, Gilbert B., P P.J.G.W. Cornwall, P.M No. 450.

Peck, M. C., Past G. Standard Bearer, Eng., Prov G. Sec. N and E. Yorks.

Pendlebury, A. A., Assist G. Sec, Eng.

Penfold, Abel, P P S G D Kent P.M No. 913,

Pigott, R. Turtle, D.C.L., P.A.G.D C. Eng.

Pinckard, G. J., Rep. G L. Eng. near the G L Louisiana.

Pocock, Dr. F. Ernest, P.M. No. 1891.

Potter, R. F., P.M. No. 749, Prov. G. Tyler, Surrey.

Powell, George, P.M. and Sec No 142.

Powell, W. A. F., Prov. G.M. Bristol.

Prior, Frederick W., P M and Sec. No 90

Pritchard, Henry, Prov. G. Treasurer, Middlesex.

Quare, Horace, S W. No. 108

RALLING, T. J , P A.G D.C Eng , Prov. G. Sec. Essex

RAMSAY, Col MARMADUKE, Dist G Master, Malta

RAWLES, JAMES, (late No. 507)

READ, GEORGE, P.M No. 511.

RECKNELL, G S., P.M. and Sec. No. 1728

REED, AUBONE S No 5

REED, Commander G H BAYNES, P.P.G Swd. B. Cornwall.

RICHARDSON, FRANK, Past G. Deacon, Eng. (2 copies.)

RICHEY, Capt W , P.P.G.S.B , Essex P M. Nos. 51 & 700

ROBERTSON, J ROSS, M W G.M Canada

ROBINSON, FRANCIS, S W. No 704.

ROBINSON, Rev THOMAS, M.A , Past G. Chaplain, Eng. (3 copies)

RONALDSON, Rev W , P M , No 844, New Zealand

ROOM, HOWARD H , Prov G. Sec. Middlesex.

ROWLEY, WILLIAM, W.M No. 2148, P.M. No 1924 (2 copies.)

ROYAL SOMERSET HOUSE and INVERNESS LODGE No 4

RUSHTON, F T., Past G. Steward, P M. No 8

RYLANDS, W. H., Past G. Steward, P M No 2 (2 copies)

SANDEMAN HUGH D Past District G M. Bengal, Sec Sup Con. 33°

SAUNDERS, Col. AUBREY, Past District G M Madras

SAUNDERS, GEORGE, jun., P.G J Warden, Somerset, P M No 261.

SAUNDERS, W J. H , P M. No 139 Michigan U S A

SAYLE, ERNEST J., No. 1351.

SCHAFER, AUGUSTUS, No 1351

SCOTT, WILLIAM G , Grand Sec and Librarian, Manitoba.

SCURRAH, W A P.P. G Sup Wks. Middlesex, P M No 1714 &c

SETON, Sir BRUCE M , Bart , Past G Deacon, Eng

SHADWELL CLERKE LODGE, No 2336

SHAW, THOMAS E , P P G D , Warwickshire, P M No 1163

SHERWELL JOHN W , I G , No. 231.

SHERWOOD, N N , P M and Treasurer No 231

SHOWERS, JAMES Treasurer No 261

SHURMUR, WILLIAM Prov. G. Treasurer, Essex, W M 2371

SILLITOE, J H., P.G Std. B Eng , &c

SKINNER, W H , P M No 395.

SMEATON, JOHN, No. 1507.

SMITH, F. MASTERTON, J.W No 162.

SMITH, HENRY, Past G Deacon, Eng , Dep P G M W Yorks

SMITH, H. PERCY, J W. No 1838, &c

SMITH General, I.C Past G. Master Illinois.

SMITH, RICHARD, P.M. No. 137

SMYTH, Rev. THOS C., D.D., Past G Chaplain, Eng.

SMYTH, Major W H., Prov. G. Master, Lincolnshire

SODEN, WALTER, late No. 1287.

SOUTHGATE, S E , W.M. No. 700.

SPAULL, W. H , Past Assist G D C Eng Prov G Sec Salop

SPETH, G W , P M No 183, Secretary No. 2076.

SPILLING, HENRY G , No 2148

SPILLING, WALTER F., I.G. No. 435.

SPINKS, Capt. G., P.P.G Std. B. Kent, P.M. No. 1536.

STEGGLES, R W , No. 1979, I.G. No. 2398.

STERRY, JOHN H , S.W. No 521

STEVENSON, GEORGE D , P.M. No. 2148.

STEVENSON, JAMES H , No. 2148.

STILES, WILLIAM M , P M No 1507, &c.

STIMSON, EDWARD, P.M. No 15.

STORR, EDWIN, P M No. 167.

STOTT, N. STANHOPE, No 4, P M No 1397.

STRADLING, Rev W LYTE, P G C Eng , D P G M S Wales

STRATTON, JAMES, No 913

STRETCH, Junr. S , P.M. No 1950

SUDLOW, R. CLAY, Grand Std. Bearer, Eng P M No 263

SWAN GEORGE F. P M No 1321, &c

TAYLOR, JAMES K., No. 1897

TAYLOR, JOHN, W M No 1402

TAYLOR, ROBERT J , P M. No 144, Sec No. 1922.

TERRY, JAS , Past Gd Swd Bearer, Eng , Sec R M B I (2 copies).

TEW, THOMAS W , Prov G M. W. Yorks, &c

THOMAS, JAMES LEWIS, F S A , P A G D C. Eng , &c

THOMAS, J. G. P.M No 871

THOMAS, HENRY, P.P.J G. Deacon, E. Lanc

THRUPP, RAYMOND H , P A G D C Eng , Dep P G M Middlesex

TIDMARSH, JOHN, W.M No. 2163, S W. No 2157.

TILDESLEY, HARRY A , I G No. 1585.

TODD, JOSEPH P P S G.W N & E Yorks, P.M. Treas. No. 236

TREWINNARD, A. H , P.M No 228 and 1693.

TRITTON, W B , P.M. No 108.

VALLENTINE, SAMUEL, Assist. G Pursuivant, Eng

VASSAR-SMITH R V , D. Prov. G M Gloucestershire, &c.

VENABLES, ROWLAND G. P A G D C Eng , Dep P G M Salop

VERNON, Hon. W. W., P. J. G. W. Eng.

VERY, JAMES, No 754

VINCENT, WILLIAM, P P G S B Middlesex.

WALKER, JOHN, W.M. No. 731

WALKLEY, ARTHUR, P P S.G. Deacon, Somerset

WALLS, Captain T. C., P P.J.G W Middlesex &c

WARD, HORATIO, P P.G. Warden Wilts, P.P G W. Kent, &c

WARNE, THOMAS S., P.P.S.G. Warden, Kent, &c.

WARRINGTON, RICHARD S., Past G. Steward, P M. No. 197.

WATKINS, WILLIAM, P P S G Warden, Monmouth, &c

WATSON, WILLIAM, P.M. No 61, Hon Librarian W Yorks

WATTS, GEORGE N., P.M. No. 194

WEBB, C W. C, W M No 2095, P.M. No 1397

WEBBER, WALTER, P.M. No 700.

WEEDEN, CHARLES, P M No. 813.

WEINEL, F. P., W M, No. 1828.

WELLCOME, HENRY S, J W No 3

WELSFORD, W. OAKLEY, D.C No 1321.

WENDT, ERNEST E., D.C.L, G. Sec., G.C. Eng.

WEST, FRED, F R G S, Past G D Eng, D P G M Surrey

WHARTON, C. L., S W. No. 706

WHILE, JOHN, P.M No. 228.

WHITMARSH, THOMAS W, Past G Pursuivant Eng

WHITTON, JOHN W., No 731

WHYMPER, H. J, C I E, P D D.G M Punjab. 6 copies.

WHITEHEAD, THOS B, G. Swd Bearer, Eng. P P S G W. N and E. Yorks

WILLIAMS, S STACKER, Past G. Master, Ohio.

WILLIAMSON, R, P.P.G.D. W. Yorks, P M. No 521

WILLIAMSON, W B, P P S G W Worcestershire

WILLEY, W. L., Sec Massachusetts Lodge, U S A.

WOOD, CHARLES F., No. 1693.

WOODMAN, Dr W R, Past G. Sword Bearer, Eng

WOODS, Sir ALBERT W, K.C M.G, C B, P G.W & G D C Eng

WOODS, CHARLES A., P.M. No. 145, &c.

WOODWARD, A. C., P.M. and Secretary No. 1538

WOOLFORD, THOMAS, P M No 1467.

WRIGHT, FRANCIS W, P M Nos 1725 and 2046

WYATT, GEORGE. P.P S.G. Warden, I.W (2 copies)

YARKER, JOHN, Past Sen, G. Warden Greece

YORSTON, JOHN C., Philadelphia

CONTENTS.

DIRECTIONS FOR BINDING THE PLATES.

THOMAS DUNCKERLEY.

INTRODUCTORY REMARKS.

"THOMAS DUNCKERLEY! who was *he?*" doubtless some of my readers will exclaim,—and to those who are unacquainted with the history of Freemasonry in England during the latter half of the 18th century, the question would be a very natural one, but to the searchers after truth; those who believe that our Order has a *history* worthy of being recorded and profited by (a daily increasing band) his name and character, are more or less familiar. These will, I doubt not, readily admit that as a Mason he held a conspicuous place in the ranks of his contemporaries, a position so remarkable that neither before his time nor since has any other person filled a similar one. A biography written nearly a hundred years after the death of the subject of it must of necessity be incomplete and wanting in details and incidents which might go far towards awakening the interest and rivetting the attention; I very much regret therefore, that notwithstanding my utmost endeavours to find something in the shape of corroborative evidence, the story told by Dunckerley

B

himself is practically the only information I can furnish as
to his parentage and birth. As, however, it is principally
with the later period of his life that I shall probably be expected to deal, I am not without hope of a fair amount of
success in this direction. In the main, I shall let him
speak for himself, being fully convinced that the series of
original letters, which now for the first time appear in
print, will furnish a far more accurate estimate of his
character, and masonic achievements than any words of
mine, as well as throw considerable light on the early
history and progress of the Order in many of the counties
over which he so ably presided.

The period between the years 1766 and 1796 was a
most eventful one for Freemasonry in England; it was a
period of consolidation and permanent improvement, for it
witnessed the total abandonment of the "happy-go-
lucky" principle which had hitherto marked the proceedings of the executive department of the Grand Lodge ; and
the adoption of measures tending to elevate the Society
and establish it on a much more respectable and solid
basis than at any previous period of its history. It is
not unlikely that a spirit of emulation may have had
some influence in bringing about this change, the
Grand Lodge being then harassed by an active and powerful rival in the shape of an opposition body of Free·
masons, which had been organised in London about the
year 1751, and which had since made rapid progress both
in prosperity and influence. Having already dealt at considerable length with the history of this Society, * I shall
have but little to say about it now, and that little will, I

---

* See "Masonic Facts and Fictions," 1887.

think, be more appropriate at a future stage. It will, doubtless, be sufficient for present purpose if I state that in the earlier portion of the period mentioned the two rival Masonic bodies were briefly distinguished by the names of *Ancients* and *Moderns;* the former being the general appellation of the opposing faction, and the latter that of the adherents of the regular Grand Lodge formed in 1717, of which Dunckerley was a most ardent supporter.

On the 29th January, 1766, a new Grand Treasurer was elected in the person of Rowland Berkeley, who appears to have commenced his duties at the next meeting of the Grand Lodge. The following extract from his Treasurer's book will show at a glance the financial position of the Society at the time of his taking office :—

		£	s.	d.
April 9, 1766.	By Cash Rec^d at Q. Com-munication	83	6	6
,,	30 Gold Mohurs, sold to W. A. Cox @ 85/- per oz. Rec^d from Calcutta, sold 24th May	45	6	8
,,	Cash Rec^d of Bro^r Geo. Clarke, late Grand Trea-surer; being the Bal. of his Acco^t	116	9	11
July 14 ,,	In^t on £1,300 Bank Ann. Consol.	19	10	0
		264	13	1

These figures represent the whole of the funded property of the Grand Lodge, and almost its entire possessions, for with the exception of two books of records, a sword, and possibly a Bible, etc., and a jewel or two, presented by former Grand Masters, it had neither furniture, jewels, nor habitation. Its general meetings were held at one of the celebrated taverns in the neighbourhood of Fleet Street, and the annual "Grand Feast" at one of the halls of the City Companies. There was but one fund and that was "The Fund of Charity" to which the lodges contributed according to their means and inclinations; occasionally nothing whatever was heard of lodges after they were constituted and placed on the official list.

The contributions received by the Grand Lodge from the various subordinate lodges between the 23rd of April and the 29th of October, 1765, only amounted to £104. 4s. 6d., while the corresponding period of 1795 gives a total of £506. 0s. 9d. During this interval there had certainly been a considerable increase in the number of lodges, but not nearly in the same proportion, for at the beginning of 1765, there were about 300 lodges on the list, and in 1795 not more than 540.

"On the 16th February, 1766, an Occasional Lodge was held at the 'Horn Tavern' in New Palace Yard" by Lord Blayney, Grand Master, when "His Royal Highness William Henry, Duke of Glocester, was in the usual manner introduced, and made an entered Apprentice, Passed a Fellow Craft, and raised to the Degree of a Master Mason." This Prince who was the third son of Frederick Prince of Wales, and consequently brother of George III., seems to have been the first to follow in his father's footsteps by entering the English

His Royal Highness Frederick Prince of Wales &c.

fraternity, his elder brother Edward, Duke of York, having been initiated in a lodge at Berlin in 1765.

Frederick, Prince of Wales, the first of the Royal House of Hanover to become a Freemason, was initiated in a Special Lodge at Kew Palace in 1737. It was to him that Dr. Anderson dedicated the Second Edition of the Constitutions, now the rarest and most valuable of any issue of that work. He describes the Prince as " Master of a Lodge," but as His Royal Highness was only initiated a few months before the book was published, it seems probable that in those days there was really a royal road to the Master's Chair. On the 9th February, 1767, H.R.H. Henry Frederick, Duke of Cumberland, entered the Order in a lodge at the "Thatched House Tavern," St. James's Street, presided over by Col. John Salter, Deputy Grand Master. At a Grand Lodge held on the 15th April following, the Duke of Beaufort (Grand Master elect), " Proposed to this Society that as a Testimony of the Sense they entertained of the Honour their ROYAL HIGHNESSES THE DUKES OF YORK, GLOUCESTER and CUMBERLAND had done the Society by becoming Members of it, That the Grand Lodge should present each of their Royal Highnesses with an Apron lined with blue Silk as worn by Grand Officers, and that they should take place in all future Processions as Past GRAND MASTERS, next to the GRAND OFFICERS for the Time being, which Proposal being unanimously agreed to. Ordered, that Brother Jaffray do make three Blue Aprons accordingly, that the Grand Treasurer do pay for them and charge them in his account to the Grand Lodge. And that their Royal Highnesses be humbly requested to accept of the same."

Among the names of the Grand Officers who attended

this meeting is that of "Thomas Dunckerley, P.G.M. for the County of Hampshire." This is the first time his name appears in the Grand Lodge records, but from another source I learn that his Patent of appointment as Provincial Grand Master was dated the 28th February, 1767. On the 27th of April following he attended the Grand Festival at Merchant Taylors' Hall. The only other meeting of Grand Lodge during this year was held on the 30th of October, which was also attended by Dunckerley, and on this occasion his name is followed by the *then* significant addition of "Esqr." This may be accounted for by the fact that an important change had taken place in his circumstances and prospects, King George III. having on the 7th of May, formally acknowledged him as a natural son of his predecessor on the Throne of England. It has been asserted that Dunckerley owed his masonic promotion to his supposed royal descent, but it is plain this could not have been the case in the first instance, his appointment having been made at least two months previous to his being acknowledged. No doubt the accident of birth and the liberality of his royal patron had considerable influence on his subsequent career, by enabling him to travel about the country in the service of the Grand Lodge and Grand Chapter, which he seems to have done year after year until his last illness. In my opinion "real worth and personal merit" had much more to do with his preferment than any other consideration, and as will be seen hereafter, several of his appointments were certainly not of his own seeking.

At a Grand Lodge held on the 28th of October, 1768, Dunckerley being present, the foundation was laid of a

" Fund to build a Hall and purchase Jewels, Furniture, &c., for the Grand Lodge, independent of the General Fund of Charity." A series of 10 regulations were adopted at the instance of the Deputy Grand Master, the Hon. Charles Dillon, in furtherance of the above laudable object The first being as follows :—

" That every Grand Officer shall contribute annually in proportion to the Dignity of his Office not less than the following sums :

	£	s.	d.
Grand Master	20	0	0
Deputy Grand Master	5	5	
Senior Grand Warden	3	3	
Junior Grand Warden	2	2	
Grand Treasurer	3	3	
Grand Secretary	3	3	
Grand Sword Bearer	1	1	

It was also enacted " That every Lodge shall pay the sum of two shillings and sixpence for every Mason they shall hereafter make, when such Brother is registered," and " That a book shall be open in every Lodge for the voluntary contributions of the Members to be applied to the purposes of the Grand Lodge."

At a later period of the evening the Grand Treasurer announced that he had received £51. 9s. towards the new Fund.

These regulations were printed and sent to the Lodges with the following circular letter :—

" Right Worshipful,

" You are requested immediately to forward to me a list of your Members on the 28th of *October* last, and from Time to Time to transmit the Names of such as may join, or be hereafter made in your Lodge, with the Fees specified in the inclosed Regulations, that they may be duly Registered. And the Contributions which voluntarily flow from the Generosity of your worthy Members, please to remit Quarterly to Rowland Berkeley, Esquire, Grand Treasurer, at No. 5, Wood Street, who will give a Receipt for the same.

" I am,

" Yours sincerely,

" THOMAS FRENCH,

" *Grand Secretary.* *

" New Bond Street,

" Nov. 12th, 1768."

Judging from the Grand Lodge register the new regulations seem to have been very well received in the metropolis, and met with a fair amount of favour from the members generally as well as from particular lodges. They were, however, quite ignored by many of the lodges situated at a distance, and this is not surprising, considering that they had never before been asked to pay a fixed sum for registering their members, or even to send a list of their names to the Grand Lodge, an institution which a large majority of them knew only by hearsay, and probably had not the remotest intention of visiting, or even applying to for assistance.

On the 5th May, 1769, James Heseltine was appointed Grand Secretary. This brother appears to have been far superior in mental capacity and educational

---

* Thomas French was a linen-draper in New Bond Street. He was appointed Grand Secretary 28th October, 1768, but only held the office for a few months. Early in the following year he became bankrupt and either retired or was superseded.

attainments to many of his predecessors. He was a Proctor in Doctors' Commons and was evidently a most worthy and highly respected member of the Society as well as an efficient and zealous Grand Secretary, which office he filled till the year 1784. The following year he was appointed S.G. Warden, and in 1786 was elected Grand Treasurer, and was re-elected annually until his decease in 1804.

At a Grand Lodge held on the 19th November, 1773.

" It was resolved unanimously :

" That in order to procure a regular and due observance of the Laws already in force relative to the Fund for building a Hall, &c., each Lodge be required to transmit to the Grand Secretary on or before the next Quarterly Communication, a regular list of their Members, with the dates of their admission or initiation, also their ages as near as possible at that time, together with their Titles, Professions, or Trades, and to continue on or before every succeeding Grand Lodge, to acquaint the Grand Secretary with the names and descriptions of any additional Members, or other alterations in the Lodges as to Members. And that for every person made a Mason five shillings be transmitted, and for each person becoming a Member two shillings and sixpence for registering the names, &c., in the Grand Lodge Books, agreeable to the regulations; and that no person made a Mason subsequent to the 29th October, 1768, at which time the regulations took place, shall be entitled to receive Charity from the Grand Lodge, or to partake of any other privileges of the Society, unless his name, &c., be regularly registered and the Fees paid as above.

" Resolved also : That this regulation shall extend to

the Lodges abroad, and that twelve months be allowed to the Lodges in Europe, America, or the West Indies, to transmit their first accounts, and two years to the Lodges in the East Indies."

Owing, in a great measure to the zeal and energy of Heseltine, to the tact and industry of the afterwards celebrated Masonic historian, William Preston, who assisted him in his Secretarial duties, and to the persistent efforts of Dunckerley in the Provinces, "the fund for building a Hall, &c.," amounted in March, 1774, to £1,422. 15s. 3d. With this sum and a loan of £2,000, the Society was enabled to acquire the freehold of two houses and a large garden, situated in Great Queen Street, Lincoln's Inn Fields, and upon the site of this garden Freemasons' Hall (now known as "The Temple") was erected. It was completed and dedicated to Masonry, Virtue, and Universal Charity and Benevolence, on the 23rd of May, 1776.

The beneficial effects of this new departure extended far beyond the original object of the promoters of the scheme, by bringing about a more regular correspondence between the Grand Lodge and the lodges in distant parts as well as those in the country districts. In the latter direction, Dunckerley's services were invaluable, and it was probably the knowledge of this fact that led to his being placed at the head of so many different provinces. No doubt, the good work done by him was the means of directing attention to the importance of the office of Provincial Grand Master, for at the time of his first appointment (1767) the office was virtually dormant in England, as were also most of those who held it. At the outside there were not more than a dozen, some of whom had not been heard of by the Grand Secretary for several years; this, however, was not of much consequence, as in the early days the appointments were generally made without the slightest regard to either expediency or efficiency, social standing and local influence being the chief considerations. The advent of Dunckerley, and the earnest and methodical enthusiasm which he immediately brought to bear upon his new duties, with the most satisfactory results, doubtless awakened the authorities to the knowledge that it was possible for a Provincial Grand Master to be a real help to the Society, instead of merely an ornamental addition to it. The reception into the Order of seven Royal Princes, with a goodly following of aristocratic recruits, would naturally have a tendency to increase the number of those considered eligible for supreme command in the counties. Hence we find, that whereas in 1770, the official list of Grand Officers only gives the names of eleven Provincial Grand Masters, presiding over as many provinces in England and Wales, the same authority for 1795 shows that twenty-four Provincial Grand Masters then represented thirty-four provinces, Dunckerley having for his share eight out of that number, viz.: "*Dorset, Essex, Glo'ster, Hereford, Somerset,* and *Southampton,* with the City and County of *Bristol* and the *Isle of Wight.*"

This large increase in the number of the provincial magnates was by no means the only sign of improvement, the men themselves, as a general rule, being far superior (masonically speaking) to their predecessors, although very few of them found sufficient leisure for the active and careful supervision of their lodges habitually exercised by Dunckerley, whose admirers may fairly claim for him the title of *father* of the present race of Provincial Grand Masters, if not that of originator of Provincial Grand Lodges.

It is no part of my present plan to repeat, or even revert to, all that has been said by previous writers on the subject of these memoirs, for their knowledge of him is generally derived from the same source, viz.: "The Freemasons' Magazine," published in the latter part of the last century, "The Gentleman's Magazine," 1795, and the records of the Grand Lodge and Grand Chapter of England. As the information therein contained will be duly set forth in the following pages, the reader will have an opportunity of placing his own estimation on its value. William Preston, a contemporary of Dunckerley, with whom he was probably well acquainted, in the "Illustrations of Masonry," 1781, says "By the indefatigable assiduity of that masonic luminary, Thomas Dunckerley, Esq., in whose favour the appointment for Hampshire was first made, Masonry has made considerable progress, not only within his province, but in many other counties in England." That Preston was not singular in his appreciation will be shewn by the following extract from a report of the proceedings of a Provincial Grand Lodge of Kent, held at Maidstone, December 28th, 1795 :—

"The Provincial Grand Master, William Perfect, Esq., was in the chair, and after dinner addressed the company on the history and merits of the Saint whose day the Craft had thus met to commemorate. After which he honoured the memory of that truly Masonic Luminary, the late Mr. Dunckerley, with due commendation, and in a pathetic speech of considerable length, enumerated the virtues of the deceased, which he concluded by observing, that the spirit of Masonry was ever grateful to departed worth, and that a good name was the best legacy that could be bequeathed to posterity."

These testimonials, from two distinguished contemporaries, will doubtless have due weight with the reader, as will also the opinions of two others who were probably more intimate with Dunckerley, one of them having been for many years his deputy in Essex, and the other, his successor in the office of Grand Master of that county; their views of the character and labours of their friend will be duly recorded at a subsequent stage of these memoirs. Many of the statements of posthumous biographers, and other writers, should be received with caution, unless supported by something in the shape of corroborative evidence.

In this category I include the remarks of a masonic historian who says that Dunckerley's "influence in shaping the course" of Royal Arch Masonry has been much over-rated; he was frequently reprimanded by the "Modern" Grand Chapter "for exceeding the bounds of his office." It appears to me, that one who exercised active supervision over eighteen different counties, must have had very considerable "influence in shaping the course" of the Order alluded to. The frequent reprimands will appear and be dealt with hereafter. Another celebrated writer, Dr. Oliver, seems to go to the other extreme. In his "Revelations of a Square," a most interesting book, but one in which *truth* and *fiction* are so cleverly blended as to render it extremely difficult to distinguish one from the other, the worthy and talented author's commendable and enthusiastic admiration of Dunckerley, apparently prompts him to credit that brother with services to which, judging from my own more recently acquired light, he appears somewhat doubtfully entitled.

For instance, he says on page 132 : " Bro. Dunckerley

was the oracle of the Grand Lodge, and the accredited interpreter of its constitutions. His decision like the law of the Medes and Persians, was final on all points, both of doctrine and discipline, and against it there was no appeal."

Now this may be very flattering, and it reads prettily, still I think it requires confirmation before being accepted as literal truth. Dunckerley was essentially a Provincial Mason, and spent most of his time in travelling about the country. The records of Grand Lodge show that although he attended its meetings fairly regularly for the first two years after his appointment as Provincial Grand Master, his subsequent attendances were much less frequent. He does not appear to have taken an active part in debates, and when he addressed the Grand Lodge it was generally on some matter relating to one of his own lodges; moreover, I do not think an "Oracle" would have been tolerated in Grand Lodge in his days. There were several brethren, more experienced masonically and otherwise, equally energetic, as well as of higher social position, who regularly attended the Quarterly Meetings, and took the leading part in the business thereof.

The Grand Lodge minutes contain no evidence in support of the statement on page 133, that "He was authorised by the Grand Lodge to construct a new Code of Lectures, by a careful revision of the existing ritual, etc.," neither is there anything in the Minutes of the Committee of Charity, or the transactions of the Hall Committee to warrant any such conclusion.* The same remark will apply to the

---

* These two bodies were equivalent to the present Board of Benevolence, and the Board of General Purposes.

correspondence between Dunckerley and the Grand Secretaries, extending over the most active period of his masonic career. Another reason for thinking that this story has no real foundation, is that Preston, who refers to Dunckerley in complimentary terms (alluding also to his several appointments) in every edition of his book which contains a history of Masonry, is silent on the subject; had anything of the kind really taken place, he would in all probability have mentioned it. Under these circumstances, I can come to no other conclusion than that this, as well as several of the other stories and incidents in which Dunckerley figures, is the outcome of the Doctor's own imagination, for he could not have personally known Dunckerley as a Mason, and I question whether he ever met with anyone who *had* known him intimately. On page 146 of the book under notice, the author gives a " reminiscence of this eminent Mason," which he says was extracted " from the private MSS." of a brother initiated by Dunckerley. It reads very like an extract from the Lodge Minutes, and will be reproduced in the portion of this book devoted to Masonry in Gloucestershire. With this single exception, I am strongly of opinion that Oliver really *knew* no more of Dunckerley than had appeared in print. It is not at all likely that he was permitted to inspect the written records of either Grand Lodge or Grand Chapter; nor is it probable that he ever had a letter of Dunckerley's in his possession My excuse for adverting to these matters is a desire that my hero should not hereafter appear with any fictitious, or even doubtful honours attached to his name; that he should be known and esteemed for what he was, and what he did in support of the Institution he loved so well. In

furtherance of this object abundant evidence will be adduced independent of tradition, hearsay, or imagination.

I shall now endeavour to answer the question
which appears at the opening of the foregoing remarks,
by first tendering the following brief account of
Dunckerley from the October part of the first volume of
the " Freemasons' Magazine," published in 1793, during
his lifetime, and doubtless with his sanction. The sketch
was written by " Brother White, of Colchester Academy,
Provincial Junior Grand Warden for the County of Essex."
It is the earliest reference to Dunckerley's parentage I
have been able to find in print, and appears to have been
generally accepted, at all events, I am not aware that the
story was ever questioned until after his decease, although
many of the personages therein mentioned, were living at
the time it was made public.

SKETCH OF THE LIFE

OF

THOMAS DUNCKERLEY, ESQ., P.G.M.

——"*of Right and Wrong he taught
Truths as refin'd as ever Athens heard;
And (strange to tell!) he practis'd what he preach'd.*"—ARMSTRONG.

R. DUNCKERLEY is a Past Senior Grand Warden of England, Provincial Grand Master for the city and county of Bristol, the counties of Dorset, Essex, Gloucester, Hereford, Somerset, Southampton, and the Isle of Wight, *under the authority of His Royal Highness the* PRINCE *of* WALES; Grand Superintendant and Past Grand Master of Royal Arch Masons for the city and county of Bristol, the counties of Dorset, Essex, Gloucester, Hereford, Kent, Nottingham, Somerset, Southampton, Surry, Suffolk, Sussex, and Warwick, *under the patronage of His Royal Highness the* DUKE *of* CLARENCE; Most Eminent and Supreme Grand Master of Knights of Rosa Crucis, Templars, Kadosh, &c., of England, *under His Royal Highness* PRINCE EDWARD, *Patron of the Order.*

"The Masonic titles of this gentleman are given to shew the high sense the Grand Lodge of England entertains of his abilities and exertions, the great trust reposed in him by the Heir Apparent and his illustrious brothers, the very great esteem and regard with which he is honoured (we had almost said adored) by several hundred Brethren in the above-mentioned counties, and to point out the amazing progress he has made in moral, social, and

(

scientific Masonry, during forty-six years, by his travels in Europe, Africa, and America, particularly in England, Ireland, France, Spain, Portugal, Italy, Gibraltar, Corsica and Sardinia.

" As a gentleman, Mr. Dunckerley is universally allowed to possess powerful mental abilities, which he has not failed to cultivate by an intimate knowledge of the Belles Lettres, and those arts and sciences that refine and exalt the human mind; and by a most extensive intercourse and acquaintance with the most illustrious and ingenious personages in this and many other kingdoms.

" With a most enlightened mind and an urbanity of manners, that endears him to everyone, he fulfils all the relative duties in a manner truly exemplary. He has naturally a taste for poetry, and exclusive of those pieces which have received the stamp of public approbation, his private friends have infinite cause to be charmed with the effusions of his Muse. Though conversant in science and philosophical researches, he is of too virtuous and vigorous a frame of mind, and too well-grounded in his religious and moral principles ever to suffer philosophy to lead to infidelity; but all the Christian Truths receive his most hearty concurrence, and all the Christian Virtues his constant practice. As a Brother, Mr. Dunckerley stands unrivalled in his indefatigable exertions in the glorious cause of Charity, and in promoting concord and unanimity, brotherly love, morality, and good fellowship, with the strictest order and decorum; witness his many private and public charities, particularly his recent donation at the Provincial Grand Lodge at Chelmsford, for the support of the ' Royal Cumberland Freemasons' School ;' witness also the many excellent Charges he has given in the Provincial Grand Lodges where he has presided, and the uniform proofs his whole life has manifested, that he ' lets his light shine before men '

" The various scenes this gentleman has experienced would require volumes to record ; the limits of our work will only admit of the general outlines of a character chequered with events, which could be sustained only by *honesty* and *courage.* ' Honestas et Fortitudo ' was a motto he took at ten years of age, when a thirst for glory, and a desire to engage in the bustle of the world induced him to leave school abruptly and enter the Royal Navy, where, during twenty-six years constant service, he had the honour and satisfaction to obtain the commendations and friendship of the following gallant commanders under whom he served, viz., Admirals Sir John Norris, Matthews, and Martin, Captains Cornish, Russell, Berkley, Coates, Jekyll, Legge, Marshall, Byron, Swanton, Peyton, and Marlow, but having no parliamentary interest, nor any friend in power, that he then knew of, to assist him, his own modest merit was insufficient to procure him a command.

" In the year 1760, upon Mr. Dunckerley's return from the siege of Quebec, an event happened which could not but fill him with astonishment ; as it placed him in a new and most extraordinary point of view,—A Lady, receiving the Sacrament on her death-bed, made a declaration in all the awful solemnity of the occasion, by which it appeared that Mr. Dunckerley owed his birth to the first Personage in the Kingdom, and Nature was determined that it never should be questioned, for those who recollect the high Personage alluded to, will require no further proof when they see the subject of these Memoirs ; but as this is a matter of much delicacy, our readers must excuse us from entering into further particulars and permit us to draw a veil over this part of the life we propose to record, which were we at liberty to illustrate, would prove a most interesting part of the history.

" Notwithstanding this discovery of Mr. Dunckerley's

descent, he determined not to quit the service of his country until the end of the war, but, unfortunately for him, in the meantime the sudden dissolution of the great Personage we have alluded to, deprived him of a friend, who died without knowing that such a person existed. In 1764 he applied for and obtained superannuation; but it was not until 1767 that his case was laid before a Great Personage, who was graciously pleased to make a provision for him.

"Possessing a strong active mind, with an easy fluent delivery, he was advised in the year, 1770, to become a student in the law, and during five years' close application, acquired such a fund of legal knowledge, that in Michaelmas term, 1774, he was called to the bar by the Honourable Society of the Inner Temple, but being fond of an active life, and still animated by a thirst for glory, when the court of France became hostile to this country in supporting American Independence, and an invasion was threatened, he accepted a commission in the South Hampshire regiment of Militia, where he greatly distinguished himself during three years service. It has been the particular good fortune of Mr. Dunckerley to be honoured with the friendship of the first and best characters of the age, from whom he has letters that would fill an octavo volume, and which reflect the highest honour upon him and them. We were anxious to obtain many of these to enrich our present work, but such is his extreme delicacy and fear of giving offence, that we could only obtain the two here subjoined; one is from a noble Viscount (now a Marquis), and the other from the late General Sir Adolphus Oughton, K.B., which we are happy in being permitted to publish, as they offer a just tribute of praise to the benevolence of our gracious and beloved Sovereign, and manifest an interest and regard for Mr. Dunckerley, worthy of their exalted rank. Gratitude is a prominent

feature in this gentleman's character,—We have felt the
luxury of doing good when we have heard him speak of
the many obligations he is under to the following noblemen and gentlemen, which he relates with a heart over-
flowing with a just sense of their kindness and favours.
In 1766 he was befriended by Lord William Gordon,
Captain Charles Meadows (now Mr. Pierpoint), and
Captain Edward Meadows, of the Royal Navy. In 1767
by the Dukes of Beaufort and Buccleugh, Lord Chesterfield,
Lord Harcourt, Lord Valentia, Sir Edward Walpole, Sir
Edward Hawke, and Mr. Worsley. In 1768 by the Duke
of Grafton, the Marquis of Granby, and Lord Townshend,
and afterwards by Lord Bruce (now Earl of Aylesbury),
Lord North, Mr. Robinson, Mr. Brummell, Mr. Richard
Burke, Mr. Blackburn a merchant in the city, and Mr.
Heseltine, our worthy Grand Treasurer; and though ' last
not least,' by General Hotham and Colonel Hulse, to
whom he expresses himself highly obliged by their kindness and personal attention.

"He married early in life, being now in the sixty-
ninth year of his age, near forty-nine of which have been
spent in wedlock; his lady, who is every way worthy of
such a valuable husband, is some few years older than he
is, and enjoys a good share of health and spirits. Having
last year, in his Masonic character, laid the first stone of a
new church at Southampton, he jocularly observed, ' that
if the structure were completed by the time he had completed fifty years in wedlock, he should think himself justi-
fied in following the practice of some nations he had
travelled in, viz.,of keeping a Jubilee year, and in that case
handsel the new church by being re-married in it.'

" Previous to the appropriation of Somerset House to its
present use, Mr. Dunckerley had apartments therein, since
then he generally resides at his apartments in Hampton
Court Palace, and by the munificence of his Sovereign,

the Prince of Wales, and Duke of York, has the honour and happiness to be in a very comfortable situation, and, to crown all, we shall add in his own words, 'that he has been blessed with the friendship of that Great Being who never faileth those that seek Him.'

"That he may long, very long, continue to enjoy these blessings, and be an ornament to a Society which has received the testimony of approbation from the good and great in all ages, is the free, fervent, and zealous wish of his humble Biographer, and thousands of others, who deem it none of the least of the prerogatives of Free Masonry to call this excellent man by the most friendly of all titles —A Brother."

The following are the two letters mentioned by the writer of the foregoing sketch to which they are appended :—

"Sir,

"The kind communication of His Majesty's benevolence and goodness made me as happy as the frequent reflections I made upon unmerited distress, before this event, gave me sincere concern.

"I cannot divine to what channel you owe that piece of good fortune ; if in any degree to one person ; * to whom I mentioned your affair (whose benevolence of heart and public virtues I know are only obscured by public prejudice). I may have possibly been in a small degree an instrument of conveying to the knowledge of one of the most generous of Princes, one of the opportunities in which I believe his soul is most delighted. By whatever means it came, blessed be the hand which confers it ; may you, sir, and your family long enjoy the comforts of such a provision.

"I am, with great regard, your obliged and faithful servant."

---

* The late Earl of Bute.

" Edinburgh, Nov. 18, 1767.

" Dear Sir,

"I very heartily congratulate you on the happy change you have lately experienced in your fortune. Lord H. and Mr. W. are men whose virtues are of no common stamp, and the bounties of our most amiable and excellent Sovereign cannot flow through channels more worthy of them. It would be a vain attempt, as well as totally unnecessary to you, to express the sense I have of the King's humanity and goodness. Instances of it frequently come to my knowledge which fill my heart with joy and add fervency to my prayers that it may please God to reward him, even in this life, by impressing on the minds of all his subjects a due sense of their obligations to him for so inestimable a blessing, and affectionate duty to so unparalleled a Prince. The attending Lord —— in Ireland, would not (in my opinion) be an advisable scheme, the expense being great and certain, the advantage small and precarious. Lord Granby may get you a commission for your son, and will, I dare say (recommended as you are), do it readily ; they advise you well not to ask a favour of him for yourself. Sir Edward Hawke's proposal is indeed very handsome, and should be gratefully accepted ; his motives for making it do honour to you both ; but as so sudden a rise will infallibly draw envy upon you, it is of importance that you should be extremely circumspect in your behaviour ; a man in adversity is a most respectable character, even a certain degree of pride becomes him, as it makes a greatness of mind superior to ill-fortune, and the world readily gives him credit for virtues which neither hurt their own pride nor clash with their interests ; but when the clouds of adversity are dissipated, and the sun of favour shines upon him, he stands in a conspicuous point of view, and the scene is entirely changed, envy, malice, and all uncharitableness, find matter to exert their malign influence upon him ; the perspective is turned, his faults magnified, his virtues diminished ; hence the justness of that Proverb, ' That it is difficult to carry a full cup even,' or, as our friend Storace [Horace] expresses it, ' *ut tu Fortunam sic nos te celse feremus.*' Humility and complacency are the armour he can put on ; but it requires judgment and address to guard against the appearances of meanness or affectation ; when those amiable qualities are inherent in the disposition and ripened by judgment, as I am persuaded yours are, the task is much more easy ; for the man who acts naturally has always the best chance of pleasing.

" I condole with you on the state of Mrs. Dunckerley's health, nor would I wish you to be such a Stoical Philosopher as not to be fully awake to all the tender feelings ; but as a Christian Philosopher you will consider that the loss of friends is the condition of life, nor can we hold it by any other tenure.—Mrs. Oughton joins me in wishing you all possible happiness, and I am,

" Dear Sir,

" Your most faithful Friend and Brother,

" JAMES ADOLPHUS OUGHTON." *

ANOTHER VERSION OF DUNCKERLEY'S PARENTAGE

The "Gentleman's Magazine" for 1795, page 973, contains a notice of Dunckerley's death, under date 19th November. " At Portsmouth, in his 71st year, Thomas Dunckerley, Esq., Provincial Grand Master of Masonry,

---

* Lieut -Col. James Adolphus Oughton was appointed Provincial Grand Master for the Island of Minorca by Lord Byron, Grand Master of England, in 1749 ; and was Grand Master of Scotland from 1769 to 1771. H. S.

and pretty generally supposed to have been a natural son of George II."

On page 1052 of the next monthly part, under the heading of "Additions to, and Corrections in, former Obituaries," appears the following:—

"The late Mr. Dunckerley was son of a servant maid in the family of Sir Robert Walpole, at Houghton, whence his father married her, and got the place of porter at Somerset House.

"His mother died when he was very young, and his grandmother took care of him till he was put apprentice to a barber. From this place he ran away, and got on board the ship of Sir John Norris, who was then going abroad, Sir Edward Walpole, informed of this circum·stance, wrote to Sir John (we do not know whether he had been knighted at that time), requesting that the boy might have such instruction given him as the ship would afford. He seems to have continued in the sea-service, as the next we have heard of him was his being at the siege of Quebec by Wolfe, where he behaved so well as to have had a recommendation to fill some employment in the Naval Academy at Portsmouth, which he did with credit. About twenty years ago he availed himself of the remark-able likeness he bore to the Royal Family, to get it repre-sented to his Majesty that the late King was in truth his father, and that he owed his existence to a visit which that King, when Prince, had paid to Houghton, and he ventured to refer to Sir Edward Walpole for his knowledge of the circumstances. His Majesty, ever attentive to charitable applications, directed inquiry to be made of Sir Edward Mr. D had apprised this gentleman of what he had done; Sir Edward expressed his astonishment that he should refer to him to support such a tale; then for the first time suggested to him who had known him all his life, and then brought forward when his father, mother, and grandmother were all dead.

" Sir Edward added, that he had at all times been his friend, that he believed him meritorious in the capacity in which he had served, but he could never be made an instrument of imposing this story as true. He, however, got a pension and apartments at Hampton Court, and was afterwards entered at some inn of court, and called to the bar, but not succeeding, soon quitted that profession."

It is somewhat strange that the anonymous writer of this version of Dunckerley's history should have waited until after his death before making it public. At first sight the story seems sufficiently plausible but it contains several statements which are pure fiction, as I shall here· after be able to prove, and certain others which may justly be described as doubtful; so that its value, from an historical point of view, is very slight. In short, it savours too much of the " penny-a-line" character to entitle it to much respect. Appearing in the "Society" periodical of the day it probably answered the purpose of the writer by creating a sensation, which no doubt gave rise to other stories of a kindred nature, although this was the only one, so far as I have been able to ascertain, that appeared in print. This cowardly attempt to blacken the memory of, and brand as an impostor, one who, whether descended from a " Porter at Somerset House," or a Prince at St. James's, had certainly made a host of friends, was doubtless the cause of considerable pain to those with whom he had been intimately associated; it was but natural, therefore that they should have adopted the readiest and most efficacious means of refuting the slander. Hence we find in "The Freemasons' Magazine" for February, 1796, the following circumstantial story, which, it will be observed, differs materially in many respects from the one just quoted.

"Further Particulars of the Late
"THOMAS DUNCKERLEY, ESQ.

"Communicated in his own hand-writing by
his Executors
"Which fully contradict the many idle stories
that have for some time been in circulation
respecting him.

"Jan. 9, 1760, soon after my return from the siege of Quebec, I received an account of my mother's death; and having obtained permission from my captain to be absent from duty, I went to London and attended her funeral.* Among the very few that I invited to this ceremony was Mrs. Pinkney, who had been many years a neighbour to my mother in Somerset-house. On our return from the burial, she desired I would call on her the next day (and not bring my wife with me) having something of consequence to tell me. I waited on her accordingly; and the following is the substance of what she related to me, as I took it in writing :—

"'Mary Dunckerley being dangerously ill with the gout in her stomach (Jan. 2, 1760), and believing it will be her death, is desirous, at the request of her friend, Mrs. Pinkney, that the following account may be made known to her son in the most secret manner, and to none but him.

"'At the latter end of November, 1723, Mr. Dunckerley went to Chatsworth, in Derbyshire, on some business for the Duke of Devonshire, and did not return till the May following. At Christmas I went to see Mrs. Meekin at Lady Ranelagh's. Mr. L——y happened to come there, and paid me the greatest respect; and hinted that I stood in my own light, or I might be the happiest

---

* Mary Dunckerley was interred in the burial-ground of the Chapel Royal, Savoy, Jan. 11, 1760. H. S.

woman in England. I knew his meaning, but made no
reply, and went back to Somerset-house the next day. A
fortnight after, I had an invitation to Lady Ranelagh's, and
her coach was sent for me. I was surprised to find Mr.
L——y there again. He handed me from the coach to the
parlour; where, to my future unhappiness, I found the Prince
of Wales, whom I had *too well known* before my unhappy
marriage. At his request (for I could deny him nothing)
I stayed several days, during which time he made me *five
visits*, and on Candlemas day I went home.

"'Soon after I found myself sick and breeding, and was
resolved to make an end of my life. I was taken very ill.
Lady Stanley came to see me; but I could not let her know
my disorder. Mrs. Meeking came to see me; and I told her
the consequence of what had happened. The next day she
came again, and brought me bank bills for £50 inclosed in a
cover from Mr. Lumley acquainting me that it was by the
Prince's command. She said Lady Ranelagh was coming to
see me; and in less than an hour her ladyship came; they advised me to go in the country, and said a house was taken
for me at Richmond; but I was obstinate, and said I would
not go out of the house until I was brought to-bed. I desired
that they would never let the Prince of Wales or Mr. L——y
know that I was with child; and I never found they did.
Dr. Mead attended me. He ordered me to be bled, and in
two days I could sit up.

"'Mr. Dunckerley came from Chatsworth in May, and
seemed not displeased to find me with child. I disdained to
deceive him; and told him what had happened. He com-
mended my conduct with so much joy, that I could not help
despising his meanness; and his barbarous behaviour to me
in the last month of my time was what I always resented,
when he threw a cat in my face, and swore that he would
mark the bastard. Our separation soon followed after my
delivery; and he kept the secret on his own account; for he

had two places, and considerable advantages, as the price of my folly.

" ' My son might have been known to his royal father, and I might have lived in as elegant a manner as Mrs. H. or Miss B. ; * but my dear mother reclaimed me from so criminal a passion ; and dread of public shame prevented my making it known. '

" This is what Mrs. Pinkney assured me was my mother's declaration on her death-bed ; for she departed this life five days after.   She also told me that my grandmother Boldnest, Mrs. Cannon, a midwife, † and herself, were present at my birth, Oct. 23, 1724; that my mother then declared the Prince of Wales was my father ; and that my grandmother and mother requested it might be kept a secret.

" Mrs. Pinkney also informed me that my mother was a physician's daughter, and lived with Mrs. W. when the Prince of Wales debauched her ; but that Mrs. W. discovered what had happened, and had her married to Mr. Dunckerley, who was then attending the Duke of Devonshire, on a visit to Sir R. W. ‡ at Houghton.

" This information gave me great surprise and much uneasiness ; and as I was obliged to return immediately to my duty on board the Vanguard, I made it known to no person at that time but Captain Swanton.   He said that those who did not know me would look on it to be nothing more than a gossip's story.

" We were then bound a second time to Quebec, and Captain Swanton did promise me that on our return to England he would endeavour to get me introduced to the King, and

---

* Probably Mrs. Howard, afterwards Lady Suffolk, and "the beautiful Mary Bellenden," maids of honour to the Princess of Wales. Here as elsewhere, where notes are added to the original text, I have marked them H S.

† " Mrs. Cannon, midwife to the royal family," died 11th December, 1754. H S.

‡ Sir Robert Walpole. H. S.

that he would give me a character; but, when we came back to England, the King was dead.

"I had flattered myself that my case would be laid before the King, and that I should have the honour and happiness to be presented to my royal master and *father;* and that his majesty, on recollecting the several circumstances, would have granted me an appointment equal to my birth; but, by the demise of my most gracious sovereign, my expectations were frustrated, and all my hopes subsided.

"In January, 1761, I waited on Sir E. W.* and asked his opinion, if I was like the late King? But, as he was pleased to say that he saw no resemblance, I did not, *at that time*, acquaint him with my reason for asking such a question.

"Soon after I was appointed by Lord Anson to be gunner of the Prince (a ship of the second rate); but being *too well* convinced that the late King was my father, I could not suppress a pride that rose superior to my station in the navy; yet I remained in that sphere till the war was ended; and, in 1764, I was superannuated by the interest of Lord Digby.

"At the siege of Louisburg, Admiral Boscawen granted me a warrant as teacher of the mathematics on board the Vanguard, in addition to my being gunner of the same ship; and, though I discharged both duties for three years to the satisfaction of my captain, yet, when I expected to have received my pay, £130, as teacher of the mathematics on board the Vanguard, it could not be obtained, because Lord Anson had not confirmed the warrant which I received from Admiral Boscawen. This unexpected loss, in addition to sickness in my family, and the expence of having my daughter's right leg cut off above the knee (which was occasioned by a fall), brought me in debt £300.

---

* Sir Edward Walpole. H S.

"Mrs. Pinkney being dead, I knew of no person living who could authenticate the story she had told me ; and, as I was unskilled in the ways of court, I saw no probability of gaining access to the royal ear, or his Majesty's belief of what I had been told concerning my birth. * Fearful of being arrested, I left the kingdom in August, 1764 ; and, having ordered the principal part of my superannuation-pension for the support of my wife and family during my absence, I sailed with Captain Ruthven, in the Guadaloupe for the Mediterranean ; and here it was that I had the happiness to be known to Lord William Gordon, who was going to join his regiment at Minorca.

"In June, 1765, I was put on shore at Marseilles, being seized with the scurvy to a violent degree ; but by the blessing of God, and the benefit of that fine climate, I was perfectly restored to health in less than six weeks, when I received a letter from Captain Ruthven, inclosing a recommendation of me to his Excellency Colonel T. at Minorca.

"I took an opportunity of sailing for that island, and waited on Colonel Townsend, who received me with great friendship. I remained there six weeks, during which time I was constantly at his Excellency's table ; but no employment offered that was in his power to dispose of.

"I had (in the confidence of friendship) acquainted several officers in the army and navy with the account I had received from Mrs. Pinkney, and they were all of opinion I should endeavour to get it represented to some of the royal family.

"Some gentlemen of the LODGE at GIBRALTAR, knowing my distress, sent me £20 to Minorca ; and on the same day I received a letter from Mr. Edward M—— at Marseilles, with an order to draw on him for £10. Thus being enabled to undertake a journey through France, I resolved to return

---

* Ann Pinkney was interred in the burial-ground of the Chapel Royal, Savoy, 15th April, 1761. II. S.

to England, and try to get my case laid before the Duke of Cumberland.

"I sailed from Minorca on the first of October, and landed two days after at Toulon, whence I went through Marseilles to Nismes, in Languedoc, to wait on Captain Ruthven and my good friend Mr. M——. Captain R. gave me a letter to Admiral Keppel [then a Lord of the Admiralty], requesting his assistance for my obtaining £130 due to me for having taught the mathematics on board the Vanguard, and after staying three days at Nismes, I set out for Paris.

"When I entered the capital of France, I had only two louis d'ors left, and a small bill which Mr. M. had insisted on my taking.

"Soon after I came to Paris I had the honour of an invitation to breakfast with Lord William G. at l'Hotel Deltragnes. His lordship knowing how much I was distressed, begged (with the greatest politeness) that I would give him leave to present me with £200, assuring me that he should receive as much pleasure in bestowing it as it was possible for me to enjoy in the possession.*

"My surprise at this instant could only be exceeded by my gratitude to this generous young nobleman.

"After staying five days at Paris I went by the route of Lisle to Dunkirk, and thence to Calais, where I arrived on the 5th of November, and was informed (to my great grief and disappointment) that the Duke of Cumberland was dead.

"I embarked the next day for Dover; on the 7th got to London, and had the happiness to discharge £150 of my debt. I removed my family from Plymouth to the apartment in Somerset-house, where my mother had resided near

---

* This gentleman who was a younger brother of Alexander, 4th Duke of Gordon, was Deputy Ranger of St. James' Park for many years. He died in 1823 H. S.

forty years; and at her decease it was continued to me by an order from the late Duke of Devonshire.

"The next year (1766) I was honoured with the notice and friendship of several persons of distinction, who endeavoured to convey the knowledge of my misfortunes to the Princess Dowager of Wales and Princess Amelia, but it did not meet with success. In April, 1767, General O.[1] (who had known me for several years) acquainted Lord H.[2] with my situation; and that nobleman, with the assistance of Mr. W.,[3] laid my mother's declaration before the King. His Majesty read it, seemed much concerned, and commanded that an inquiry should be made of my character from Lord C.[4] and Sir E. W.[5] who had known me from infancy. The account they gave of me was so satisfactory to the King, that he was graciously pleased to order me a pension of £100 a-year from his privy purse, May 7, 1767.

"The next morning I received the following letter from Lord H.

"'Sir,

"'I saw General O. last night, and am happy to find that we have not been unsuccessful in our attempt to serve you, and hope it will be an earnest to something better. My friend Mr. W. had the happiness to lay your case before a King, possessed of every virtue that can adorn a crown. Don't call on me to-morrow, for I am going to Chatham with the Duke of Gloucester; any other time I shall be happy to see a man possessed of so fair a character, which I value above everything in this life.

"'Your friend and humble servant,

"'H———.'

"I had also congratulatory letters from the Duke of Beaufort, Lord Viscount Townshend, General Oughton, and many of my friends."

1, General Oughton; 2, Lord Harcourt; 3, Mr. Worsley; 4, Lord Chesterfield, 5, Sir Edward Walpole   H S.

D

There is one circumstance in connection with the foregoing story which I cannot quite understand. According to Mrs. Pinkney's statement there were certainly *four* women in possession of this very interesting *secret* of Dunckerley's paternity, one of whom was a midwife. How many of the other sex shared it with them we have no means of ascertaining. Bearing in mind Mr. Dunckerley's "joy" on being informed of the result of his partner's frailty, it seems scarcely credible that he should have been able to withstand the temptation of making others acquainted with his extraordinary good fortune. Moreover, I fail to see how he could have had (as Mrs. Dunckerley tells us) "two places, and several considerable advantages, as the price of my folly," unless that folly was known to those who were instrumental in getting him the appointments. In view of these facts and certain others which will be hereafter noted, I find it extremely difficult to believe in the inviolability of the supposed secret, although the facts might not have been known to Dunckerley himself. With this exception I see nothing improbable or inconsistent in the story. The Royal personage referred to was I believe more remarkable for courage than for conjugal fidelity.* And as for the lady—judging from her own confession—she appears to have been more decent and much less mercenary than many others who have been similarly distinguished.

Whether she was " a servant maid in the family of Sir Robert Walpole" or "a physician's daughter, and lived with Mrs. W." is not of material import. She may have been a governess, lady's-maid, or what is now described in the advertisement columns as a "Lady-help," or companion. I must, however, confess my inability to swallow the first paragraph of the anonymous version with the readiness of

---

* George II. is celebrated as being the last King of England who commanded in person on the battle-field. His final appearance in this character was at the battle of Dettingen in 1743. H. S.

I. Highmore Pinx.   I. Faber F. 1744.

Georgius II. D. G. Mag: Brit: Fran: et Hib: REX F. D.

Brun: et Lunen: Dux S.R.I. Arch: Thesau: et Princeps Elector &c.

Inauguratus 11 die Octobris 1727.

Sold by I. Faber at the Golden Door in Craven Buildings Drury Lane.

some of its recent supporters. It seems to me most unlikely that a mere porter's wife separated from her husband should have been allowed free quarters in a Royal Palace for " near forty years "—for the remainder of her life in fact—for that she ended her days there I have not the smallest doubt, having recently seen the record of her burial, at all events, the burial of a " Mary Dunckerley " in the Register of the Chapel Royal, Savoy, the date of which interment agrees with that given by Dunckerley as the period of his mother's death.

We may, therefore, reasonably conclude that the story of his mother having " died when he was very young " has no foundation.

At the period of which I am writing Somerset House was used for precisely the same purpose as Hampton Court Palace is used at the present time; it was a Royal alms-house or home for pensioners of the Crown.

Stow, in his "Survey of London," says that Somerset House was formerly the property of the Duke of Somerset, " but he being attainted soon after the building was completed, it fell to the Crown and has usually been assigned for the residence of the Dowager-Queen, as it was to Queen Catherine, Dowager of King Charles the Second; but as none of the Royal Family reside there, several of the nobility and officers of the Court are permitted to have lodgings in it."* The present Somerset House was erected

---

* It may possibly interest some of my readers to know in what manner this "fine property" came into the possession of the Crown. If I rightly remember my history the original owner was a wealthy nobleman whose power and importance in the State were so great as to have earned for him the distinctive title of " Lord Protector " He seems to have been very fond of pomp and pageantry, and one fine morning while taking a prominent part in a grand public ceremonial on Tower Hill, he met with a serious accident, which so altered his condition, that his new palace in the Strand was deemed too large for his future requirements. His friends, therefore, removed him to a much smaller

on the site of the old building described by Stow, between
the years 1776 and 1780, since which period it has been
used for the purposes of the Government. On the demoli-
tion of the former structure the residents (among whom
was Dunckerley) were allotted apartments in Hampton
Court Palace; his anonymous biographer was not, therefore,
strictly accurate in stating that "he got a pension and
apartments at Hampton Court" I mention this merely to
show that the writer in question could not have been very
familiar with his subject or he would have been more pre-
cise in his statements Indeed the whole of his story
savours more of hearsay or gossip than of actual knowledge.

At a future stage I purpose placing before my readers
such particulars of Dunckerley's naval career as I have
been able to glean from the Admiralty Records. I shall not
therefore now examine in detail the account of his boyhood,
given by the writer just referred to. I may, however, mention the fact that the said Records disprove the story of
Dunckerley's having been employed in the Naval Academy
after the siege of Quebec, while they confirm his own
statement, that he was obliged to resume his duty on board
his ship, then about to return to the North American
station. It has been a matter of surprise to certain writers
that Dunckerley should not have endeavoured at once to test
the accuracy of Mrs. Pinkney's information ; but for my
part I see nothing extraordinary in the omission. Bearing
in mind the onerous and important services then required
from the gunner of a ship of the size of the Vanguard,

---

tenement, but one in every way suited to his reduced circumstances.
In order to prevent the noble building from falling into decay the Government of the period kindly undertook the charge of it; and probably
with the view of preventing any unseemly disputes amongst his relatives the
said Government retained possession of it, and in due course handed it over
to their successors together with the rest of the Crown properties   H. S.

carrying seventy guns, only just returned from a cruise, and being about to sail again immediately "with stores," it is rather a matter of surprise to me that he got permission to be absent from his post even for the few days necessary for the interment of his mother ; and it is highly probable that, had he exceeded his leave for his own private purposes, he would have been severely punished. It will be seen that the anonymous writer frequently mentions Sir Edward Walpole in a way that might lead to the inference that his information came direct from him, which is hardly likely, Sir Edward having been dead about ten years when the article was written.

It is impossible to reconcile the two versions of the part taken by this gentleman, as both before and after Dunckerley's death he is referred to as one of his chief benefactors ; indeed it would appear that it was owing to the good offices of Sir Edward Walpole and Lord Chesterfield that his recognition was ultimately brought about. On the other hand we are told that the gentleman in question was strongly opposed to Dunckerley's claims, although both accounts agree in stating that he had known him from infancy. It seems to me that probabilities are decidedly in favour of the Dunckerley story. Sir Edward Walpole, K.B., second son of the celebrated statesman, Sir Robert Walpole, was born in 1706, and died unmarried in 1784. He was evidently a person of considerable importance at the Courts of both George II. and his successor, having filled the post of Chief Secretary of Ireland, under the Duke of Devonshire, who, according to Dunckerley, had ordered that the apartment in Somerset House formerly occupied by his mother, should at her decease, be continued to him, and which order is said to have been given several years before the question of Dunckerley's paternity came to the front.

It is rather curious also, that Dunckerley's nominal father should have been in attendance on the Duke of Devonshire at the time of his marriage and still have remained in the service of that nobleman. Had he been merely a " porter at Somerset House " it is hardly probable that he would have been sent in the country " on some business for the Duke of Devonshire " which occupied him for a period of six months.

In Mrs. Dunckerley's confession a Mr. Lumley figures somewhat prominently, and it is but fair to state that this name is frequently mentioned in the lists of promotions, &c., during the early period of the reign of George II. In 1731, John Lumley, Esq. (brother of the Earl of Scarborough), was appointed Colonel of a Company of Grenadiers.

In 1733 he was appointed " a Commissioner for executing the office of Master of the Horse." In 1737, John Lumley, Esq. is mentioned as " Gentleman of the Horse to his Majesty."

" The Hon. John Lumley, Esq., brother to the Earl of Scarborough, member for Arundel, Groom of the Bed-Chamber to the Prince of Wales, Col. of a Company in the 2nd Reg. of Foot Guards," died on 16th Oct. 1739. These notices apparently refer to the same person, and it is not unlikely that it was this gentleman who made himself so peculiarly useful to his future sovereign on the occasion referred to.

DUNCKERLEY IN THE ROYAL NAVY.

It will be remembered that Dunckerley's biographer says that suffering from a thirst for glory he left school abruptly at the age of ten, and entered the Royal Navy, but the ship in which he first endeavoured to cure himself of his rather precocious complaint is not mentioned. As, however, the name of Sir John Norris heads the list of commanders under whom Dunckerley says he served, there may be some truth in the subsequent statement, that " he got aboard the ship of Sir John Norris, who was then going abroad." As a matter of fact Sir John *did* go abroad about the time that Dunckerley is said to have entered the sea-service, and it was in command of as fine a gathering of the "old wooden walls" as ever left our shores.

Early in the year 1735, big Spain endeavoured, with a fair amount of success, to pick a quarrel with little Portugal, who pluckily showed fight, at the same time appealing to England for assistance. Sir Robert Walpole, who was then at the head of the government, immediately responded by sending a fleet into the Tagus, consisting of twenty-five ships of the line with several fire-ships, together mounting 1,716 guns. Sir John Norris carried his flag as Admiral of the Fleet on board the Britannia, 100 guns. I have searched the pay lists of the period of several ships of this fleet, but no such name as Dunckerley is to be found therein, so whether our very young sailor took part in this magnificent demonstration I cannot now determine. For my own part I am inclined to think he did, as the fleet sailed in May, and he would then have been ten years and six months old. Possibly he may have been too young for a place on the ship's books. The appearance on the scene of this formidable squadron produced a speedy and most salutary change in the aspect of affairs. The King of Spain suddenly discovered that there were no real grounds for quarrelling with his neighbour, and that it was quite a mistake to imagine that he had the remotest intention of enlarging his own territory. The best course, therefore, he thought, was to shake hands and be friends, intimating that if there was one person he really liked better than another, that favoured individual was his little brother Portugal.

Matters being thus amicably settled, "Foul weather Jack," as he was called by the sailors, weighed anchor and returned to England, having had no occasion to use a single one of the hundreds of solid and weighty arguments he was quite ready to bring to bear on the subject.

The earliest mention of Dunckerley to be found in the Admiralty Records is on the 19th February, 1744, when he was appointed schoolmaster of the Edinburgh, a seventy gun ship in the Channel Squadron; he would then be twenty years of age, and must have made very good use of his time to have qualified himself for the position. England was then at war with France and Spain, and preparations were in rapid progress on the other side of the channel, having for their object a descent on our shores with a view to the restoration of the Stuarts, so that with watching the enemy's ports and chasing his cruisers, our "jolly tars" would, probably, have had rather a lively time. We can well imagine that the boatswain's pipe, or the roll of the drum, would occasionally relieve the monotony of scholastic studies and send the pupils scampering off to their posts in pursuit of far more congenial occupations. As an illustration I give the following item of news from the "London Magazine" for August, 1745:—

"An express arrived at the Admiralty from Plymouth on the 15th with Advice, that on Monday last Admiral Martin arriv'd there in his Majesty's ship the Edinburgh, with three other Men of War of 70 guns each, from a cruize, and brought in with them a French Man of War of 24 guns, a Privateer, and a very rich ship from St. Domingo."

Dunckerley remained in the Edinburgh until the 4th March, 1746. On the 20th of May following he was appointed gunner of the Fortune sloop, his warrant bearing date 22nd of April; in this vessel he served till the 1st of March, 1747, and on the 17th of June we find him gunner of the Crown. While in this ship he wrote a number of letters to the Earl of Chesterfield descriptive of various ports and places of interest in the Mediterranean, several of which will appear hereafter. He subsequently served in the same capacity in the Nonsuch, Tyger, Eagle, Vanguard, and, lastly, in the Prince of 90 guns, from the 27th of March,

1761, to the 31st of May, 1763. On the 18th of June, 1764, he was superannuated. The Vanguard seems to have been his favourite ship, his period of service in her extending over six years. From October the 1st, 1757, to March the 26th, 1761, he is described as acting in the double capacity of Gunner and Schoolmaster of the Vanguard, which, it will be seen, confirms his own statement.

Some years ago a well-known masonic writer alluded to Dunckerley as a "mere gunner" probably under a wrong impression; it may be as well therefore to mention that a gunner in the Royal Navy is an officer appointed by warrant after a very strict examination. He takes prior rank to the boatswain and carpenter, he must have been fairly well educated, have a general knowledge of seamanship, and be thoroughly efficient in the science and practice of gunnery. The armament, ammunition, warlike stores, and everything relating thereto are under his immediate care, and he must keep an account of their receipt and expenditure. In short, he is responsible for every article required for either offensive or defensive operations being in perfect order and ready for use; and when I state that the duties of a gunner, as laid down in the Admiralty Regulations, fill nearly eight closely printed pages, it will readily be understood that the office must be one of considerable responsibility. It is hardly likely to have been less important in the days when war was the rule and peace the exception, and when instead of a small number of heavy guns, worked chiefly by mechanical appliances, the gunner had a much more numerous family whose daily wants demanded his unremitting attention. To have been appointed to a post of this description before he was twenty-two years of age, Dunckerley must have been a man of exceptional merit and uncommon abilities, and that he should have attained no higher rank in the service appears most extraordinary.

It would have been exceedingly gratifying to me, and probably interesting to the reader, could I have furnished some account of the engagements in which, during his long period of active service, he doubtless took part, but as he with becoming, although to me, provoking modesty, only mentions the two which have a bearing on the personal narrative of his parentage, we must be content with a brief notice of these.

With the exception of the Fortune, sloop, and the Guadaloupe, all of Dunckerley's ships, of which we have any record, appear to have been of the class coming under the category of ships of the line; vessels of heavy tonnage, usually carrying not less than sixty guns, and as these were not so well adapted for cruising purposes and independent action as the smaller vessels, our naval histories contain but few references to their doings, while they abound with descriptions of the daring exploits of the smart frigates and ships of a lighter draught.

About the middle of the last century, Louisburg, Cape Breton, was held by the French, who, having lost it to a party of English colonists from Massachusetts in 1745, materially improved the town and strengthened its defences after its restoration to them in 1748. Ten years later it was considered an important stronghold, and the English naturally wanted it back again, its possession forming a part of the programme for the conquest of all North America. Early in 1758 Admiral Boscawen was dispatched from England with a strong fleet carrying a well-equipped army, under the command of two daring and sagacious Generals, Amherst and Wolfe, "Men of Kent," and soldiers from boyhood, each having entered the army at the age of fourteen. The fleet anchored before Louisburg on the 2nd of June, and having captured or destroyed the French ships left to protect the place, the Admiral landed the troops in the face of tremendous opposition from the elements as well as the enemy, Wolfe, it is said, being the first to spring from the boat into the raging surf.

By avoiding dissension (invariably the source of disaster) and acting strictly in concert, the British naval and military forces soon compelled the enemy to capitulate, and by the 27th of July the whole island was in possession of the English.

Whether Dunckerley's having distinguished himself in any way at this siege was the reason of Admiral Boscawen's notice of him it is impossible to say, it is plain however, that the Admiral must have had a high opinion of his conduct as well as of his capacity, or he would not have granted him "a warrant as teacher of the mathematics" in addition to the post which he already held as gunner of the Vanguard.

The siege of Quebec at which Dunckerley is said to have "behaved so well" was a much more important business. It was an example of military daring and skill which I feel sure that all readers of English history must look upon with mingled feelings of pride, pleasure, and regret, and although battle scenes may possibly appear somewhat out of place in these pages, I am of opinion that a brief description of so memorable an event, in which qualities ever dear to the English heart were displayed to their fullest extent, cannot be too widely spread, and will not be without interest to many of my readers, particularly as Dunckerley took part in the labours and shared in the honours of the victory.

In the spring of 1759 Admiral Saunders sailed from Portsmouth with a powerful fleet, having on board a comparatively small but well-appointed body of troops under the command of General Wolfe, the main object being the reduction of Quebec, hitherto deemed impregnable. It had been arranged that Generals Amherst and Prideaux, then engaged in the interior, should join forces with Wolfe at Quebec, but various delays and difficulties prevented the execution of this design, and on Wolfe's arrival in the St. Lawrence at the latter end of June, he found himself thrown upon his own resources. He however disembarked his troops on the Isle of Orleans, a little below Quebec, on the 27th of June. The Marquis de Montcalm, the French Governor of Canada, and commander of the forces at Quebec, a man of great courage and experience, immediately adopted vigorous measures for the defence of the capital. He first endeavoured to prevent the British from landing, and then from erecting batteries which they had commenced as soon at they reached the shore, but in this he failed. On the same night a terrible storm blew down the river, driving several of the large ships from their anchors and sinking some of the smaller ones. In the midst of the storm the enemy sent down a number of fire-ships intended for the destruction of the fleet, and had the attempt been successful, disaster and defeat would doubtless have been the portion of the invaders, but fire-ships and British seamen were old acquaintances from the days of the " Invincible Armada."

With characteristic coolness and intrepidity they intercepted the blazing craft in their boats before they could reach their own ships and towed them to the river banks, where those who sent them had the equivocal satisfaction of seeing them burn to the water's edge without doing the least injury. From the heights of Quebec this fiery fleet under weigh must have presented a magnificent spectacle, well calculated to infuse hope and enthusiasm into the bosoms of the besieged, and to strike terror and confusion into the hearts of the besiegers ; but however pleasing the sight may have been to the French inhabitants the result was pro·bably not quite what had been anticipated.

Montcalm was not, however, the man to be disheartened by a single failure, but finding that fully-rigged ships made rather costly bonfires, and vessels being probably scarce, he hit upon a plan somewhat less expensive. A month later, the tide being favourable, he sent down a number of huge rafts laden with burning timber and other combustibles, which our gallant tars, animated no doubt by a desire that the spectators should have the full benefit of the grand display, obligingly treated as they had done the ships. Quebec was at this time strongly fortified, and its natural situation always rendered it extremely difficult to carry by assault, for it stands on a steep rock at the junction of the rivers St. Lawrence and St. Charles, whose rocks and shoals gave additional security, so that it was virtually inaccessible on three of its sides—a second Gibraltar, in fact.

The French had availed themselves of every point of vantage for erecting batteries and entrenchments, out of which Wolfe vainly endeavoured to draw them; but he had to deal with an opponent equally shrewd, and not a whit less brave and determined than himself. In the midst of a hostile population and harrassed by bands of savages in the pay of the enemy, Wolfe was compelled to depend on the fleet for supplies, and knowing that when these were exhausted his position would be untenable, he determined upon attacking the enemy in his intrenchments. His plans were well laid, but the force at his command was far too weak for so desperate an enterprise, and owing to the difficulties of landing, and the impetuosity of a portion of the attacking party, who the moment they reached the shore, rushed up towards the entrenchments instead of waiting for their supports, they were nearly annihilated by the guns of the enemy. Night coming on with a storm brewing, the attempt was abandoned, and Wolfe made the best of his way back to the camp, his comparatively small force having been weakened to the extent of about 800 men.

This failure had a most depressing effect on the spirits of the British, for the situation was becoming desperate, and even Wolfe himself took a desponding view of the enterprise. This may in some measure be accounted for by approaching illness, for he was shortly afterwards stricken down with fever which compelled a cessation of active hostilities. On his recovery he renewed his efforts to draw the French from their entrenchments, but to no purpose. Despairing of success in this direction, he consulted the naval commanders and a plan was agreed upon, which from its very audacity gave hopes of success This was to scale the heights of Abraham at the back of Quebec where the defences were weakest. The troops were therefore re-embarked unobserved by the enemy, and taking advantage of a favourable wind and tide, the Admiral sailed up the river as if bound on a surveying expedition or a pleasure trip, not even wasting a passing shot on the fortifications.

A suitable spot having been selected for the landing, the ships continued their course several leagues higher up the river, and when the night was at its darkest, the Admiral dropped quietly down with the tide with all his boats out in readiness for the daring attempt. Owing to the skill and caution of the sailors and the excellent discipline of the soldiers, the French sentinels posted along the banks of the river were all passed without an alarm being given.

The first to land were some Highlanders, who began to climb the face of the rocks, using their hands more than their feet, and grasping at every bush and projection that could facilitate their ascent; they were followed in a similar manner by the remainder of the troops. The French guard above their heads hearing a noise, but seeing nothing, fired down the precipice, but did no further harm than arousing the sentries adjacent. Some of our men who evidently did not appreciate being shot at for nothing, returned their fire at random, which so terrified the French that they bolted, and left their captain, who being wounded and taken prisoner, begged our officers to sign a certificate to the purport that he really was wounded and had not run away, lest he should be punished as corrupted, believing that this bold enterprise would be deemed impossible without corruption.

Wolfe now stood on the heights of Abraham; but excessive fatigue and disease, the French and their confederates had reduced his army to less than 5,000 men. He had no artillery, but his men seized four guns in one of the enemy's batteries, and the English seamen managed to haul up one small gun from the landing-place. Fortunately for our people, Montcalm came on in so great a hurry that he had only time to bring two small field-pieces. At first he could hardly believe the evidence of his senses—so impossible did it seem for an army to ascend those dangerous cliffs. After lining the bushes with detachments of Indians, the French and Canadians came on in fairly good order, but they opened an irregular fire at too great a distance to be effective.

The English reserved *their* fire until the enemy was well within range, and then they poured in a terrible discharge. This first volley was succeeded by a most steady and deliberate fire, and, in less than half-an-hour the French began to waver. But as Wolfe stood in the front line cheering his men, a musket ball struck his wrist. He wrapped a handkerchief round the wound, and put himself at the head of his grenadiers, who had fixed bayonets for the charge, when he was hit by a second ball in the groin; but he seemed scarcely to heed this more serious injury, and continued giving his orders, until he received his death wound, for a third ball struck him in the breast and brought him to the ground. His men, stricken with grief, at once carried him to the rear. As his eyes were growing dim, he heard a wounded officer near him exclaim, " See how they run !" Who run? faintly inquired Wolfe. "The French !" replied the officer, " they give way in all directions." " Then," said the hero, " I die content ! " and after ordering Webb's regiment to move down to Charles River and secure the bridge in order to cut off the enemy's retreat, he expired

General Monckton, the second in command, was dangerously wounded, but Townshend completed the victory. Montcalm received a mortal wound in attempting to rally the French, and his second in command was made prisoner and conveyed on board an English ship, where he died the next day of his wounds. In this fierce contest the French lost 1,500 men and the British 640. The city of Quebec capitulated on the 18th of September (five days after the battle), and the possession of Canada was finally secured to Great Britain by the treaty of 1763.

Thus fell, at the early age of thirty-three years, and at the moment of a glorious and hard-won victory, one of England's bravest and noblest soldiers. A monument has since been erected at Quebec appropriately inscribed with the names of the two brave leaders who fell on that memorable day —Wolfe and Montcalm—worthy antagonists, and an honour to their respective nations; although, so far as the former is concerned, the dominion of Canada might well be deemed a sufficient memorial.

The death of Wolfe was regarded as a national loss. Mourning was worn for him by all classes, and a monument in Westminster Abbey was voted to his memory by the House of Commons; but his body was interred in the parish church at Greenwich beside that of his father, who died only a few days before the news arrived of the death of his son. " General Wolfe was not more distinguished for his military genius and bravery, his ardent and fearless spirit of enterprise, his thorough knowledge of his profession, and his skill as a disciplinarian, than for his religious principles, high-souled generosity, amiability, humanity, and exemplary conduct in private life. His name is one of the purest, as well as highest, on the roll of our country's military heroes." *

I regret my inability to account for the encomium passed

---

* "The Imperial Dictionary of Universal Biography."

on Dunckerley's conduct at the siege of Quebec. As will have been seen the military did most of the fighting, the ships being chiefly engaged in the transport duties. The Vanguard is not mentioned as having been in action at all on the occasion. It is, however, not unlikely that a naval force landed on the heights and assisted in the final struggle, indeed the fact of the sailors having dragged a gun up the face of the cliff points to this conclusion. If so, Dunckerley may have been one of the party, although I believe it is very unusual for a gunner to be sent on land service under such circumstances. He certainly may have volunteered, having a desire to take part in the expected battle, and not being required on board, but even this is somewhat doubtful.

Soon after the fall of Quebec, the Vanguard was sent to England, where she arrived early in January, 1760, as stated by Dunckerley. She was ordered to return as soon as her stores could be got on board, in company with several other ships of war, their object being the relief of the capital then besieged by the French, Captain Swanton, in the Vanguard, being senior commanding officer, and Dunckerley, occupying his former post as gunner of the same ship.

The squadron arrived in the St. Lawrence early in May and was fortunately able to ascend the river, but only just in time to prevent Quebec falling again into the hands of the enemy who had invested the fortress with much spirit both by land and sea. The English ships made short work of the frigates left to defend the approaches, capturing or destroying them under the eyes of the French commander, who seems to have suddenly arrived at the conclusion that after all Quebec was undesirable as a place of permanent residence, for the very same night he hastily left the neighbourhood with all his belongings, forgetting even to leave his address.

In the month of June following, Dunckerley installed the Provincial Grand Master of Canada, so that the story of his having been "appointed to some employment in the Naval Academy" is evidently unfounded.

One of the many loose statements about Dunckerley is that he sailed in a merchant vessel for the Mediterranean in order to escape arrest for debt. How this notion got into the head of the writer I cannot conceive, but there is certainly no truth in the first part of the statement. The Guadaloupe, the ship referred to, was a 32-gun frigate, commanded by Captain the Hon. John Ruthven, with whom Dunckerley appears to have been on very friendly terms. This officer, who was the second son of James, third Lord Ruthven, was made a Mason at the age of twenty-two in the Royal Navy Lodge, Deal, on the 7th of September, 1762. He was then captain of the Terpsichore frigate, taken from the French in 1760. In connection with the name of this brother there appears a slight discrepancy between the Grand Lodge Register and the naval records, which, at first sight, is somewhat puzzling. The column in the former which is headed " Remarkable Occurrences " contains the curious information that he died on the 7th of September, 1762, the very day on which he is said to have been initiated. This must have been a *very* remarkable occurrence indeed, but " Charnock's Biographia Navalis " tells a different story ; it informs us that he continued in the Terpsichore till 1764, when he was appointed to the Guadaloupe, and employed on the Mediterranean station till 1767 ; that he was subsequently appointed to the Glory frigate and was supposed to have died in the year 1771. From another source I learn that in the latter part of 1762, while in command of the Terpsichore he fought and captured a French ship of war, and was wounded in the action. This, at all events, does not seem a very ghost-like proceeding ; under the circumstances, therefore, I feel bound to admit the possibility of a mistake having in this instance *really* been made in the Secretarial department of the Grand Lodge.

THE ORIGIN OF ENGLISH FREEMASONRY IN QUEBEC.

Having frequently mentioned Quebec in the preceding pages, I probably cannot do better than finish this part of my undertaking by presenting the following verbatim extract from a long letter addressed to the Grand Secretary on the subject of early Masonry in that Colony.

At first sight it does not appear to have much connexion with Dunckerley, but to my mind his handywork is plainly visible in the ready and systematic organization of the scattered forces into a compact and united body.

It is copied from an old letter-book, the original being written by Brother John Gawler, who belonged to the Royal Artillery, but in what capacity I am unable to ascertain.

                        " Woolwich,
" Sir,   " 9th Feb. 1769.

    " As by the death of our late Brother Spencer, his office of Grand Secretary has fell to you, and as you may not be so well acquainted with the state of Masonry at Quebec as he was, so as rightly to understand the accounts you may receive from thence, I beg liberty to give you a brief account of its origin and progress in that province, and how it comes that the lodges there are not entered on the printed list

    " In the winter of the year 1759, when conquest had added that capital to His Majesty's dominions, the Masters and Wardens of all the Warranted Lodges held in the Regiments garrisoned there (to the number of eight or nine) assembled together and unanimously agreed to choose an acting Grand Master to preside over them, the better to advance Masonry, regulate their proceedings, and unite them in one common band of brotherly love.

    " Agreeable thereto they made choice of Brother Guinnett, Lieutenant in the 47th Regiment, and drew out, sign'd and seal'd a Warrant, empowering him and his successors elected, to congregate them together as a Grand Lodge for the intent before mentioned, they having the Constitutions as their chief guide.

"This regulation together with the charitable collections made and given to the poor widows and orphans of the army and the distress'd Canadians, brought the Craft into such universal esteem that numbers applied to the different Lodges, and was made Masons, inasmuch as to make them so numerous, as to oblige the Grand Master to grant Warrants from under his present authority, until opportunity might offer for them to apply for a greater.

"The 24th of June, 1760, Brother Simon Frasier, Colonel of the Highland Regiment, was elected to preside over the Lodges, and Bro. Dunckerley, of His Majesty's ship the Vanguard, who was possessed with a power from the Grand [Lodge] of England to inspect into the state of the Craft wheresoever he might go, honoured them with his approbation of their conduct and installed Brother Frasier in his high office.

"The brethren amongst the merchants being united together under a warrant of the above Grand Lodge, considering themselves as likely to reside there, made application to the Grand [Lodge] of England, and obtained a Warrant.

"The office of Grand Master was afterwards successively filled by the following persons.—

"27th Dec., 1760, Bro. Augustus Spaner, Capt. in the 28th Regiment.

"27th Dec., 1761, Bro. Milbourne West, Capt. in the 47th Regiment.

"About this time many of the above Lodges with their regiments having left Quebec, the whole province conquered, and many of the Lodges under the above sanction remaining, it was resolved to apply to the Grand [Lodge] of England for a Provincial Grand Warrant. Accordingly abstracts of their whole proceedings, and a letter praying their Grand Authority together with a considerable sum towards the General Fund of Charity, was sent and graciously received, and their prayer granted; but through the neglect of the Brother who was the bearer of it, the Warrant was not taken out to the great disappointment of the Brethren.

"The following year another sum was sent by the then acting Grand Master (Bro. West) who took out the Warrant, but never sent it to Quebec. The Lodges still continued to assemble, as they understood by the late Grand Secretary's letters that their former proceedings was approved of, and was presided over by Bro. Turner, Lieut. of the 47th Regiment, Bro. Walker, and Bro. Collins, Esqrs., and still continued to send to England what they could spare from the many calls for charity they had there, which was always entered by the Grand Secretary as coming from the Merchants' Lodge, though it was the united contributions of all the Lodges at Quebec. The bearers of this was often impowered to inquire for Bro. West and send them the warrant, or apply for another, but from some neglect it never was sent out. At my leaving Quebec, the brethren honoured me with a particular confidence, and gave me letters to the Grand [Lodge] praying for another warrant, which I presented in November 1767. The then D.G. Master, Bro. Salter, Esq., was pleased to grant their prayer, and in consideration of the many sums sent on that account, ordered that I should have it for paying the Clerk's fee; and as the Lodges then warranted at Quebec, had paid large sums at their embodying, part of which had been sent to England to the General Fund of Charity, granted that the Lodges then subsisting under the former sanction should be admitted on the list of regular Lodges, on paying for their engraving. And as I did not know the exact number then subsisting in Canada, was ordered to write them to know, which I did and understand they have sent you a list thereof, together with the names of the members of each Lodge.

"This, Sir, is as true an account as my memory will admit me to give, and the reason they hope to be admitted on the List of Lodges as granted by Brother Salter.

"My duty called me at Quebec from the time of its conquest till July, 1767, most part of which time I had the honour to be a member of the Grand Lodge, and sure I am, that no body of men could be more desirous to live and act up to the Character and Constitutions of Masons, than they have been, though they were so unhappy thro' the neglect of Brethren to be so many years without the warranted sanction of the Grand [Lodge] of England."

The remainder of Brother Gawler's letter is not of sufficient historical import for reproduction. I may, however, mention that his story was in a measure confirmed in 1789, when a list of the members of the " St. Andrew's Lodge, No. 2, Quebec " (No. 178 on the English register) was received by the Grand Secretary of England. This document is headed "List of the Members of St. Andrew's Lodge, No. 2. Quebec, acting under a warrant of Constitution, dated at Quebec 20th October, A.L. 5760, granted by the Honourable and Right Worshipful Colonel Simon Fraser, then Provincial Grand Master of Masons in Canada, who was installed into that office in virtue of a special authority by the Right Worshipful Thomas Dunckerley, Esqr., then an officer of His Majesty's Vanguard man-of-war, now Provincial Grand Master of Essex.

"Quebec, 25th October, 1789."

The list comprises 70 names, and is very carefully made out, giving the " age when admitted " of each brother, his " Business or Profession," " Residence," " When made," " When admitted a Member," and has a broad marginal column headed "Remarks," which contains a number of notes and additional information relative to many of the members, nine of whom have the initials P.M. appended to their names. As may well be imagined nearly every trade and profession is represented, as well as nearly every part of the colony; military and naval officers make a goodly show, gentlemen, merchants, Indian traders, mariners, farmers, and many others are designated, all apparently of the well-to-do description. The first name on the list is that of "James Thompson, Overseer of work for Quebec," made a Mason in Scotland in 1754, and admitted a Member on the 20th October, 1760. "S. Warden of the Lodge when constituted, now Master."

No. 2 on the list is Lauchlan Smith, Lord of the Manor of St. Ann's, made 5th November, 1760. In the "Remarks" column he is described as "P.M., attending the duties of the Lodge while in the city." These two brethren were evidently living at the time their names were returned to Grand Lodge in 1789, and it is therefore probable that the information as to the origin of the Lodge came from them or from the Lodge records. At the end of the list of names is the following note.

"The above list of members are stated as they appear on the Records of the Lodge, omitting the dead, some who for conveniency have joined other Lodges, and such as have removed to other climates at so an advanced age that we believe them not to exist, and a few, who, from their conduct in the society do not merit our attention."

This appears to have been the last return of members made by the St. Andrew's Lodge, although it was retained on the official list until 1813.

DUNCKERLEY'S LODGES.

THE LODGE OF ANTIQUITY, PORTSMOUTH.

FEW years ago I had the good fortune to find in the archives of the Grand Lodge the following letter in the handwriting of Dunckerley, which conclusively settles the till then open question as to which of the two rival Masonic bodies (Ancients or Moderns) first received him into the Order. The letter is addressed to James Heseltine, Esq. (the Grand Secretary), Doctors' Commons :—

"Portsmouth, Decr. 19th, 1773.

"My Dear Friend and Bro^{r.}

"You will not be surprised when I acquaint you that we have troublesome Brethren at this place, who I think are equal in obstinacy to any we have formerly met at the Qua. Com.* You are no stranger to the regard I have always express'd for my Mother Lodge at the Three Tonns in this Town, and that it was my repeated requests which has prevented it being struck off the List for some years past; and you are sensible that when I was in Town, five weeks ago, I acquainted you with my hopes that I should be able to revive the said lodge, and establish it on a very respectable footing; but as it was not *then* in my power to give you a regular List of the Members (for not one is to be found that has paid any Subscription for more than three years past) nor has any Lodge been held. You

---

* Quarterly Communication.

very justly observed that they were subject to the resolutions of the Committee, and that paying any money on their account to the fund of Charity would not prevent it; but that they would certainly be restor'd if they made a proper request to me for that purpose, and it came with my recommendation, before the Grand Lodge. I then paid five Guineas to the fund for building the Hall, together with the names of those (to be register'd) which I had made Masons at this place in a P.G. Lodge.

"Judge my surprise when after having summon'd the oldest Brethren of the said Lodge, five only came to attend me at P.G. Lodge last Friday, when I had the pleasure of Sir Peter Parker's company & several other very respectable beside my Grand Officers. After acquainting them with my proceedings as above, and that it was proper they should write to me requesting to have their Lodge restored; all (except Captn. Robinson) rejected it with disdain—said they would not write to me for any such purpose, nor feed my vanity in any such manner—that I had no Right to make Masons—that I had Pocketted the Money—and Mr. John Tucker, a Watch-maker, threaten'd me—that he would shake my Provincialship, and write against me to my Grand Seigneur; surely he did not mean the King? However, supposing he meant Lord Petre; I have this happiness that my general character, together with my situation and connexion in life set me above his low malice and detraction; for if I am rightly inform'd he intends to impeach me of high crimes, which if he cannot prove, I am determined to bring an action on the case for Slander against him and all who joyn with him in the said Impeachment or Accusation. In short, Sir Peter Parker, the P.G. Officers, and my Friends that were present were astonished at his indecent behaviour. I expect to be in Town by the middle of next month; but shall hope to hear from you as soon as convenient, and that you will acquaint me when the next

Qua. Com.* is to be held. Sir Peter unites with me & Chez
Moi in sincere regard for you yourself and all friends.

　　　　"I am, Dear Sir,

　　　　　　　"Yours, with the greatest affection,

　　　　　　　　　"Thos. Dunckerley."

It is not surprising that Dunckerley, whose early training
in the Royal Navy had doubtless given him very strict ideas
of discipline and respect for lawfully constituted authority,
should have felt considerable anger at the mutinous conduct
described in his letter, and it is but natural to conclude that
the delinquents were at once punished by the deprivation of
their warrant, and the irrevocable erasure of the lodge.
Notwithstanding, however, the contemptuous treatment he
had received at the hands of those whom he had endeavoured
to benefit, Dunckerley seems to have kept steadily in view
the first Grand Principle of our Order—*Brotherly Love*—
and to have displayed to the last that affectionate regard for
his mother lodge, which he mentions in the first portion of
his letter.

The lodge was certainly erased from the list, but it was on
the 27th of April, 1773, nine months before the very lively
meeting so graphically described in the foregoing letter.
This summary proceeding on the part of the authorities, or
some other cause, evidently brought the malcontents to
reason, for on the 25th of February, 1774, the lodge is credited
by the Grand Treasurer with £1. 1s., and reappears in the
list for 1775 under its former number, having doubtless been
restored at the intercession of the Provincial Grand Master. In
the Grand Secretary's list for this year it is credited with
£2. 2s., against which amount is written "Dunck," probably
as a reminder that the sum was paid by Dunckerley on behalf of the lodge. For some years after the settlement of
the differences between the Provincial Grand Master and the

---

* Quarterly Communication.

Portsmouth brethren, the progress of the old lodge appears to have been fairly steady, although the official records evince considerable irregularity in the matter of payments and returns to Grand Lodge. It must be borne in mind, however, that this was a very critical period for Masonry in England, many of the old lodges were strongly inclined to rebel against the new regulations for compulsory registration and payment for members, and evidently did not see the justice of being taxed for the purpose of building a hall which they were not likely to see, let alone make use of, unless at a great expense of both time and money.

This lodge seems to have taken the name of "The Lodge of Antiquity," * about 1788, and, though in a declining state at the time of the Union in 1813, it was brought forward on the list of the United Grand Lodge as No. 28.

It may seem strange that Dunckerley's name should not be found among those returned to Grand Lodge. I account for it in this way—compulsory registration was only resolved upon in 1768, and was not strictly enforced until five or six years later. Doubtless our old friend, who was then residing in Hampton Court Palace, had left the lodge many years before.

The first list of names in the register after the passing of the before-mentioned regulations, appears to have been returned about 1780 ; it is headed by that of Mark Robinson, Captain in the Navy, made a Mason in November, 1747. He was probably the only member of the lodge, to whom Dunckerley was personally known, and of whom he makes honourable mention in his letter. I need hardly say that the name of the wicked watchmaker who had dared to use such atrocious threats against the person of his superior officer, and that officer a scion of Royalty, is *not* in the list of members.

---

* Probably suggested by Dunckerley himself; previous to this period it had only been distinguished by its number on the list, or the name of the tavern at which it was held. H. S.

There is one item in connection with this list of names which strikes me as being rather peculiar. In the column of the Register which is headed " Remarkable Occurrences," against the name of George Cuthbert, Clergyman, is written : " Discontinued a member by his own request."

This old lodge was very appropriately named, for it seems to have been the pioneer of Freemasonry in Hampshire and the parent of several lodges at Portsmouth. It first appears in the Grand Lodge Records in what is known as the Second Manuscript List of Lodges, which gives the names of the members of most of the constituted, or "regular" lodges existing in the year 1725. The lodges had not yet been arranged in numerical order, but the list comprises 79 lodges, and the one which occupied the seventy-second place is described as being held at the "East India Arms," at Gosport, Mr. Timothy Raggett, 27th Febry., 1726."

> " FRA. MAXWELL,   Master.
> ROBERT SPICER, } Wardens.
> TIM. RAGGETT, }
> JOHN MASLIN,
> JAMES CLARK,
> BISTON MARTIN,
> SAM^L. PITMAN,
> ANDREW NAIRNE."

Whether " Mr. Timothy Raggett" was the proprietor of the "East India Arms," or merely the person from whom the list was received, I am unable to determine. A Grand Lodge was held on the 27th of February, 1726, but the record of the proceedings is of the most meagre character, and it contains no reference to the lodge in question. It is evident, therefore, that this lodge was in existence early in 1726, but how long it had then been working it is quite impossible to say. Warrants were then unknown, and fees for registering members had not been dreamt of. The expenses of the Quarterly Communications were shared between the Grand

Master and his Wardens, and all petitions to the Grand
Lodge for charitable aid were met by "sending round the
hat."

The Engraved List for 1729 (printed in 1728) is the first
in which the lodges are distinguished by numbers. In
this list Dunckerley's mother lodge figures as No. 35, but
the space in which the date of constitution usually appears is blank, and so it remains in all subsequent lists
until the year 1740, when "1724" is introduced, probably because it was first given a place on the roll among
the Lodges constituted in the latter year. By the various
alterations in the numbers it became in 1740, No. 31;
1755, No. 21; 1770, No. 20; 1781, No. 18; 1792, No.
17; 1814, No. 28; 1832, No. 26.

John Lane, in his invaluable " Masonic Records," gives
the following table of the various places of meeting and the
years of removal, from the time it first appears in the
Grand Lodge books until its erasure in 1838.

"East India Arms, Gosport, Hampshire ...	1729
Two Posts,* Portsmouth	1736
Vine...	1738
Three Tuns...	1752
King's Arms	1790
Three Tuns	1794
George Inn	1799
Mitre Tavern, Portsea	1804"

The Grand Lodge register makes no mention of the trade
or calling of the original members, and owing to some extraordinary laxity or want of foresight on the part of the
authorities, there is a gap in this register from about
1730 to 1768. Judging, however, from the description

---

* This was probably the celebrated tavern immortalised by Captain
Marryat, "*The Blue Postesses*, where the midshipmen leave their
chestesses, call for tea and toastesses, and sometimes forget to pay for
their breakfastesses." H. S.

of the members returned after that period, and the fact of Captain Robinson and Dunckerley having been initiated therein, it seems highly probable that this venerable lodge had been from its infancy the favourite resort of the naval brethren whose avocation brought them into the neighbourhood of Portsmouth. Doubtless, it was rather an exclusive lodge, for most of the members seem to have been either naval or military officers of a superior grade, or the higher class of tradesmen.

Captain Mark Robinson, the "father of the lodge," was an officer of distinction, whose intimacy with Dunckerley may be accounted for by the fact of his having been for a short time in command of the Vanguard. From 1775 to 1779 he was Captain of the Worcester, 64 guns, and took part in the indecisive action off Ushant on the 27th of July, 1778, between the Brest fleet under the Comte D'Orvilliers and our Channel fleet under Admirals Keppel and Palliser. The Worcester led the rear division and got plenty of knocks but not much honour, for the affair caused much dissension, afloat as well as on shore, and the two Admirals were tried by court-martial for allowing the enemy to escape; but as the latter took advantage of a fair wind and a dark night and declined to remain to be beaten, it was considered that the French were more to blame than our commanders, consequently they were let off easily. Early in 1779, Captain Robinson was appointed to the Shrewsbury, 74 guns, and while cruising off Scilly on the 4th of April, he fell in with two large French privateers who at once made off in different directions. After a smart chase one of them was captured, the other getting clear away. His next important engagement was off the Chesapeak, on the 5th of September, 1781, when the English fleet under Rear-Admiral Graves had rather a sharp encounter with that of the French under the Comte de Grasse. This affair terminated in a similar manner to the action off Ushant, for although the enemy had the advantage both in the number of ships and weight of metal, he sheered off in the night, and made no attempt to renew the battle next day. The Shrewsbury was the first to come into action, and she was severely punished for her temerity, receiving more injury and losing a greater number of men than any other ship in the fleet. She had fourteen killed and fifty-two wounded, one of the former being her First Lieutenant, and among the latter her Captain, who had one of his legs shot off. Being thus unfitted for further service he was soon afterwards placed on the list of superannuated Rear-Admirals. Captain Robinson frequently distinguished himself in the service of his country, and on several occasions led the British fleet into action. He was one of the earliest friends of the immortal Nelson, and was the chief instrument of that hero obtaining his first step, the latter being placed with him as Acting-Lieutenant on board the Worcester in December 1776. He died in November 1799.

Another justly celebrated member of this lodge was Captain Robert Roddam, R.N. He first distinguished himself about the year 1744, on the Spanish coast near Cape Ortugal, when in command of the Viper sloop, by destroying in one day thirty-two sail of merchant vessels; he then captured and brought out from under the batteries a privateer whose force was much greater than that of the Viper. He was subsequently appointed to the Greyhound frigate, and rose steadily in his profession, each command being more important than the preceding one. In 1778, he was promoted Rear-Admiral of the White, and appointed Commander-in-Chief at the Nore. He was Senior Admiral of the Red when he died at the age of 89 on the 31st of March, 1808.

One cannot repress a feeling of surprise and regret that so old and respectable a lodge should have been permitted to die out. It was virtually in abeyance from 1803 to 1821, during which interval the warrant, minute books, &c., are said to have been lost. In 1822, an attempt was made to resuscitate the lodge and a warrant of confirmation was granted, which only served to prolong its life for a few years.

Among the last of its members were :—

> Archibald Low, solicitor, Portsea.
> William Prince, watchmaker, Portsmouth.
> George Martell, surgeon,   ,,
> Francis M. Clarke, merchant   ,,
> *Henry Besant, gentleman, Portsea.
> John Ediss, merchant,   ,,

The last payment was made to Grand Lodge in 1831, and it was finally erased in 1838.

LODGES HELD ON BOARD SHIPS OF WAR.

In the present day the popularity of Masonry in the Army and Navy is proverbial; but judging from our lists of lodges, and registers of members, and considering the enormous increase of the Order generally, it is not nearly so popular as in the old fighting days when most of the regiments on active service as well as those of the militia had lodges attached to them; and there were few of our seaports but had a particular lodge favoured and supported chiefly by the men who "go down to the sea in ships." Full information as to army warrants issued by the Grand Lodges in Great Britain and Ireland may be found in "Gould's History of Freemasonry," the author having made this subject his especial study. My present purpose is to offer a few remarks on the lodges directly connected with the sister service.

It is unlikely that the name of the enthusiastic soldier who first conceived the idea of having a Freemasons' lodge

---

* The last Secretary of the lodge, and uncle of Walter Besant   H. S.

restricted to the members of his profession in his own regiment will ever be known; but I think there can be little, if any doubt, that Thomas Dunckerley was the first to hold a regular lodge under the Union Jack in the broad dominions of Father Neptune. It will be remembered that he himself states that he came to London early in January, 1760, to attend the funeral of his mother (which took place on the eleventh of that month), and the " exigencies of the service " necessitated his immediate return to the Vanguard. The records of the Grand Lodge show that a Warrant bearing date 16th of January, 1760, was issued for a lodge to be held on board His Majesty's ship Vanguard. Two days previously, viz., on the 14th of January, a Quarterly Communication was held at the "Crown and Anchor" in the Strand, which Dunckerley is not likely to have omitted attending, if he was still in London. Whether or no, it seems highly probable that during this visit he had an interview with the Grand Secretary or someone else at head quarters which resulted in the Warrant being granted for the Vanguard Lodge, and also an authority to regulate Masonic affairs in the newly conquered Canadian provinces, or in any other part of the globe he might visit, where no Provincial Grand Master had been appointed. The next meeting of the Grand Lodge was on the 14th of May following, and in the statement of monies received in the interval appears the item " Constitution of a Lodge on board his Majesties ship the Vanguard £2. 2s." this sum being the amount then payable for a Warrant or " Constitution." On the 5th of June, 1761, the lodge is credited with the same amount to the Fund of Charity; after which no further mention of it is made for several years, although it retained its place in the Engraved List of Lodges. The Vanguard sailed for the West Indies in October, 1761. Meanwhile Dunckerley had left her and had been appointed to the Prince, a larger ship, or, as he terms it, " a ship of the second rate." For this vessel a

F

Warrant bearing date 22nd of May, 1762, was granted, and the lodge was credited with the usual fee on the 27th of July. The money column of a meeting held on the 29th of April, 1763, contains the following :—" His Majesty's Ship Prince, 90 Guns £2. 2s." This item reads very like what Dunckerley himself would have written had he remitted the money, as in all probality he did.

On the 23rd of April, 1764, the lodge is credited with a guinea, which appears to have been the last payment made while it was held on board ship. Two months later Dunckerley retired from the service, and he appears to have taken the Warrant with him, indeed I do not see what else he could well have done with it as the ship was paid off, and her crew probably dispersed in all directions. He was then much pressed for money, or, as he would probably express it, "on a lee-shore, and almost on his beam ends." In fact he was suffering from a troublesome complaint, very common in those days and not entirely unknown in the present, generally referred to as " red tapeism." What name it went by in Dunckerley's time I know not, probably several, especially when it interfered with the payment of wages and prize-money.

Fortunately for himself, he seems to have had a natural facility for making friends with people in a higher social position than *he* occupied ; among whom may be reckoned the Captain of the Guadaloupe, who, in order to enable him to escape the degradation of a debtor's prison, the prospect of which to a person of Dunckerley's temperament must have been terrible indeed, kindly took him for a trip up the Mediterranean, ostensibly as an A.B., for as such his name appears on the ship's book, probably on account of the pay and rations, but he really went as a passenger. In this ship he would doubtless have had plenty of time to practise the rites of Masonry and impart some of his enthusiasm to those about him. He evidently had something of the kind in view when he joined the ship, for in a second edition of the Engraved List for 1764, No. 279, which in the previous issue had been represented as on board the Prince, is described as being held on board the Guadaloupe, on the 4th Wednesday, " A Masters' Lodge at Plymouth," so that he must have communicated with the Grand Secretary directly he had arranged to take the trip. Many of the incidents of this, his last sea voyage have been duly set forth in his personal narrative in which he is so provokingly reticent on masonic matters as to create an ardent wish that spiritualism were a reality, that we might have him " rapped up " occasionally to give an account of himself and gratify our curiosity on the subject of his nautical lodges. There are many points which, if light could be thrown on them, would, I feel sure, be most interesting to the fraternity. For instance, I should like to know in what part of the ship the lodge was held? Whether the members were summoned in the ordinary way, or by the shrill pipe and stentorian cry of the boatswain's mate, something after this style—" D'ye hear there fore and aft? All you Freemasons 'll muster in the after-cockpit at seven bells " or some other bells.

I should like to know too, whether the lodges met regularly on the days stated in the by-laws? It seems to me that some kind of reservation would have been desirable, such as " wind, weather, and the exigencies of the service permitting." I have also a little curiosity on the subject of the ceremonies. Were the brethren ever startled in the midst of the third degree by such orders as, " Clear lower deck," " Hands make sail; " or by the sharp command, " General quarters for action? " and, if so, what became of their aprons, collars, jewels, and other paraphernalia? Did they stay to " un-rig? " or did they run up " all standing? " There are many other questions which I should like to ask, but as I am not likely to have an opportunity, it is scarcely worth while enumerating them.

In July, 1761, the Prince sailed from Spithead for a cruise on the coasts of Spain and Portugal (on an errand of a similar character to Sir John Norris's expedition in 1735), returning to England in the autumn of the same year, and was then employed in the Home service until the 25th of June, 1762, when she was ordered to Lisbon with the fleet under the command of Sir Edward Hawke. It seems, therefore, quite feasible to suppose that Dunckerley was in England at the time the Warrant for a lodge on board this ship was granted, and from his subsequent action in removing the lodge to another vessel, we may reasonably infer that he was the person who had applied for it.

A not improbable reason for his having relinquished the former Warrant is that there were a sufficent number of Masons on board the Vanguard to hold a lodge when the ship left for the West Indies in 1761. Considering his intimacy with Dunckerley it is highly probable that her commanding officer, Captain Swanton, was a member of the Order; his son, Colonel Swanton, was "made" in the Lodge of Friendship No. 3 in 1783.

We have no evidence of the existence of more than three of these sea lodges, and it has been generally supposed that Dunckerley was in some measure responsible for the formation of each of them.

With regard to the two already mentioned, I think there cannot be much doubt on that point. I shall hereafter show that his interest in their welfare did not cease with his retirement from active service.

The third lodge has been to me a source of considerable perplexity, as it did not make its appearance until several years after Dunckerley had established himself on shore, and then it appeared in a quarter with which he had long ceased to be actively connected. In the official list for the year 1770, six new lodges are entered, five located at Quebec and one at Montreal, numbered consecutively from 221 to

226.   No. 220, the "Merchant's Lodge, Quebec," had been on the previous lists from 1763, having the date of constitution 2nd March, 1762, affixed.   In 1770, the lodges were re-numbered, and an entirely new set of plates was engraved.   For some inexplicable reason, or for no reason at all, the date of constitution of the Merchants' Lodge was omitted from the new list, as was also that of the six new lodges, but they were placed in a batch among the other lodges constituted in 1762   No. 224 is described as meeting "On Board his Majesty's Ship Canceaux at Quebec." In the year 1775, the first "Freemason's Calendar" appeared, printed in ordinary type.   Up to the year 1778, the Engraved List and the Calendar were published concurrently, but in this year the former was discontinued, leaving the field entirely free for its modern rival.   The Calendar had never given the date of constitution of any of the lodges, and so it continued until the year 1784, when this omission was rectified; the Quebec lodges were still in the same order, and all represented as having been constituted in 1762.   I have long had an idea that Dunckerley was in some way implicated in these lodges being entered on the list, but having learnt that he was not at Quebec in 1762, I could not quite understand it.   However, recent research has furnished an explanation.

The following letter supplies an approximate date of the constitution of three out of the six new lodges.

"Quebec, 2nd Aug., 1769.

" Right W. Brother the Grand Sec⁷ of England,

"Since our Letters of 5th Septr and 9th Feby last we have none of your brotherly favours.   At our last Quarterly Communication so many matters came before us relative to the Craft here that we had not time to write you ; and as the ensuing meeting happens at a season when the Brethren here are in the hurry of Business, we take this occasion to acquaint you that the Lodges in this Province are in the same situation as advised in Septr last, only with the addition of three new ones, viz., one held on board his Majesty's Ship Canceaux, No. 5, another in this city, the Select, No. 6, and a third in his Majesty's 52nd Regiment of Foot, No. 7,* whose dues for their Warrants (Three Guineas each) we cannot at present remit, our Right Worshipful Brother Collins, the Provincial Grand Master being in Acadia on his private affairs.   And here we cannot help remarking to you, that this confirms the necessity of what we have so long sought for in vain; we mean the Grand Lodge of England giving the Lodges here authority to elect a Provincial Grand Master to preside over them in case of the death of him to whom you have granted a Warrant, or his being obliged to quit the Province, which we pray may be taken into consideration by the Grand Lodge at its next meeting.   We now remit you Two guineas for the General Charity by brother Aylwin, which please to enter in the Printed list as coming from the Lodges in Canada by the hands of the Provincial Grand Master, more you may perhaps expect, but the present distress'd condition of this colony occasions more calls on us than the contributions, generous as they are, enables us to pay.

" We are, very respectfully,
        Right Worshipful Brother,
            Your faithful and Loving Brethren,
                JOHN AITKIN, D.P.G.M.,
                THOS. AYLWIN, G.T.,
                JAS. THOMPSON, G.S.,
        " A Committee appointed to answer Letters."

The letter referred to under date " 5th Sept. last " is an acknowledgment of the receipt of the Prov. Grand Warrant ("transmitted to us by our worthy Brother John Gawler ") with the Grand officers' thanks for the same, and an ex-

---

* These numbers refer to the Provincial register. H. S.

pression of regret that the said Warrant does not give them the authority to elect their Provincial Grand Master annually as they had been accustomed to do. It also requests the acceptance of Two Guineas for the Grand Charity, and contains the following reference to the lodges in the Province. "Inclosed is a list of the lodges under our sanction, as also of the Itinerants * now here, with the members contained in each." At that time foreign and colonial members were not registered, and unfortunately, I have been unable to find the enclosure referred to.

It would thus appear that the Canceaux Lodge was constituted by the Provincial Grand Master between September, 1768, and August, 1769.

Another letter from Quebec, dated 23rd of Sept., 1771, says, " We have the pleasure to acquaint you that Harmony and Unanimity reigns among us—no alteration necessary to advise you of has lately happened, except the removal of our Brethren on board His Majesty's Arm'd Ship Canceaux, who are now in one of the New England Provinces, and we doubt not will get themselves enregistred there and contribute as usual if their numbers are sufficient to form a regular Lodge."

The Canceaux was a comparatively small ship, carrying only six guns, and a crew of about forty-five men. She left Woolwich in April 1764, under the command of Lieutenant Henry Mouat, for North America, on what I should imagine to have been a surveying expedition, which frequently took her into the neighbourhood of Quebec. During the troubles between the English Government and the American colonists, she was very busy on the New England coast in pursuits of a nature hardly likely to ensure her crew a masonic welcome in any of the ports she visited. In October, 1775, Captain Mouat in the Canceaux, having under his command several

---

* Military, or travelling Lodges   H S

other small war-ships, appeared off the town of Falmouth in Massachusetts.   The inhabitants of this place had opposed with violence the loading of a mast-ship, in consequence of which act of hostility the Admiral on the station despatched Captain Mouat with his squadron to demolish the town unless all the artillery and small arms were delivered up to him forthwith, and four gentlemen sent on board as hostages. These conditions being refused, Captain Mouat, having given the inhabitants a few hours' grace to enable them to remove their families, proceeded to bombard the town, and in a short time destroyed 130 houses, 278 store and warehouses, a large new church, the court-house and public library.

At the time this ship-lodge was constituted Dunckerley was residing in London, and could not therefore have had anything to do with its formation.   The probability is that some of the Canceaux's officers were made masons at Quebec, where the remembrance of Dunckerley's lodge on board the Vanguard must have been still fresh, and so have been taken as a precedent by the Provincial Grand Master.

So far as I can learn this lodge never paid for its Constitution, nor returned a list of its members to the Grand Lodge of England.   It was struck off the roll in 1792.   These facts alone, are, in my opinion, fairly reliable evidence that Dunckerley was not responsible for its formation nor interested in its subsequent career.

As the lodges on board the Vanguard and Prince were constituted during what may justly be described as the dark period in the history of Masonry, nothing is known, or probably ever will be known of them beyond what is here set forth.   The names of their members were not returned to Grand Lodge, and if minutes of their proceedings were kept—which, from Dunckerley's methodical habits, is highly probable—they would most likely have been in his possession, and were either lost or destroyed after his decease.

Probably owing to the respect in which their founder was held the lodges were not erased although they may be said to have "died at sea," for no payment is recorded on the Grand Lodge books from the Vanguard Lodge after 1761 until its resuscitation in 1768; nor from the lodge on board the Prince and Guadaloupe from 1764 until it was re-opened at Somerset House in 1766. Both, however, retained their original numbers on the roll and their old Warrant or "Constitution."

THE LONDON LODGE No. 108.

This lodge may justly be considered the lineal descendant of the first lodge constituted on board a man-of-war, notwithstanding the gap in its history previously referred to. By the kindness and courtesy of the Secretary (Br. Henry W. Green), I have been permitted to inspect the old minute books which are fortunately intact, from its resuscitation in 1768, and are, as may well be imagined, of a most interesting character. They contain many references to Dunckerley to whose masonic zeal and personal influence the lodge undoubtedly owes its existence. As is usually the case with old lodges the earliest minute book commences with the laws and regulations signed by the members, and headed as follows:—

"**Bye Laws and Regulations** to be observed by the Lodge of Free and Accepted Masons No. 254 removed from on board his Majesty's ship Vanguard to the Queen of Bohemia's Head in Wych Street, in the parish of Saint Clement Dane in the County of Middlesex, made and agreed to the first day of May A.D., 1768. A. L. 5772."

Here follow fifteen Articles or Rules very carefully drawn up in legal phraseology, and clearly written, a briet summary of which will suffice for present purposes:—

"**First.**—That every member of this Lodge shall observe and keep all the Laws, Rules and Regulations laid down in the last Edition of the Book of Constitutions." . . .

"𝔖𝔢𝔠𝔬𝔫𝔡.—That this Lodge shall consist of one Master, two Wardens, one Treasurer, one Secretary, two Stewards, and a number of Brethren not exceeding thirty in the whole, . . . and that the 1st and 3rd Saturday evenings in the months of October, November, December, January, February, and March, and the 1st Saturday evenings in the months of April, May, June, July, August and September shall be deemed public L. [Lodge] nights." . . .

The annual subscription was two guineas, to be paid within three months after each general election of officers or the defaulting brother to be struck off the list (after having been written to by the Secretary) " and no longer deemed a member or admitted as such " . . .

"𝔗𝔥𝔦𝔯𝔡.—That a Master shall be elected out of those who are of the exalted Degree of Master Masons, by Ballott, on the first Lodge night in January, annually, who immediately after his Election shall be invested with the Master's Jewell by the then late Master, and installed, . . . and upon every Election and in every Nomination, Regard shall be had to the Qualifications of the Members only and not to Seniority or place." . . .

Every Master, who had not filled the office before in that lodge, to pay for a bottle of claret "to entertain the Brethren," every Warden or Treasurer a bottle of port, and any officer declining or refusing to accept an office to which he had been elected or appointed was fined 10s. 6d., but was not compelled to serve more than two successive years, "if there be any other member of the lodge duly qualified." Every officer who failed to attend in his place at or before 8 o'clock was fined one shilling.

" Nor shall any profane, immodest, political, or religious Discourses, or Wagers, or any eating, drinking, or smoaking be permitted in the lodge."

The initiation fee was three guineas, the joining fee one guinea, and the visitor's fee 5s.

" **Fifteenth.**—That every member of this Lodge shall subscribe these Laws."

" I do agree and promise to obey, fulfil and keep all the foregoing Laws, Rules and Orders, and all such as shall hereafter be made in this Lodge agreeable to the 13th Article.

" (Signed)   Thos. Dunckerley, Somerset House.

William Guest, near Half-moon-Street, Piccadilly.

Jno. Rigge, Inner Temple.

Roger Simpkinson, Fleet Street.

Geo. Garrick, Somerset House.

William Latimer, Somerset House.

Samuel Hooper, Strand.

Jas. Skene, Cursitor Street.

*Jas. Urquhart, Cursitor Street.

†Thos. Viguers, Strand, woollen draper."

The first seven of these names represent the total membership of the lodge at the time of its resuscitation in London, Bro. Skene being a visitor on the 5th of November, 1768, from Calcutta; he joined the lodge January, 7th, 1769. The leaf which probably contained the minutes of the first meeting is unfortunately missing, but the names of the brethren who attended are recorded on the opposite folio, viz. :—

" Br. Dunkerley, R.W.M.

„   Rigge, S.W.

„   Hooper, J. W.

---

* Initiated and passed to the second degree 16th December, 1768. H. S.

† Joined the Lodge 16th December, 1768.   H. S

"Br. GARRICK, Treasurer.

   „ LATIMER, Secretary.

   „ GUEST.

   „ SIMPKINSON."

The next two meetings were presided over by Br. Guest as Deputy Master, but no business was transacted, and the meetings which should have been held in August, September and October were omitted because " the majority of the Brethren being out of town, those who attended could not proceed to Business."

On the 5th of November, Dunckerley was in the chair, and "proposed Mr. Alexander Maxton, of the Royal Navy, to be made a Mason in this Lodge." * He was initiated, passed, and raised at a lodge of emergency on the 10th of November (having to go to Scotland before the next lodge night), Dunckerley presiding.

January 7th, 1769, Bro. Rigge was elected master and installed by Dunckerley, who was present as P.M. on 4th of February and the 4th of March. At this meeting, " The Brethren present were unanimously of opinion that the Company would be better entertained with a few promiscuous songs from the Brothers than by any lecture or further proceedings in masonry, wherefore the Lodge was closed without such Lecture."

During the next three years the lodge appears to have been at a very low ebb, and was frequently not opened on the stated nights for want of members. Meanwhile Dunckerley had resigned, although there is no record of his resignation in the minutes, the only intimation of that fact being the word " declined " written against his name at the end of the By-Laws. On the 13th of December, 1771, he

---

* This gentleman was on board the Prince as a supernumerary at the time Dunckerley was gunner of that ship. He joined the Guadaloupe as an A.B., but was promoted during the cruise to the rank of Master's Mate. H. S.

was present as a visitor, when it was unanimously agreed to remove the lodge to the London Coffee House, Ludgate Hill. The lodge accordingly held its next meeting at this house on the 20th of the same month, Dunckerley again attending as a visitor. On this occasion he was "requested to become a Member of this Lodge in order to take upon himself the charge of Master, to which he, having given his consent, the proposition for that purpose was made and seconded." He was elected and installed at the next meeting, January 3rd, 1772, and presided as Master at the following sixteen consecutive meetings.

From the time of his resuming the chair the prospects of the lodge improved materially, it is not therefore surprising that on the next election night it should have been "proposed by Bro^r Simpkinson and seconded by Bro^r Tomlinson that Bro^r Dunckerley do take upon himself the Office of Master of this Lodge for the year ensuing."

"Proposed by Bro^r Dunckerley, that Brother Simpkinson do take upon himself the Office of Master of this Lodge for the year ensuing, but the proposal was not seconded."

At a Lodge of Emergency on the 5th of February, 1772,
"Bro. Dunckerley, R.W.M.

  „ Taylor (Past Grand Warden) Senr. Warden.

  „ Heseltine (Grand Secretary) Junr. Warden.

"The R.W.Master proposed the following Gentlemen to be made Masons, viz., Joseph Hamer, Esq., Mark Dyer, Esq., William Ryan, Esq., and John Greathead, Esq."

These gentleman were forthwith elected, initiated, and passed to the second degree.

On the 20th of March following, the R.W.M. proposed several alterations in the Laws, one being, "That every Mason appointed an Officer in this Lodge, pay a Bottle of Claret instead of Port." *

---

* Old Port was then 2s. 6d. per bottle, Claret, 5s.   H. S.

The last transaction recorded at this meeting is rather curious—"Bro^r Hooper was fined a Bottle of Port for a Ludicrous Expression ; a Lecture was given." This seems very severe, but whether the "Ludicrous Expression" had reference in any way to the "Lecture" or whether the "Lecture" was the outcome of the "Ludicrous Expression" we can only conjecture. We may, however, be pretty sure that the "fine" was satisfactorily disposed of.

On the 3rd of December, 1773, James Heseltine, Grand Secretary, and several other Grand Officers were elected members of the Lodge on the proposition of the R.W. Master.

January 7th, 1774, being the night for the election of officers, "Bro^r Heseltine was unanimously elected Master, and duly installed." Among the visitors on this occasion were the two Grand Wardens, and Bro. Thomas Parker, Prov. Grand Master for Surrey.

On the 21st of the same month it was "Proposed and unanimously agreed to, that Brother Dunckerley be admitted an honorary Member of this Lodge." On the 2nd of December, Bro. Rowland Holt, Deputy Grand Master, was a visitor.

About this period Dunckerley removed from Somerset House to Hampton Court Palace, and his attendances became less regular, indeed, his name does not appear in the book for several years. Meanwhile, under the able guidance of Heseltine, the lodge continued to prosper, and was frequently visited by Grand Officers and other distinguished brethren, many of whom ultimately became members of it.

The following extracts may possibly be of some little interest to the members of the two lodges mentioned, as they clearly indicate the kindly feeling which then existed between the brethren.

April 6th, 1779, " Proposed by Br. Rowley and seconded by Br. Pritchard, that Capt. Wm. Stukeley, of the Lincolnshire Regiment, having been made a Mason by Br. Dunckerley, the FATHER of this Lodge, be admitted a member on the same footing as if made herein or in the Somerset House Lodge. The same was agreed to unanimously."

March 6th, 1781.—"A very friendly and social intercourse having long subsisted between this and the Somerset House Lodge, calling each other sister lodges and reciprocally visiting without fee, a motion was made by Bro. Const, and seconded by several Brethren, that that part of the law of this lodge (No. 10) respecting the admission fine of Two guineas, be dispensed with when any Brother who is a subscriber to the Somerset House Lodge shall become a member of this—agreed to unanimously."

The minutes of April 16th, 1782, contain the following: "Bro. Dunckerley, father and founder of this lodge, which was first instituted at his expense on board His Majesty's ship the Vanguard, in the last war, removed by him on board the Guadaloupe, from thence to the Queen of Bohemia's Head, Wych Street, since to the London Coffee House, most obligingly requested the lodge to accept of the constitution, This favour was accepted of by the Master and Brethren. and the unanimous thanks of the lodge were voted to Bro. Dunckerley for this polite compliment."

There seems to be a slight mistake here with reference to the lodge having been removed from the Vanguard to the Guadaloupe. The account does not agree with the heading to the Bye-Laws, and it is opposed to the evidence contained in the Grand Lodge Records.

According to the latter, it was the lodge constituted on board the Prince, in 1762, that was subsequently held on board the Guadaloupe, and this, as will hereafter be seen, is borne out by the records of the Somerset House Lodge. It is not improbable that Dunckerley in his speech—for he was present at this meeting—made some allusion to his having held a lodge on board the Guadaloupe, and the Secretary in writing up his minutes from memory or from notes, introduced the two ships instead of one, and as Dunckerley was not present when the minutes were confirmed, the error was allowed to pass unchallenged. Although the London Lodge had its occasional periods of depression—as has been the case with all old lodges—its career during the closing years of the eighteenth century, judging from its records, was marked by general prosperity and increasing importance. For many years it enjoyed the proud distinction of being one of the eight or nine "red apron" lodges having the privilege of sending a steward to the Grand Festival, and from one or the other of which the Grand Officers were invariably selected. It was one of the earliest subscribers to the Hall Fund, in conformity with the following resolution.—

"Grand Lodge, Extraordinary, June 21st, 1779.

"That a subscription be entered into of a sum not less than £25 each to be lent to the society without interest, upon an engagement of the Grand Lodge to pay off the debt in equal proportion, and at such times as the Hall Fund will admit; but that the Grand Lodge shall be obliged to make a dividend whenever the cash in hand will amount to £20 *per cent.* upon the money advanced. That as a mark of distinction for the service thus rendered, by relieving the society from the annual payment of a large sum for interest upon the present debt, each subscriber shall be complimented with a medal, of such form and value as the Grand Lodge determine, with a motto suitable to the occasion; and that the names of the subscribers shall be enrolled in the books of the Grand Lodge, as an honourable testimony of their services; and if any lodge should subscribe to this plan, a like medal shall be presented, to be ever after worn by the master for the time being."

The medal referred to is still in the possession of the lodge, which was one of the first to change the loan into a gift, for on the 6th of March, 1787, we find the following entry:

"A motion was made by Bro' Bottomley, and met with the general approbation of all the Brethren present, that this lodge do relinquish its claim on the Grand Lodge for a debt of £25, which was lent 28th February, 1782. Ordered that the R.W.M., Bro' Prichard, do attend on the next Quarterly Communication to present the same to the public fund of Masons."

The printed report of a Quarterly Communication, held on the 4th of April, 1787, at which Dunckerley and several of his friends were present, contains the announcement "That the following Brethren and Lodges declared their intention of giving up the whole of their subscription to the Hall Loan, and requested the Society to accept of the same, viz. :—

Sir Herbert Mackworth, Bart., P.S.G.W., and P.G.M., for South Wales.

Thomas Dunckerley, Esq., P.S G.W., and P.G.M., for Dorset, Essex, &c.

George Hesse, Esq. } P.J.G.W.
James Meyrick, Esq. }

Stephen Lushington, Esq

Robert Ingram, Esq.

The Stewards' Lodge.

No. 23, St. Alban's Lodge, Thatched House Tavern.

  „ 114, Rose and Crown, Crown Street, Westminster.

  „ 162, London Lodge, London Coffee House.

  „ 474, Harmonic Lodge, Hampton Court.

(The last named was another of Dunckerley's creations of which more hereafter.)

"It was then RESOLVED UNANIMOUSLY That the Thanks of the Grand Lodge be given to the above named Brethren and Lodges for the liberal and generous present of their subscriptions."

At the preceding Grand Lodge, on the 7th of February, a similar presentation had been announced, which included the names of several of Dunckerley's intimate friends, and also the two other lodges which he had assisted in forming and of which he was an honorary member, viz., the Somerset House, No. 2, and the lodge of Friendship, No. 3. Indeed, the lodges with which he was connected were undoubtedly by far the most liberal in England with their contributions to the General Charity and the Hall Fund. To the former, the London Lodge contributed from 1768 to the end of 1813, £74. 6s., and to the latter during the same period, £124. 19s. 6d. Bearing in mind the paucity of members from which the lodge had occasionally suffered, these figures speak well for the genuine masonic feeling by which the brethren were actuated, although they by no means represent the full amount of their contributions, for many of them had made liberal donations to the Hall Fund independently of the lodge subscriptions. The lodge continued to meet at the "London Coffee House" (whence its name is probably derived) until 1812, when it was removed to the "Queen's Arms Tavern," in Cheapside. It was afterwards held at the "Freemasons' Tavern," in Great Queen Street. In 1871 the lodge again migrated citywards, and for the second time took up its quarters in a ship; but one of quite a different character to the old Vanguard, she being more noted for hard knocks than for hospitality. For the last twenty years the home of the London Lodge has been the well-known "Ship and Turtle," in Leadenhall Street, a house dear to all who can appreciate a good dinner, and justly celebrated for the excellence of its *cuisine*, as well as for the artistic beauty and noble proportions of its various public rooms.

THE ROYAL SOMERSET HOUSE AND INVERNESS LODGE, No. 4.

The following brief sketch of this lodge forms an introduction to a code of thirteen bye-laws printed in 1783, when doubtless some of its members had actual knowledge of its early history, and the peculiar circumstances under which it bade farewell to a roving life and settled on shore.

" BYE-LAWS for the Regulation of the LODGE,

No. 2, distinguished by the Title of the

SOMERSET-HOUSE LODGE,

Of the Most Ancient and Honourable Society of FREE AND ACCEPTED MASONS, being the united lodges of the OLD HORN LODGE, No. 2, and the SOMERSET-HOUSE LODGE, No. 279; the former constituted Time immemorial, and the latter on the 22d day of May, A.L. 5766, A.D. 1762, and was first held on board His Majesty's ship PRINCE; from thence removed on board His Majesty's ship GUADALOUPE; afterwards to SOMERSET-HOUSE; then held at the KING'S-ARMS Tavern, in *New Bond-street;* afterwards at the TURK'S-HEAD in *Gerrard-street;* where the Union of the two lodges took place the 10th day of *January,* 1774; then held at ADELPHI TAVERN in the *Strand;* and now held at FREE-MASONS' TAVERN, *Great Queen-street, Lincoln's Inn Fields.*"

Want of space precludes my reproducing these bye-laws in full, they contain nothing, however, of a special character, the most striking features being their brevity and simplicity; the whole of the matter occupying less than three sides of a sheet of foolscap.

The initiation fee was five guineas, the joining fee two guineas, exclusive of the registration fee; and the annual subscription two guineas.

The regular meetings were held " on the second and fourth Mondays in January, February, and March, the second Mondays in April and May, the fourth Mondays in October and November, and the second and fourth Mondays in

December, in each year, at seven o'clock in the evening, precisely."

The visiting fee for Honorary Members was four shillings; for other brethren, when introduced by a member, five shillings; but any brother "casually visiting this lodge without such introduction shall pay half-a-guinea for every such visit, except present and past Grand Officers, Members of the Stewards' Lodge, or Foreign Brethren, who out of respect to their Situation are to be exempt from paying any visiting fee."

The 13th and last bye-law is rather curious, "That the Master or Mistress of any Tavern or other House where this Lodge may be held, shall subscribe his or her name to an Inventory of the Furniture and other Property belonging to the Lodge, in his or her Custody, thereby declaring the Property thereof to be in the Treasurer of the Lodge for the Time being."

"The above Bye-Laws having been originally framed and agreed to the 25th November, 1776, are now revised, corrected, and confirmed, at a lodge held the 24th November, 1783"

A complete history of the three celebrated lodges now represented by the Royal Somerset House and Inverness Lodge, No. 4, would, no doubt, be most interesting, but would far exceed the limits of the present volume. I must, therefore, content myself with briefly noticing two of them, reserving my remarks more particularly for the one which Dunckerley established at sea, and subsequently re-established on shore.

This lodge is undoubtedly indebted to him for its distinctive name, as well as for the very prominent position which for a long period it has occupied in the annals of English Freemasonry.

According to the present enumeration it should have been first on the list of Dunckerley's lodges, but I have placed it third, conformably with his connection with it, and the date of its constitution, for it will be remembered that his "Mother Lodge" was constituted about 1724; the lodge on board the Vanguard—afterwards the London Lodge— in 1760, and that on board the Prince—afterwards the Somerset House Lodge—in 1762.

According to Dr. Anderson, "the father of Masonic historians," the lodge referred to as the "Old Horn Lodge," was one of the four lodges that assisted in organizing the Grand Lodge of England in 1717.

At this time it was held at the "*Rummer and Grapes Tavern, in Channel-Row, Westminster,*" but about 1723 it was removed to the *Horn Tavern, Westminster.*

There are no means of ascertaining its actual age, but as its existence was anterior to the formation of the Grand Lodge, it has always been described as "Constituted Time Immemorial," which simply means that it was never constituted at all, according to the present acceptation of the term. Its first appearance in the Grand Lodge Records is in the 1723 MS. list of lodges, "with the names of the Masters, Wardens and Members of each lodge." At this time it was probably the most numerous, as well as the most aristocratic lodge in the whole craft.

The name of the Duke of Richmond Grand Master in 1724, heads the list as Master of the lodge, followed by that of Mr. George Payne, Past Grand Master, as Deputy Master, and seventy other brethren of high rank, including Lord Paisley, Grand Master in 1725; the Duke of Queensborough, Sir Richard Manningham, Lord Waldegrave, Sir Adolphus Oughton; and quite a formidable array of Honourables, Colonels, etc, etc. In short the lodge seems to have been composed of the very *élite* of the fraternity. The list of members returned in 1725 included most of those in the previous list, with several additional names of a similar character.

On the 24th of June, 1723, the first Grand Secretary was appointed, in the person of "William Cowper, Esq., a Brother of the Horn Lodge at Westminster." He filled the office of Deputy Grand Master in 1726.

The next return of members of the various lodges took place about 1730, but as registration was not then compulsory, there are a great many blanks in the Register, and unfortunately the "Horn Tavern in Westminster" is one of them; but as the Grand Secretary left two folios with the above heading, on which to enter the names whenever they should come to hand, the natural inference is that the lodge had considerably increased in numbers since the last registration.

The first contributions to the General Charity (now the Fund of Benevolence) were collected in Grand Lodge on the 25th of November, 1729, and amounted to £9. 8s. 6d. from four lodges. "The rest of the Lodges excused themselves for their Default and promised to bring in their Charity on St John's Day."

"The Deputy Grand Master, at the Desire of his Grace the Duke of Richmond, Master of the Horn Lodge, acquainted the Brethren that he was but lately come from France, and by reason of most of the Members of his Lodge were out of Town, being for the most part persons of Quality and Members of Parliament, the General Charity had not yet been proposed. But that his Grace had it much at Heart, and would recommend it in the strongest Terms at their first meeting."

We may fairly assume that "his Grace" fulfilled his promise, for the contributions received at the next Grand Lodge amounted to £41. 0s. 6d. from seventeen lodges, the "Horn Tavern in Westminster" heading the list with £22. 2s.

At a Grand Lodge held on the 21st of April, 1730, the collection amounted to £31. 2s., £15 of which came from the "Horn Lodge"

On the 13th of December, 1733, "Bro^r· Edwards, Warden of the Horn Lodge informed the Grand Lodge that our Rt. Worshipful Brother, Capt. Ralph Far-Winter, Provincial Grand Master of East India, &c., had sent over a Chest of Arack for the use of the Grand Lodge, and Ten Guineas to the General Charity, being the Contribution of our Brethren in East India."

"The Healths of Br. Winter and the Brethren in East India were drank with Thanks for their handsome Present."

At a subsequent meeting, the Earl of Crawfurd, Grand Master, in the Chair. "His Lordship was pleased to order a large Quantity of Rack that was made a present of from Bengall to be made into Puuch and distributed among the Brethren."*

"All Business being over the Grand Lodge was closed with an uncommon appearance of Harmony."

The Grand Lodge Records indicate a falling off in the attendances, as well as in the contributions, from the "Horn" from about 1733, although in both respects it compares favourably with many other lodges of that period. Various reasons may be assigned for the decline of the lodge. The members may have let in a "black sheep" who made things uncomfortable all round. The newly formed Stewards Lodge and several other aristocratic lodges constituted about this time may have absorbed the best of the old members. Whatever the cause, there is no doubt that this fine old lodge declined rapidly, and for several years was practically non-existent.

On the 21st of November, 1745, the "Horn at Westminster" and seven other lodges were summoned "to attend at the next Quarterly Communication to answer for their not attending the Grand Master at the General Meetings of the Society for a considerable time past." Four of the

---

* "Why don't they do it now?" H. S.

lodges summoned were erased at the next meeting, but the
" Horn " was allowed a year's grace, although it does not
appear to have responded to the summons. Probably the
good work done in the past was not forgotten, or some of
its former members among the Grand Officers may have
induced the Grand Lodge to take a lenient view of its
recent omissions. However, no advantage appears to have
been taken of this respite, and on the 3rd of April, 1747, it
was " Ordered that the Lodge No. 2, at the Horn at Westminster, not attending according to the Order of the last Q C.
be erased out of the Book of Lodges." No further mention
of the lodge occurs until the 4th of September, 1751, when
" Bro^r. Lediard informed the Brethren that the Right
Worshipful Bro^1 Payne, L.G.M., and several other members of the Lodge lately held at the Horn, Palace Yard,
Westminster, had been very successful in their endeavours
to revive the said Lodge, and that they were ready to pay 2
Gs. to the use of the Grand Charity, and therefore moved,
that out of respect to Bro. Payne and the several other
L.G.M.* who were members thereof, the said Lodge
might be restored and have its former Rank and place
in the List of Lodges, which was ordered accordingly."
Having been thus rescued from oblivion, the old lodge
seems to have lived a life of comparative mediocrity until
it was united with the young and vigorous Somerset House
Lodge, No. 219, with the indefatigable Dunckerley at its
head ; the latter giving its name in exchange for the old
number and place on the Register ; an arrangement no
doubt satisfactory to all concerned.

The records of the " Old Horn Lodge " have probably long
since gone the way of many other records, at any rate they
are not now available ; but judging from the official register
of members and payments, the lodge must have been in a

---

* Late Grand Masters.   H. S.

very weakly condition for some years prior to the amalgamation, and there is every probability that Dunckerley was well aware of that fact The Grand Secretary, Heseltine, was his intimate friend, and in the person of William White, another of his friends, who was initiated in this old Lodge in 1770, and succeeded Heseltine as Grand Secretary, he no doubt found an able coadjutor in bringing the lodges together.

The Grand Lodge Register shows the relative strength of the two lodges at the time they were united. The " Old Horn Lodge" is represented by fifteen members only, and, with the exception of White, there is not one among them of any masonic importance

On the part of the Somerset House Lodge seventy-two names are recorded under the heading of " A member prior to 1768 ; " no register fee being chargeable for those who joined or were initiated previous to that year. From 1768 to the end of 1773, forty-six additional names were placed on the Register, which shows a proportionate increase year by year until it greatly exceeded most of the other lodges in the number of its members, many of whom were persons of the highest standing, both socially and masonically.

A few of their names will suffice to indicate the character of the whole. Dunckerley of course heads the list, as being the oldest member. He is followed by James Galloway, J.G. Warden in 1781 ; James Heseltine, Grand Secretary, afterwards S.G.W , and subsequently Grand Treasurer ; Rowland Berkeley, Grand Treasurer ; Rowland Holt, D.G.M., 1775-86 ; Hon. Charles Dillon, D.G.M , 1768-74 ; the Duke of Beaufort, Grand Master, 1767-71 ; and the Duke of Buccleugh. Lords Wenman, Foley, Gormanstone, Tyrawley, and Effingham (Acting Grand Master), Sir Joseph Banks, Admiral Sir Peter Parker, D.G.M., 1787-1811 , James Neild, the philanthropic visitor of prisons, and many other celebrities, both titled and untitled, too numerous to mention. In short, I may safely say that the list of members includes nearly all the earnest workers and "leading lights" in English Masonry from about 1768 to 1800, although many of them only subscribed to the lodge for a few years.

As the oldest minute-book now in the possession of the lodge extends no earlier than 1783, I must fall back on the official records to prove the connection between the lodge constituted on board the Prince and the one after-wards held at Somerset House. I have already stated that the last payment while it met on board ship was made in April, 1764, and that shortly afterwards Dunckerley was in financial difficulties, also in ill-health, and actually depen-dent on charity. According to his story, he landed in England from his Mediterranean trip in November 1765, and subsequently removed his family to Somerset House.

A meeting of the Committee of Charity was held " at the Horn in Fleet Street, January 22nd, 1766," which was attended by the Masters of 38 lodges, whose names are not given, but the names of their lodges are, and the second lodge on the list is "Majesty's Ship Guadaloup." Now, as the Guadaloupe was at this time in the Mediterranean, a reasonable inference would be that Dunckerley himself attended as Master. A week later (January 29th) a Quar-terly Communication was held at the "Crown and Anchor" in the Strand, which was attended by two members of a lodge held in a " Private Room, Somerset-House," the same lodge being credited with a guinea to the General Charity. A like amount was received on the 9th of April, and two guineas on the 17th of October ; on this occasion the lodge was repre-sented by the Master and Wardens. An engraved official list of lodges for 1766—the property of the then Grand Secretary—contains a marginal note opposite No. 279 (the Guadaloupe Lodge), " A Private Room, Somerset - house, Strand," and in a similar list for 1767, No. 279 is " Sommer-set-House Lodge, at yͤ King's Arms, New Bond Street."

It is evident, therefore, that Dunckerley must have set about re-organizing the lodge shortly after he had taken up his residence in London. His efforts in this direction were probably so warmly seconded by some of the eminent brethren previously mentioned, that it soon became necessary to seek for more commodious quarters, for in the Grand Treasurer's list of receipts from the various lodges, under date 28th of January, 1767, the "Somerset-House Lodge, King Arms, Bond Street" is credited with £3. 3s. to the General Charity, so that the removal probably took place at the latter end of 1766.

Without entering into further details, I may state that from this period the progress of the lodge is marked by the most regular and liberal contributions to the various funds in connection with the Grand Lodge. In this respect it was only second to one lodge in the whole Craft This was a lodge of a similar character, and composed chiefly of the same members, viz., the Lodge of Friendship No. 3, the present No. 6 Between these two distinguished lodges a spirit of emulation or friendly rivalry seems to have existed for many years. From 1766 to the end of 1813 the Somerset House Lodge contributed, in fees and donations to the Grand Lodge for the General Charity and for building purposes, upwards of £1,140, exclusive of thirty guineas to the fund for presenting a jewel to the Earl of Moira on his departure to India, and several liberal donations to the Girls' School; while during the same period the Lodge of Friendship is credited with upwards of £1,190. It is only fair to mention that although these sums are the highest on record, they are not greatly in advance of the contributions of several other well-known metropolitan lodges, which did their utmost to assist in establishing the Society on a firm and respectable basis by enabling it to acquire "a local habitation" in addition to its time-honoured name.

In its prosperous days the "Horn Lodge" had been one

of the earliest lodges to send a steward to the Grand Festival How long it retained this privilege it is impossible to say, but it probably lapsed in consequence of the decline of the lodge after 1740. Nor can we ascertain whether it regained this distinction as well as its former place on the roll in 1751. The absence of the early records of the Somerset House Lodge leaves us somewhat in doubt as to whether it merely inherited the "red apron" on its union with the older lodge, or whether it had been in possession of that privilege some years earlier. Unfortunately from about 1730 to 1775 we are left almost in the dark as to the "red apron lodges," but in the last named year we find the Somerset House Lodge in the enjoyment of the unique distinction of having *three* red aprons at its disposal, whilst its sister lodge, the "Friendship" had but two, as was also the case with another aristocratic lodge (the Royal Lodge), which subsequently fell into abeyance and was erased from the list. So far as I have been able to learn these three were the only lodges that had the privilege of being represented by more than one Grand Steward at the same time. A probable reason for the "Somerset House" having one more than the others, is that it may have had two on its revival in 1766, when as previously noticed, it was joined by the upper class in such large numbers, and distinguished itself by the liberality of its donations. Also that the "Old Horn Lodge" had preserved its privilege down to 1774, when the two were amalgamated, thus conferring a third red apron on the united lodges.

Thanks to the courtesy of the Secretary, Bro. Frederick West, Past Grand Deacon, I have been permitted to inspect the oldest minute book now in the possession of the lodge, which commences with a statement of its financial position on the 8th of January, 1783, being a Committee Meeting for auditing the accounts. The result shows that the lodge was indebted to the Treasurer to the extent of "Twenty-five

Pounds and four pence, exclusive of the Expences of this Night" which amounted to £2. 3s. 6d. At first sight this seems an unsatisfactory state of things but the next regular meeting January 13th being subscription night, places the balance on the other side, showing £19. 2s. 2d. to the good after all expenses were paid.

This was also Installation night and from the fact of the "minutes of the last lodge" having been "read and confirmed," it is evident that the earlier records had not then been lost sight of. The business at this meeting was the appointment of officers, by Bro. Heseltine who had been re-elected Master at the "preceding Lodge," the initiating and passing to the second degree of Mr. Charles Stafford Smythe, and balloting for three candidates, who were "unanimously approved of."

Dunckerley, it seems, had resigned his membership; for the first time his name appears in the book is on the 12th of May following, when it is placed with the names of the visiting brethren.

At this meeting "Henry Harford Esq. was Initiated into the first Degree of Masonry, and, by Dispensation from his Royal Highness the Duke of Cumberland, Grand Master, signified to the Lodge, by the Grand Secretary, was passed to the Second Degree, and raised to the Degree of Master Mason, on account of his intending in a short time to go to Maryland." This gentleman was shortly afterwards appointed Provincial Grand Master for Maryland.

Dunckerley's next visit to the lodge was on the 27th of February, 1786, when his name appears in the list of members present but as there is no record of his having rejoined the lodge in the interval I am of opinion that he was really an honorary member, as at this time he was much occupied in travelling about the country and looking after his numerous lodges and chapters. His last appearance in the lodge was on the 8th of February, 1790.

On the 12th of February, 1787 "It was moved by the S.W. and seconded by the J.W. that the £25 subscribed by this Lodge towards discharging the Debts of the Hall be presented to the Grand Lodge for the Augmentation of the Hall Fund, which was unanimously agreed to." The old "Freemasons' Tavern" being in a ruinous condition the Grand Lodge appealed to the Craft for assistance to rebuild it. Several of the London lodges responded with more or less liberality but the Somerset House Lodge came nobly to the front on the 14th April, 1788 with a gift of one hundred guineas, being the largest amount given by any lodge for that purpose; the Britannic Lodge (present No. 33) coming next with a donation of fifty guineas. During the rebuilding of the Tavern the lodge was held at the "Shakespear Tavern," Covent Garden, and subsequently at the " Crown and Anchor," in the Strand. On the completion of the building operations it returned to its old quarters in February 1790, and from that time to the present its meetings have been held on the Grand Lodge premises. The first meeting held at the "Shakespear" was on the 8th of December 1788; when " Mr. John Guichard an Ancient Mason was proposed to be re-made under the Constitution of England, and to become an Honorary Member of this Lodge on account of his Musical abilities, which was duly seconded and referred to a Ballot next lodge night."

On the 28th of December following, " Brother Guichard, an Ancient Mason, received the several obligations according to the Forms of the Grand Lodge of England, a Masters' Lodge being opened in due Form for that purpose "

The records of this celebrated lodge are full of interest, and are well worthy of reproduction in their entirety ; but as they have little or no reference to the subject of these memoirs, I am reluctantly compelled to restrict myself to the selection of a very few items of more or less historical import, which will serve to confirm my estimate of the character of the lodge at this period.

On the 8th of November, 1790, we meet with an old friend (John Maclean), who played rather an important part in the formation of the Grand Chapter in 1766. of which he is styled " Father and Promoter." A vote of thanks was given him, together with a " Gold Plate " " for his Instructions and careful Attendance." The " Gold Plate " was probably what is now known as a R.A. jewel of the old pattern. These jewels or " Plates" appear to have been designed with a view of being plainly visible to the naked eye at the farthest possible distance On the date before mentioned, " the R.W. Master informed the Lodge that he had received a Petition from Br. Maclean, formerly a member of this Lodge, soliciting their recommendation to the Grand Lodge for relief; but on examination, he found that he had a few years since been relieved, on the recommendation of another Lodge, to the full extent of what is ever given from the Fund of Charity, and, therefore, such recommendation would be informal. The R.W. therefore proposed, if it met with the approbation of the Brethren, that on account of the great age and infirmities of Br. Maclean, he be relieved from the Fund of this Lodge with five guineas, and that it be paid him at 5s. a week towards his support, which proposition was unanimously assented to, and Br. Cuppage was desired to pay it him weekly."

John Maclean is said to have been made a mason in the year 1740, but in what lodge has not yet been ascertained. His name is not in the list of members of the Somerset House Lodge in the Grand Lodge Register; if, therefore, he ever belonged to it, it could only have been for a very short time, or his name would have been returned with the names of those who were members in 1768. It is not unlikely that he had been a member of the Horn Lodge, and had left it previous to its union with the Somerset House Lodge. At all events, it is certain he was held in great respect by the brethren with whom he had been associated in his more prosperous days.

The 27th of December, 1790, being election night, was largely attended by members as well as visitors, five of the latter hailing from the London Lodge. On this occasion there seems to have been some little opposition to Br. Heseltine, who had been *unanimously* re-elected to the Master's Chair for many years, certainly ever since 1782. At this meeting, however, he is stated to have been elected " by a considerable majority."

The next meeting, the 10th of January, was Installation night, when 43 members and eight visitors were present. The ordinary business having been disposed of, " A motion was made, seconded and agreed to. That no visitors be admitted into the Lodge during the hours of Business on the Night prescribed by the Bye-Laws for the Election of a Master, nor the Night succeeding, unless such visitor shall chuse to pay Two Guineas as his Visiting Fee."

This reads as though something unpleasant had occurred with reference to the visitors on one or both of the meetings mentioned. At this period the lodge was celebrated for the excellence of its vocal entertainments, having a large number of professional brethren among its members.

" Jan. 2, 1792. A Letter was received from the Secretary of the London Lodge enclosing a Resolution of the said Lodge on the 6th of December last, an Extract whereof is as follows :—

" 'Resolved that this Lodge (anxious to preserve that honour and liberality by which it has been its constant aim ever to be distinguished) do admit the members of the Somerset-House Lodge to visit the London Lodge without Fee, notwithstanding the present Custom of the Somerset-House towards the members of the London Lodge.'

" Whereupon it was Resolved that the Secretary do inform the R. W M. and Brethren of the London Lodge that their Letter containing the above Resolution was this night communicated to the Brethren in open Lodge, and that thereupon the Thanks of the Somerset-House Lodge were voted."

Notwithstanding the large sums given from the funds of the lodge, the Audit Meeting for 1792 showed a balance in the Treasurer's hands of £288. 14s. 4d. Br. Heseltine continued in the Chair till the end of 1793, when he declined further service. In June, 1794, a silver cup, value £21. 3s. was presented to him by the lodge.

8th of April 1793. ' John Tubbs, Esq., of Stephen's Green, Dublin (an Ancient Mason), was proposed, and duly seconded, to be initiated into the Mysteries of Masonry."

25th of May 1795. "Bro. Blackstone informed the Brethren that the Jacob's Ladder Lodge (lately held at the *New London Tavern*, Cheapside), and which Lodge had hitherto enjoyed the honour of a Red Apron by sending a Steward to attend the Grand Master at the Annual Grand Feast, had recently forfeited that honour by their omission to send a Steward at the last Grand Feast. In consequence of which the Board of Stewards (of which Br. Stafford Baxter, a member of this lodge, was President) had been pleased to nominate him to fill up the vacancy ; and having served the Office, he had nominated Br. Mackintosh, the Secretary of this Lodge, as his successor."

From the time these minutes begin (1783) the lodge had only two red aprons at its disposal, this incident placed it again in possession of a third, which privilege it retained until the Union (1813) since which event, only one Grand Steward has been nominated annually from each of the red apron lodges.

Heseltine's successor in the Chair, James Galloway, was one of his intimate friends, who had for many years filled the office of Senior Warden, and being a Past Master of the lodge, as far back as 1767, he invariably presided as Master in Heseltine's absence. He was on most friendly terms with Dunckerley, with whom he was associated in several other lodges.

I regret that space will not admit of my doing full justice to the merits of this truly eminent brother; suffice it to say, that, for a period of forty years, he was foremost in every good work appertaining to Masonry.

The following incident bespeaks his character as a Mason and a Gentleman. The 22nd of December, 1794, "being Election Night; the Brethren proceeded to Ballot in the accustomed manner for the choice of a Master for the ensuing year, when on casting up the votes there appeared to be an equal number for Br. Galloway, the R.W. Master now in the Chair, and for Br. Lionel Darell, Esq. On which the R.W. Master gave the casting vote for Br. Darell, who was thereupon declared to be duly elected Master for the ensuing year."

Bro. Darell was installed on the 12th of January, 1795. At this meeting "A Letter from the Grand Secretary was read, stating that the Grand Lodge having occasion to borrow £900 on the Credit of the Society towards discharging Two Loans of £500 each. £500 in part thereof had been already advanced, and requesting to know whether the Lodge, or any of the Brethren were inclined to lend any part of the remaining £400 still wanting to complete the said Loan ,whereupon The R.W. Master declared that he would lend the Grand Lodge the £400 wanting and requested the Secretary to inform the Grand Treasurer thereof." "Lionel Darell Esq., Dean St., Soho" is registered as having joined the lodge on the 12th of May, 1777. He was created a Baronet during the first year of his mastership (1795), and seems to have been held in great esteem by the brethren, who re-elected him to the Master's chair annually, during the remainder of his life. On the 23rd of May, 1803, he attended the lodge for the last time. From his first installation, to this date, ninety-two meetings were held and at seventy-one of these he presided in person. He died in harness, October 30th, 1803. Sir Lionel Darell, M.P., for Heydon was chairman of the

Court of Directors of the East India Company, and Colonel of the first regiment of East India Volunteers. He was Grand Steward in 1784-5, Junior Grand Warden in 1785-6, and a subscriber to the Hall Loan in 1783. In January, 1784, he joined the Lodge of Friendship No. 3 (present No. 6), but resigned in 1786, "his attendance on Parliament and the India Board preventing his attendance at the lodge." His loss was keenly felt by the members generally and is thus referred to in the records.

28th of Nov. 1803.

"It was with deep regret that the Brethren at this their first Meeting after the Summer Adjournment had to lament the serious loss the lodge in general and every individual Member had sustained by the recent death of that most truly respectable and beloved Brother and R W. Master, Sir Lionel Darell. And after deliberating on what manner they could best adopt to perpetuate his memory and to show the high sense they entertained of his unexampled care and unremitting attention for the welfare and prosperity of the lodge, Resolved Unanimously. That a Copy of the best Portrait in the possession of the Relations of our late revered Master be obtained and placed in the Lodge Room at their respective meetings, and that the Officers of the lodge, together with the Earl of Mount Norris and the Revd. Br. Coghlan be appointed a Committee to carry this Resolution into effect."

A portrait was accordingly painted, but from the following references to the subject it does not appear to have been deemed a good likeness.

27th of May 1805. "Br. Byfield observed to the lodge that Mr. Owen who had painted the portrait of Sir Lionel Darell had not been paid. After various remarks, Br. Ashton proposed that the consideration of it should be postponed to the next Meeting as many Members were absent who might have objections to make.

"The R.W.M. proposed, as Br. Byfield was so very

pressing, that a Special Committee be appointed and that the Assist. Secretary do summons the Officers for Thursday 30th Instant at 12 o'Clock to the Freemasons' Tavern. It was observed by some Members that the Portrait in question had been took from the Tavern. The head waiter was called in to inform the Lodge who had called for the portrait, he said a person had called in a Coach and brought a Note for it, but he did not inquire who he was nor did he know where it was took, neither had he the note that was brought for it "

At the subsequent Committee Meeting the Secretary stated "that the portrait had been called for by one of Mr. Owen's people by his orders, and at this present was at Mr. Owens' waiting for the R.W.M. calling there. The R.W M. having signified that he could point out to Mr. Owen some alterations which might give a more striking likeness.

"Br. Hunter observed that Mr. Owen ought to be paid for the painting notwithstanding so many objections had been thrown out against it. He aver'd that no painter could have done more justice to a picture than Mr Owen had done, from so imperfect a copy." The lodge ultimately paid the artist Twenty Guineas for the portrait, but I find no further reference to it in the minutes nor is it mentioned in the inventories of the lodge property taken in the years 1815, 1834, and 1840. It seems therefore, probable, that, as the likeness was not satisfactory, the brethren took no further steps in the matter but left it in the hands of the artist.

ROYAL INVERNESS LODGE.

The first Warrant granted after the Union in 1813, was for the Royal Inverness Lodge No. 648, so named after the second title of the Duke of Sussex, then Grand Master.*

---

* Earl of Inverness.

This lodge was consecrated at the Freemasons' Tavern, February 2nd, 1815, by the celebrated Dr. Hemming, Senior Grand Warden, and Master of the Lodge of Reconciliation, assisted by several other eminent Grand Officers, and supported by the Duke in person who performed the ceremony of Installation on the occasion. Judging by their names nearly all the founders of the lodge appear to have come from "over the border," although their subsequent conduct does not strike one as being remarkable for the prudence and frugality which we are taught to believe is characteristic of the "Canny Scot." The original members were seven, viz, James Hamilton, Simon McGillivray, D. McKinnon, Alexander Sinclair-Gordon, Alexander Grant, Andrew Robertson, and H. J. da Costa. After the lodge had been duly constituted, Messrs. Wm. Anderson, Alexander Lamb, Wm Munro, and Alexander Gray Davison, " Were proposed as candidates for the first degree, balloted for and approved ; and by especial command and dispensation of the M. W.G.M., in consideration of the peculiar circumstances of the case, were all initiated into the first degree of the Order."

This was a very fair start, although opposed to our present usages ; and it seems to have fostered a " vaulting ambition " which contributed largely to the rapid downfall of a lodge brought into existence under such distinguished auspices.

The second meeting of the lodge was on the 23rd of March, 1816, when the Bye-Laws were agreed to. The fee for Initiation was fixed at Twenty-five Guineas if the candidate became a member of the lodge, but this was reduced to ten guineas if he did not join. For a brother initiated in another lodge the joining fee was Twenty Guineas.

In view of the fact that there were several old and highly respectable lodges meeting in the metropolis at this period, whose fees were much lower although composed of brethren of a higher grade in the social scale, the adoption of these prohibitory fees appears little less than suicidal. The lodge, however, had for several years a fair accession of new members, but somehow the attendances were from the first very small in numbers, while owing to the large amount of arrears (the annual subscription was fixed at five guineas) the lodge was heavily in debt to the proprietors of the Tavern, and on October the 12th, 1820, five members only being present, a discussion took place on the advisability of dissolving the lodge and surrendering the Warrant.

The next meeting was held on the 24th of May, 1824, when several candidates were initiated, " and the revival and probable prosperity of the Lodge seemed to afford universal satisfaction." At this meeting it was determined to remove the lodge to the Argyle Rooms. This was very like going " out of the frying-pan into the fire," for in March, 1827, the proprietor of that establishment sent in a claim for £360 for banquets and hire of rooms, &c., the latter being charged at the rate of *Ten Guineas* for each meeting of the lodge To meet this bill there was about £300 *of arrears* and £100 *owing by the late Treasurer.*

Under the circumstances it was deemed advisable to suspend the meetings of the lodge in the hope that some of the money due from the members might be collected and thus enable the few brethren who had stood by the lodge to discharge a portion of its liabilities. This hope was fallacious, and the lodge remained in abeyance till April, 1828, when a meeting was held, and it was determined to take steps, to incorporate the lodge with the Somerset House Lodge, communications having already been opened for that purpose. All preliminaries and difficulties having been adjusted the union was formally consummated on the 25th of November, 1828, the united lodges being now known as " The Royal Somerset House and Inverness Lodge No. 4. Acting by Immemorial Constitution."

THE LODGE OF FRIENDSHIP No. 6,

AND THE LODGE HELD AT "THE CASTLE," HIGHGATE.

Some authorities ascribe the date of the constitution of the Lodge of Friendship to the 17th of January, 1721, while others place it one year later, viz., 17th of January, 1722.

The following copy of the Title Page of a manuscript book in possession of the lodge must, therefore, be taken for what it is worth, but as it was evidently written in 1736 it is entitled to a certain amount of consideration.

"The General & Bye-Laws to be observed in yᵉ Lodge of Free and Accepted Masons, Constituted at yᵉ Lord Cardigan's Head at Charing Cross, Jan. 17, 1722; re-mov'd to & held at Shakspear's Head in little Marlborough Street, St. James.

"Ordain'd Augt. 7, 1736.

Mⁿ· CLARE, Master.

THOS. JEFFERIES, Senr. W.

FRANCIS BLYTHE, Juni. W."

It ought not to be taken for granted that either of the dates mentioned, correctly represents the actual age of the lodge, for it may have been in existence many years before it was constituted, or acknowledged as a regular lodge.

By the special favour of the lodge I have been permitted to examine its old records, and as they extend some years beyond any other original private lodge records that have come under my notice I need scarcely say that I am deeply grateful for the privilege. The first minute book begins in 1731, with an account of the constitution of a lodge which has for a considerable period been something like a "bone of contention" between various Masonic writers on both sides of the Atlantic. Being under an impression that the constitution and transactions of a lodge at this early period cannot fail to be generally interesting, as well as valuable from an historical point of view, and in order to ensure their preservation I venture to insert them although they form no part of the original plan of this volume.

THE LODGE AT "THE CASTLE," HIGHGATE.

" Att a Meeting of the following Gentlemen it was agreed to Petition The Right Honourable The Lord Lovell, the Grand Master of the ancient & Honourable Society of Free and accepted Masons, to Constitute them into a regular Lodge to be held att the house of Brother Richard Brusby att the Castle att Highgate, which said Petition was signed accordingly, Vizt. : by

" Thomas Jeffreys, Master of the Crown Lodge, Snow Hill.

John Bridges, Esq., Junior Warden of the University Lodge.

John Pollexfen, Esq , of the same Lodge.

Humphrey Primate, Master of the King's Arms, Cateaton Street.

John Pluymert, Esq., Senr. Warden of the Crown, Snow Hill

Edward Price, Junr Warden of Do.

Henry Stonestreet, a Member of Do.

Thomas Moore, Esq., of the University Lodge.

Thomas Crawford, of the Bear & Harrow Lodge, Butcher Row."

" Which Petition being regularly Presented, the Right Worshipful the Grand Master Granted & ordered the Constitution to be Perform'd on Saturday, the 27th Day of June, in the Year of Masonry, 5731.

" Upon this order the above mention'd Petitioners attended, But the Grand Master not being able to attend att the Constitution gave orders to his Deputy Grand Master, Thomas Battson, Esq., to attend in his stead, who accordingly did attend with his Grand Wardens, Vizt :

George Douglas, M.D., Senr Grand Warden.

James Chambers, Esq., Junr Grand Warden.

Assisted by the Reverend Dr. Desaguliers, formerly Grand Master, and the following Gentlemen, Vizt.:

George Payne, Esq , Do.

Nathl Blackerby, Esq., Late Deputy G.M.

Alexr. Chocke. Esq., Formerly D. Grand Master.

—— Philips, Esq.,

Dr. Hall, of Greenwich.

" The following Brethren assisted at ye said Constitution, Vizt ·

Bro. Millwart, *Crown*, on Snow hill.

Bro. Delvall, *Paul's head*, Ludgate Street.

Bro. Parker Do.

Bro. B. Adolphus. } *Crown*, of Cripplegate.
Bro. M. Adolphus

Bro. Haynes, *Crown*, on Snow hill.

Bro. Oates, *Anchor & Baptist head*, Chancery Lane.

Bro. Calcott, *Castle & Legg*, Holburn.

Bro. Hawkins, M^r· of 3 *Cranes*, in Y^e Poultry.

Bro. Houghton, M^r of Richmond Lodge, in Surrey.

Bro. Rogers, *Paul's head*, Ludgate Street.

Bro. Wood, *Paul's head*, Do.

Bro. Brown, *Crown*, Snow hill.

Bro. Elliott, *Crown*, Do.

Bro. Misaubin, M^l of Y^e Swann, Hampstead, Mddx.

Bro. Bignell, *Half Moon*, Cheapside.

Bro. Attkins, *Crown*, Snow hill.

Bro. Coward, *Crown*, Do.

" And the lodge was then constituted, and Bro. Edwd Price appointed Master.

Thos Moor, Esq., } Sr. Wardens.
Bro. Thos Crawford, } Jr.

" The Petitioning Brethren of ye Lodge having form'd themselves into a just and perfect Lodge, on June y^c 19th,

1731, the Day intended for ye Constitution, rec'd the petition of Thomas Clypperton well recommended by Bro. Brusby, at whose house this Lodge is held, to be admitted a Member of this Right Worshipfull Lodge, he was accordingly balloted for, & accepted. (Nem. Con.). In pursuance of which Ballott he was made a Free & accepted Mason, in the quality of an Enter'd prentice, at which time assisted Brothers

Thos. Jeffreys as Master.

John Plymert, Esq^{r .} Senr Warden, ⎫ for y^e
John Polexfen, Esq^{r .} Junr Warden, ⎭ time being

with several other Brethren.

"Then the Petition of John Pawlett, Esq., recommend'd by Bro Bridges to be made a Free and accepted Mason and admitted a Member of this Lodge, was read & was accordingly accepted, on ballott, by ye Brethren then present (Nem. Con).

"The Lodge upon Consultation agreed to meet on July ye 2nd at Brother Crawford's, at ye Bear and Harrow, in Butcher Row, where were present

Bro. Price, Master.

Bro. Moor, ⎫ Wardens.
Bro. Crawford, ⎭

Bro. Bridges.
Bro. Jeffreys.
Bro. Clypperton.
Bro. Pollexfen.

when the following orders and resolutions were agreed to, vizt. :

"Bro. Brusby's bill of expence at ye Constitution being read, and amounting to Nineteen Pounds & 6 shillings, was approv'd of, Nem. Con. Bro. Moody's bill for cloathing, & ye Grand Officers' expences, amounting to Three Pounds, 3 Shillings; & 5 Shillings order'd for ye Servants were likewise propos'd and agreed too, Nem. Con.

"Order'd that a sett of jewells of ye same make and price

of those belonging to the University Lodge are bespoke for
yᵉ use of this Lodge, and that Bro. Carpenter, of yᵉ Crown
Lodge on Snow hill, doe prepare yᵉ same, and that Brother
Crawford, the Jun. Warden, doe take care to gett them
forwarded.

"Order'd likewise that Bro. Clypperton doe bespeake the
wooden Jewells, in Cedar, and gett them forwarded in the
neatest manner for the use of the Lodge.

"Mem'dum July 10th,

"Order'd and agreed, that no Gentleman being proposed to become a Member of yᵉ Lodge be accepted, under
paying Three Guineas for his making, and 5 Shillings
admittance money, and that no Brother belonging to any
other Lodge and desirous of becoming a Member of this,
be admitted, but by a ballott, and upon his paying One
Guinea admittance money, and it was further agreed too,
that no Brother, being a visitor and desirous of being a
Member of yᵉ Lodge, be admitted while present, and it
was further order'd that no Brother or any other person
willing to become a Member hereoff be admitted but by
a Ballott, and if there be one negative it shall be sufficient
to refuse them.

"Phillip Hubert, Esq. and Michaell Hubert, Esq.,
being recommended by Bro Bridges to be made Free and
Accepted Masons, & become Members of this Lodge, they
were accordingly (on a ballott) accepted by the Brethren
then present. Nem. Con."

There were present at this meeting ten members and
nine visitors, but the names of the two gentlemen who were
elected are not among them nor is there any record of
their having been initiated subsequently.

The lodge appears to have been held fortnightly, the
next meeting being on the 24th of July, when eight members
and six visitors attended. "Order'd & Resolved that
Brother Jonson do attend this lodge on all occasions, to

be heard of at St. Luke's head in Church Lane near St. Martin's Church at 2. 6. per Lodge Night & five Shillings at the Makeing."

On the 14th of August, " Bro. Richard Brusby Master of the Castle Tavern att Hygate, out of his great esteem for Masonry, made a present of the Chair for ye Rt. Worshipfull ye Master of ye Lodge to sitt in, his health was drank accordingly, with thanks by the Brethren then present."

The subsequent meetings during this year were on the 28th of August, 8th and 25th of September, and the 9th and 23rd of October. These meetings were all very thinly attended and no business appears to have been done.

" April ye 22nd, 1732.

Being Lodge Day, the following Brethren mett.

Vizt.   Edward Price, Master.

        Thos. Moor, Esq., Senr. Warden.

        John Pollexfen, Esq.

        John Bridges, Esq.

        Thos. Jeffreys.

        Richd Brusby.

" Visitors :

        Bro. Robert Dyer, *Bear & Harrow*, in Butcher Row.

        Bro. John Bristow, *Three Tunns*, Smithfield.

        Bro. Claudius Crespigny, Master of the *Devil* *

        Bro. Harry Waltho, of the *Rose* by Temple Barr.

        Bro. John Wells, of the *Paul's Head*, Ludgate-hill.

" Upon the meeting of the Brethren above mentioned, some of the Lodge being absent, it was unanimously agreed to summons a Lodge on Saturday, the 29th instant, in order to consult further for the Benefitt of this Lodge."

----

* He was only Master of a Lodge held at the *Devil* Tavern H S.

" April 29th, 1732.

" According to the Order made on the 22nd of April, 1732, the Master, Wardens, & most of the Brethren of the Lodge mett, & John Pawlett, Esq., attended & was made a Brother of this R^t W^L Lodge.

" The Lodge then present took it into consideration that the order that no Brother Mason should be accepted in this Lodge unless he payd one guinea for his admission, and finding it necessary, as the circumstances of the Lodge then stood, that the admission money should be only five shillings till the number of the Lodge amounts to Twenty & one.

" Bro. Bridges recommended Bro. Crespigny as worthy to be accepted, who was Balloted for & recd. Nem. Con.

" Bro. Shearwood, recommended by Br. Pollexfen as worthy to be accepted in this Lodge, was Balloted for & accepted, Nemine Con."

Ten other brethren were proposed and elected at this meeting, including " Br. Alexander Chocke, Esq, formerly Deputy Grand Master; Br. James Moor Smith, Esq., Present Jun. Grand Warden; Br. Blackerby, Esq., Late Deputy Grand Master; and Br. Dr. Nathaniel Cotton." *

" The Election for Master being fixt for this day, our Bro. Thomas Moor, Esq., Senior Warden, was duly Elected for the ensuing Half-year as Master, who appointed Bro. Thomas Crawford to be his Sen. Warden, & Bro. Chandler his Jun Warden."

" The Lodge Being Adjourn'd from Michaelmas Day 1732 to Lady Day 1733, mett on the 7th day of Aprill following, when were present the following Brethren :

---

* Probably the celebrated physician and man of letters of that name, author of " Visions in Verse," etc., etc, who at one time kept a house at St Albans for the reception of the insane, in which the poet Cowper passed nearly two years of the maddest portion of his life Cowper refers to him in very kindly terms, and says that he was chosen for his guardian not only for his skill as a physician, but his well-known humanity and sweetness of temper. H. S.

" Vizt.   James Moor Smith, Esq., Jun. Grand Warden.
          Thomas Crawford, Sen Warden of this Lodge.
          John Bridges, Esq.
          George Fage, Esq.
          Harry Waltho.
          Thomas Jeffreys.
          Joshua Lewis.
" Visitor.   William Allen, Esq., of the *Duke's Head,*
          Lynn Regis.

" The Lodge Being then acquainted By Brother Brusby that it did not suit his Interest & Conveniency to accommodate the Lodge with the room they were used to meet in of a Saturday, it was Unanimously Agreed to Incorporate ourselves with the right Worshipfull the Lodge, who meet att the Swan on the first & third Saturday att Hamstead."

The lodge held at the Swan at Hampstead in 1733 is now the Lodge of Friendship ; and although the book contains no record of the actual incorporation of the two lodges, there is no doubt as to its having taken place, as the lodge at Highgate (No 79) was removed from the Engraved List for 1734, and among the names of the members of the Hampstead Lodge in the latter part of 1733 are the names of some of the former members of No 79   Other evidence tending to confirm this view is not wanting, although it is unnecessary to give it here.   The book contains no further transactions of either lodge until the 9th of January, 1738.   The lodge was then held at the *Shakespear's Head,* Marlborough Street, and the day of meeting had been changed from Saturday to Monday.   The minutes of both lodges are well written, and the accounts kept in a most business-like manner.   The Master appears to have performed the duties of Treasurer and Secretary, in addition to those appertaining to the Chair.   At this time the leading spirit in the lodge seems to have been Martin Clare, A.M., F.R.S., who was appointed Junior Grand Warden in 1735, and Deputy Grand Master in 1741. He kept the records of the lodge from January 1738 to December 1749. There being only five members remaining on the books on the 10th of November 1749, including the proprietors of the Tavern (Bro⁸ George Shakespear "and his son John ") it was agreed to dispose of the furniture and utensils of the lodge to the highest bidder, and to share the proceeds ; but no offer having been made by the 27th of December, St. John's Day, it was resolved that Martin Clare should " take all the properties at the rate of Five Pounds Sterling." The brethren dined together at this meeting, and " Mr. William Shakespear is invited to dine with the Brotherhood." This is the last appearance of Clare's handwriting in the book ; he died on the 19th of May, 1751. The next folio contains the minutes of a meeting of the lodge at the "*George*, Grafton Street, near Newport Market, on the 23rd of April, 1751," wherein reference is made to the removal of the lodge from the *Shakespear's Head* to the *George;* James Wild (a former member), who is described as W. P Master, being present. This brother joined the lodge in 1740, and as he frequently presided in the absence of the Master, he had probably been elected to the Chair in another lodge.

Before proceeding further in the examination of these very interesting records, I wish to direct attention to certain peculiarities in the proceedings of the lodge during the ten years immediately preceding its last removal. An occasional extract from the minutes will probably be sufficient for this purpose.

The first minutes written by Clare are the records of a meeting held at the *Shakespear's Head* on Monday, January 9th 1738, and are as follows.

" The lodge was this Evening opened at ½ past 7. The Weather being tempestuous, the Sʳ W. was present but Bro. Jackson acted as J.W. The Minutes of the last Meeting were read from the Chair and confirm'd by the Members.

Several of the Members present paid in their arrears and Contributions to the Expenses of the Current half year.

"The Laws of the Society were read from the Chair.

"The Master's Acct. of the last half Year's Rec'ts and Payments was publickly read and audited, on Balance whereof it appear'd that there was £8. 13s. 7d. due to the Credit of this Society. His Account was regularly signed in full Lodge.

"An Examination was passed between the Master and his Acting Wardens alternately. Business being then over, at ½ an hour after 9. Adjourned." It will be observed that the word "Society" in this instance refers to this particular lodge, and not to the Craft generally.

At the next Meeting, February the 13th,

"The Master requested Br. Clare to entertain the Society at the next Conference on some laudable subject, in which he was Seconded by the Members."

March the 13th. "Bro Clare according to his undertaking read the Society a Lecture on the Subject of Education, wherein in favour of the Masons' Sons, he described the Qualifications of the Instructor and the Pupil's Disposition and Demeanour of the Pupil in order to give the Business of their coming together the expected Success."

This appears to have been the introduction to a practice, which was probably not unusual among the higher class lodges in the "olden time," although it has not hitherto come under my own observation; very few lodges having a record of their proceedings at this period. I allude to the practice of the members and visitors entertaining their brethren at the various meetings with lectures or readings on scientific subjects.

For several years this was the custom of the Shakespear's Head Lodge, and when no brother was prepared with a lecture, a part of the History of Masonry was generally read from the Chair.

The following were the subjects of discussion during the year 1738.

May the 8th :—" Bro. Jackson read his Lecture on the nature of Stones and their efficacy and showed several natural curiosities in that way."

June the 12th :—" Bro. Robertson appeared as a Visitor and Lectured the Society in a learned, elegant and agreeable manner, on the principles of Astronomy, to this the Society paid a strict attention and drank to his health in the most affectionate and grateful Manner." As the vote of thanks and the drinking of the lecturer's health invariably followed the lecture, it will probably be deemed sufficient if I merely give the subject of the discourse in future.

July the 10th :—" A discourse concerning the Reflexion and Refractions of Light by the Master."

August the 14th :—" Part of the Architecture of Palladio was read and a Lecture on the Structure of the Eye delivered by the Master."

Sept. the 11th :—A Discourse on the Origin of Writing, by the Master."

Oct. the 9th :—" The Master continued his course of Lectures and showed the Wonders that happen unobserved in the Article of vision."

Nov. the 13th :—" A continuation of the foregoing."

Dec. the 11th :—" An Introduction to the properties of Colours, by the Master "

Sept. the 10th, 1739 :—" It was moved that in consideration of the multiplication of Lodges, and the Commonness of the Craft in and about this neighbourhood; that the Admission Fees in this Society be reduced from Three to Two Guineas, in hopes that this may be an inducement to acceptable Men to enter the Craft by means of the eldest of the Constituted Lodges here assembled. This was thought reasonable in our present Circumstances and it passed for the first time, Nem. Con."

I

The Joining Fee was reduced at the same time to half-a-Guinea. Both these reductions were confirmed at the next meeting.

Jan. the 14th, 1740:—"The late Master's Accounts were Audited and passed with great Credit, for a Lawyer, and he received 4s. 3d. Balance with the Cordial Thanks of the Society for his Just and Prudent Administration during the last Six Months." It must not be inferred that the Master had misbehaved himself during the *first* six months; he had only occupied the Chair during the period named, the officers being then elected half-yearly, and in some lodges quarterly.

July the 14th, 1740:—"A Letter from the Grand Officers summoning the Officers of this Lodge to a Qy. Communication on the 23rd Instant was read from the Chair. But the Society judged that at this warm Season of the Year the Health of the Members of the Grand Lodge might be affected if the press was too great and therefore hoped their presence might be dispensed with." *

Jan. the 25th, 1742:—"The Master proposed the Revival of the Lectures in this place and this seeming universally agreeable to the Society, his Worship requested the D.G.M., to entertain the Lodge this Day Fortnight at 9 o'Clock and the Subject was left to his own choice. After him Bro. Wagg promised to read this Day Month."

The scientific lectures had been omitted for several months past. The word "Revival" was originally written *Revisal* by Clare, but as the proceedings were transcribed by him, from rough minutes, probably taken by someone else, he doubtless mistook the word and afterwards altered the s into a v, although at first sight and taken without the context the word might now easily be mistaken for *Revisal.*

---

* How *very* considerate! H. S.

This trifling error may have given rise to the tradition that Clare revised the Craft Lectures by request of the Grand Lodge; I am not however aware of the existence of the least evidence or indication that he did anything of the kind.

Aug. the 8th, 1743 :—"The Contributions this Night came to £2. 5s. and were deposited in the Treasurer's absence with our Sister Shakespear."

"The Society requested Br. Clare to post up their loose Minutes to this place, which he hath here done."

It is with a feeling of regret that I now take leave of the early records of this celebrated lodge. In my humble opinion every word contained therein is worthy of preservation, as being reliable and indisputable Masonic History; and I sincerely trust that, in the interests of the fraternity at large, the members may ultimately see their way to sanction their being printed in their entirety. The withdrawal of Martin Clare and the other old members seems to have reduced the lodge to a somewhat lower position in the social scale than it had previously occupied. This descent however was balanced by increased activity and more numerous attendances. From 1751 to 1767 the records are little more than a register of the brethren present at each meeting, with the names of new members and the receipts and expenses of the evening.

An incident, however, is recorded in the minutes of the 22nd of July, 1755, which doubtless gave rise to no little excitement. Fortunately for the lodge Bro. James Wild was still a member and it is probably owing to this circumstance that it retained its position on the list of lodges

At the meeting referred to a letter was received from the Grand Secretary "Citing the Lodge to appear at the Committee of Charity to answer the Lodge at the Fish & Bell, they making Demand to be placed on the List of Lodges prior to ours, Viz. in No. 3. The Rt. Worshipful Master of this Lodge, Br. Wild attended the said Committee. When the Question being put, Br. Wild spoke to it and defended our Rights, with the Spirit natural to himself and well becoming the honour he assum'd—when, after several Debates (they not being able to make their demands appear any ways Legall), it was Declared in Favour of us & this Lodge was order'd to be placed as No. 3. & the Lodge at the Fish & Bell was order'd never to make any such Demands for the Future. The Rt. W. Master making this Report this Evening, his health was drunk to, in Form, and he had the Thanks of the whole Lodge for his Regard and Care in Executing the Trust Repos'd in him."

The Lodge at the *Fish and Bell*, Charles Street, Soho (now the Fortitude and Old Cumberland Lodge No. 12), was one of the old lodges in existence prior to the formation of the Grand Lodge, and but for some difference among its early members, it would have been considered a "Time Immemorial Lodge," taking rank before the Lodge of Friendship instead of after it, but having accepted a "Constitution" in 1723, its proper place was among the lodges warranted in that year. Probably some of the Members had read Anderson's account of this transaction in the Book of Constitutions (1738), and knowing that the lodges were being re-numbered in 1755, thought the time favourable for making an effort to regain their former position.

In 1761 the Lodge No. 3 removed from Grafton Street to the *Sun and Punch Bowl*, High Holborn, at which house it met regularly for several years, although the attendances were much smaller than formerly, indeed it seems to have been again on the decline.

On the 5th of February, 1767, seven members and three visitors were present, one of the latter being " Br. French of the Stewards Lodge." This brother was Grand Steward in 1767 and probably a member of the Somerset House Lodge, he having nominated a brother of that lodge to succeed him as Grand Steward for the following year. On this occasion the "House bill" came to 8s. 5½d., leaving a balance of £1. 5s. 0½d in the hands of the Master. The following was added to the minutes after the lodge was closed.

"N.B. Br. Grinnard proposed exchanging this Constitution for another and a Convention Night to be summoned the 8th Instant to consider the same. Agreed to, N.C."

No doubt this proposition was the result of a conversation between French and Grinnard the Master, over a social pipe and glass.

The "Convention" meeting was attended by thirteen members, probably the whole strength of the lodge, and four visitors, including French, and "Galloway of the Somerset House Lodge."

"The Members after Little Altercation, Unanimously Agreed to Exchange this Constitution for a New one in Favour of some Honourable Gentlemen Newly Made."

On the 22nd of the same month, "Br. Giddins the R.W.P.M. Moved that the following Brethren be admitted Members of this Lodge, Viz :—

> Br. The Honble. Charles Dillon.
> ,, Rowland Holt, Esq.
> ,, Thos. Dunckerley, Esq
> ,, Thos. French,
> ,, Captn. Barnard
> ,, James Galloway.
> ,, Robert Brown, Esq.
> ,, John Errington, Esq.
> ,, Henry Errington, Esq.

Which proposition being properly seconded, the Question was put in the usual manner, and they were admitted with unanimous consent."

On the 4th of March, Br. French proposed "that this Lodge be removed to the *Thatched House* in St. James Street, and that a consideration be paid for the Regalia of the Lodge, which Question being put was unanimously approved of, and accordingly Thirty Guineas were paid into the hands of Br. Grinnard on that Acct., to such Members as do not choose to remove with the Lodge. The R W Master signified his inclination to resign his Office, which, having received the assent of the other Officers and Brethren," Br. Dillon was elected in his place, who appointed French Senr. Warden and Galloway Junr Warden. All business being over, the Lodge was closed in due form and adjourned during the Master's pleasure.

A week later the lodge was opened at the *Thatched House* by the new officers, with Dunckerley as " P.M." The Duke of Beaufort being present, he was proposed, "Balloted for, and admited unanimously."

Fourteen other brethren were also elected at this meeting; twelve of whom were designated " Esq "the remaining two being the Duke of Buccleugh and Lord Wenman.

Br. Dillon then resigned his brief mastership, and on the proposition of Dunckerley, the Duke of Beaufort was elected in his place.

" Resolved that this Lodge shall be called for the future *The Lodge of Friendship,* and that notice be given thereof to the Grand Secretary, as also of the removal of the Lodge to this House."

The brethren who had agreed to "exchange the Constitution " resigned in a body " as the places of their abode are too far distant from this House." A few months later they received a new Warrant, which only cost them four guineas, for a lodge to be held at their old house, thus making a clear profit of Twenty-six Guineas over the transaction. This lodge is now The Lodge of Honour and Generosity No. 165, and although Dunckerley's name is not in the list of its members I have not the smallest doubt that he suggested its distinctive title as well as that of The Lodge of Friendship; the former probably in allusion to the honourable and generous conduct which led to its formation. Nearly all the lodges constituted by him bore names of a similar character, such as Harmony; Benevolence; Good Will, Unanimity; Good Fellowship; Love and Honour; Urbanity; Unity and Friendship; &c. Briefly told, this is the origin of the celebrated Lodge of Friendship, No. 6. At first sight it would appear that French was the person principally concerned in the transfer of the "Constitution," and a complaint was made against him and the former members of the lodge on that account, at a Committee of Charity on the 8th of April, 1767. Dunckerley, Galloway, French, and a number of their friends were present at this meeting. Indeed, it looks very like "a whip up," Fifty-five masters of lodges attending, as against Thirty-three at the previous Committee. After considerable discussion, and on the recommendation of the Grand Master in the Chair (Col. Salter, D.G M.), it was "Resolved, that as a mark of high respect to his Grace the Duke of Beaufort and the other noblemen and Honourable Gentlemen who meet under the Name of the Lodge of Friendship, and in consideration of their being *very young Masons*, that the Constitution, No. 3 shall remain with them, even tho' it should appear upon future enquiry that this affair hath been transacted contrary to the constitutions—but at the same time resolved that this shall not be looked upon as a Precedent for the future on any account whatever."

The subject cropped up again upon the reading of the minutes of the Committee of Charity at a Quarterly Communication held on the 15th of April. "The minutes of the last C.C were Read and Confirmed, except that part of them which related to the Brother French, which were not read for Confirmation as he declared in open Q.C. that as he found he had been concerned in a Transaction relative to the removing of a Lodge by which he had given Offence to the Grand Officers and the other Members of the Grand Lodge. He was sorry that he had so done."

At this meeting the Duke of Beaufort was nominated as

Grand Master, and on the 27th of the month was Unanimously Elected   On the 28th of October, 1768, on the decease
of the Grand Secretary, he appointed French to the vacant
office.   As will have been seen, French had all the kicks;
although, in my opinion, his real part was merely that of a
"go-between," or "cat's paw," and that the idea of secur-
ing this famous old lodge exclusively for themselves and
their friends, was conceived by Dunckerley and Galloway.
The ingenuity displayed at the outset of the business is on a
par with the effective simplicity of its conclusion.

Having achieved their desires, and obtained absolution,
they are astounded at the enormity of their crime, and promise "never to sin again," evincing the sincerity of their
penitence by agreeing to a resolution prohibiting all others
from following in their footsteps.

The complainant in the case represented a very select
lodge, held at the same house as the "Friendship," and
having recently initiated two Royal Dukes, it had in consequence adopted the title of "The Royal Lodge," (No. 313).
It is just possible, therefore, that the "virtuous indignation"
aroused by seeing a few brethren who were comparatively
speaking outsiders, in possession of the oldest "Constitution,"
was not entirely disinterested.   Indeed, it is highly probable
that, had the members of the complaining lodge "only
known it in time" they would have acted in a somewhat
similar manner.   Doubtless the result was not quite what
had been hoped for, as by their action they had cut the
ground from under their own feet and effectually debarred
themselves from doing likewise, should an opportunity occur.
If fears for the future of their lodge had anything to do with
their opposition, subsequent events proved their justification,
for in proportion as the "Friendship" increased in prosperity
and influence so the "Royal" decreased; no new members
were registered after 1801 and the last payment was made to
Grand Lodge in 1806.   For my own part I fail to see

either harm or illegality in the transaction; and there cannot be a shadow of doubt that much good resulted therefrom, for whereas No. 3 at the Sun and Punch Bowl was probably in a fair way to extinction, No. 3, at the "Thatched House" prospered and increased exceedingly, materially contributing to the elevation of the Craft both socially and financially.

The Royal Alpha Lodge, No. 16, was preserved, in a similar manner by the Duke of Sussex and some of his friends. This lodge, which was constituted in 1722 had been in a declining state for several years, and in 1823 could only muster five or six members. It was also in debt to the Treasurer; whereupon the Duke and twenty other eminent brethren, all Grand Officers or Past Grand Officers, were proposed and elected in a body; the old members resigned, and the lodge has ever since been considered the private lodge of the Grand Master for the time being.

In its new quarters the Lodge of Friendship rapidly increased in strength, and by the end of 1768 upwards of sixty new members had been enrolled. For the first few years Dunckerley attended nearly every meeting, frequently presiding as Master in the absence of the Duke of Beaufort and the Hon. Charles Dillon, who succeeded to the Chair on his Grace's assuming the Grand Mastership. When not acting in this capacity his name appears among the officers as a "P.M." and he is the only member so designated.

I regret that I can only find space for a very few extracts from the records of this period. On the 27th of May, 1767, "Her Grace the Dutchess of Beaufort having been nominated last meeting as *Lady Patroness of this Lodge*, was now unanimously Elected as such. Order'd that the same be notified to Her Grace, and that she be requested to do the Lodge the Honor of her *Patronage*, and that a pair of Gloves be presented to her Grace."

The price paid for these gloves was Five Guineas, so

that they were doubtless something quite out of the common, and really fit for a " Dutchess."

Dec. the 9th, 1767, The Duke of Beaufort being present, " The Lodge requested the Grand Master to indulge the Members of this Lodge with the Privilege of wearing their swords in *Lodge Hours*, Which His Grace was pleas'd to comply with."

At a Committee of Charity, held the 22nd of April, 1768, " Brother Edwards, the S.G.W. inform'd the G.M. in the Chair, that he had sufficient Reasons to believe that some Lodges under the Constitution of the G M. of England permitted the Brethren thereof to appear arm'd during Lodge Hours, which he was in his own mind convinc'd was an Innovation in, & contrary to, the antient Usages and Customs of the Society, but begged Leave to take the opinion of his Worship and the Committee on that occasion.

" After some debates had thereon, & the Question being put whether such a practice was or was not an Innovation . . . . it passed in the Affirmative by a large Majority.

" Resolved, that the D G.M be desired by the Committee to wait on the Rt Worshipfull the G.M. his Grace the Duke of Beaufort and acquaint him with these their sentiments, and humbly to request his Grace to forbid the Practice."

At a meeting of the Lodge of Friendship on the 12th of May following, " A Letter was received from the Grand Secretary intimating the pleasure of the M W G. Master to withdraw his dispensation lately granted to the Brethren of this Lodge for wearing Swords in Lodge Hours."

On the 28th of April, 1768, the Duke of Buccleugh was elected Master of the lodge on the recommendation of the Duke of Beaufort, who " assured the Brethren that the Duke of Buccleugh would undertake the Office with great pleasure." His Grace, however, does not appear to have been a very zealous Mason, for he was not present when he was elected, nor did he attend the lodge during his mastership. I need scarcely state that the noble Duke was not re-elected, neither was he presented with a Past Master's Jewel.

On the next election night, March the 8th, 1769, "The R.W.D.G M. Moved, that a Letter of thanks be sent to our Br. the Duke of Buccleugh, late Master of the Lodge for his Grace's services and attendance during the past year. Order'd; and that the same be wrote by our said R.W.D.G.M."*

On the 9th of November, 1768, "Br. Dunckerley represented to the Lodge that Br Thos. Dibdin (late commander of the Antigallican Privateer) was reduced to great want and misery, and now confined for Debt in the King's Bench Prison, with Wife and five children. Order'd, That this Lodge do send Three Guineas towards his relief."

At a meeting of the Committee of Charity on the preceding 21st of October, Dunckerley acting as Junior Grand Warden, Br Dibdin was relieved with Five Pounds, and on the 16th of November, 1770, in response to another appeal the Committee voted him Twenty Pounds; an unusually large grant in those days

On the 10th of January, 1770, " A Letter was received from Br. Dunckerley, desiring leave to decline being any longer a Member on account of his residence in the Country, but that he may be admitted an Honorary Member, which was agreed to."

From this date Dunckerley's name appears in the book only at long intervals; his friend Galloway, however, continued to act as Secretary down to 1802, having served the lodge in that capacity for a period of thirty-five years. He died in 1805 at the age of seventy-six.

---

* This reads very like sarcasm on the part of the Proposer, with a smart rejoinder, probably emanating from either Dunckerley or Galloway wh. . . . . . H. S.

THE LODGE OF HARMONY, No. 255.

This, the last of Dunckerley's creations, was also the last lodge of which he was master. At his request, a Dispensation dated June the 2nd, 1785, was granted to him " for holding a Lodge at Hampton Court," a Warrant being shortly after-wards issued bearing the same date, and numbered 474.

A very concise little history of the lodge from the year 1801* tells us that its earliest minutes have unfortunately met the fate of the records of many other old lodges. It would appear, however, from the accompanying list of mem-bers copied from the Grand Lodge Register, that the lodge did a fair amount of good work down to the year 1792.

About this period its promoter, for the benefit of his health, passed most of his time in the Southern counties where his Masonic work chiefly lay.

The first meeting, by virtue of the Dispensation, was held on the 11th of July 1785, when, according to the Register, the two gentlemen were initiated whose names appear on the Warrant as the first Wardens. The absence from the list of the names of all Dunckerley's old friends in town, favours the inference that the burden of the work fell upon his own shoulders, and that his genial qualities, Masonic zeal, and ability, formed the cement which held the lodge together. From the end of 1792 to the beginning of 1802 no payments are recorded in the Grand Lodge books from the Lodge of Harmony, hence it would appear that it was practically dormant during that period. I learn from the little book previously mentioned that on the 16th of July, 1801, a number of brethren assembled at the *Toy Inn* with the intention of reviving the lodge. Their efforts were success-ful, and Brother Thomas Haverfield, the first Senior Warden, was unanimously elected Master in his absence. He, how-

---

* "A Short Account of the Lodge of Harmony, No. 255 [from 1801 to 1868]. By Gordon W. Clark, P.M. Continued to 1885 by Raymond H. Thrupp, P M. and Secretary, P.A G D.C and Dep. G.M. Middlesex."

ever, accepted the office, and was followed by a long list of brethren of various degrees of eminence, whose successive efforts have resulted in firmly establishing the lodge in the prominent position which it now occupies, a position well worthy of its distinguished founder. As I understand, the records of the lodge are intact since its resuscitation in 1801, I have much pleasure in supplying the names of those who were members previously, together with some of Dunckerley's letters referring to the lodge, and I much regret that I cannot also furnish the names of the different office-holders during the same period. With regard to the offices of Master, Treasurer, and Secretary, I have no doubt that they were practically filled by one person, and I think I should not be far wrong were I to suggest that the name of that person was *Thomas Dunckerley*.

MEMBERS NAMES.	AGE.	BUSINESS OR PROFESSION	RESIDENCE.	WHEN MADE MASONS
Thomas Dunckerley	30	Barrister ..	Hampton Court	Jan 10th, 1754
Thomas Haverfield	34	Esq .	Do .	July 11th, 1785
William Bowater	29	Captn Marines .	Do	Do
Thomas Branson .	54	Operative Mason	Do ..	July 18th
Robert Brawn . .	24	Esq	Kew ..	
Maurice Jones	40	Surgeon . ..	Hampton	Aug 31st
Robert Tunstall .	25	Architect	Kew	Do
Richard Dupuis .	22	Surgeon ..	London .	Do.
Gillery Pigott .	24	Captn Militia .	Kew	Do
John Haverfield .	41	Architect ..	Richmond	Sept. 14th
William Ramus .	34	Esq .	St James' Palace	Do
Rev Harry Paxton	26	Clerk	Mortlake	Do
John Railton .	38	Merchant ..	Hampton ..	Oct 19th
Charles Brown .	41	Architect	Richmond	Do
George Ramus .	37	Esq ..	St James' Palace .	Do
James Sayer .	26	Esq	Richmond	Do
James Christopher	18	Innholder	Hampton Court	Do
W J. Griffenhoofe	22	Surgeon	Hampton	Nov. 16th
John Price..	24	Mate of E I Ship		Do
Richard Tickell . .	34	Comr of Stamps	Hampton Court	Do
Charles Rowles .	25	Esq	Kingston .	Decr 23rd
Rev George Dupuis	25	Clerk .	Hoddesdon	Jan 18th, 1786
Rev Henry Waller ..	24	Clerk		Do
Thomas Boone . ..	24	Surgeon	Sunbury	Feb 15th.
Rev J D Raincock	24	Clerk	Hampton	Do
Rev George Belgrave .	30	Clerk . ..	Hampton Court	Mar 15th
Rev Arthur Owen .	25	Clerk .	Hanover Square ..	April 19th
James Powell .	23	Esq ..	Inner Temple	Aug 21st
William Clark .	40	Servant ..	Kingston, Surrey .	Do
Samuel Lewin .	25	Esq ..	Twickenham	April 4th, 1787
John Randall .	26	Coachmaker ..	Long Acre . .	Aug. 1st
Anthony Steventon .	31	Atty at-Law ..	Ely Place .	Aug 29th
Rev Hugh Totty .	30	Clerk .	Maidenhead, Berks	Oct 31st
George Edward .	40	Captn Navy .	Richmond	April 12th, 1791
Rev Thos Wrench .	25	Clerk .	Camberwell .	Do
John Pusey Edwards .	22	Student . .	Oxford .	May 17th
John Thos Harbridge .	21	Gentleman ..	London .. .	Aug 12th, 1792

The age of the brother when he was initiated H S.

"Hampton Court Palace,
                 "July 21, 1785.

"Dear Brother,

"I shall hope to give you a very good account of the several Lodges under my care before November next; as my Grand Lodge for the County of Somerset will be held in the City of Wells about the middle of October. I am now to desire a Warrant may be made out for the Lodge of Harmony No —, to be held at the Toy, Hampton Court, on the Wednesday *on* or preceding the full Moon of each Month.

Thos. Dunckerley	⎫	⎧	Master.
Thos. Haverfield, Esq.	⎬ to be the ⎨		Sen. Warden.
Captn. Wm. Bowater	⎭	⎩	Jun. Warden.

We beg you will get it framed & Glazed & put in a deal case, the cover to slide in a Groove, with two brass rings to the frame for it to be hung up each night in the Lodge Room.

"The Royal Cumberland Lodge at Bath are ready to subscribe £25 to the Hall; if Bro. Berkley will send me a Medal for them, I will be accountable to him for the same.

"When our Lodge is increas'd, & can work, which I hope will be very soon; we shall be happy to see you and any *serious* Brother. A man named Tombs has behav'd very ill at Bristol: of which you will have a particular account in my annual state of Lodges.

"Mrs. Dunckerley unites with me in sincere regard, & am

                 "Y^r affect. Brother,
"Mr. WHITE,   "THOS. DUNCKERLEY."
      "Sion Gardens,
          "Aldermanbury,
                 "London."

" Hampton Court Palace,
" Aug. 19th, 1785.

" Dear Sir,

" I was duly favour'd with Yours of the 16th, Our Lodge is greatly obliged to you for the enquiry concerning the Frame & Glass, but think it too great an expence & for the present will keep it roll'd up in the Pedestal. — On the other side is the state of the Lodges under my care you will perceive there are two removals marked* for which I have paid you Fees & shall have a large sum to pay you for Constitutions, Contributions, &c., after I have held my Grand Lodge for Somerset at Wells the beginning of October. I shall then make up the Account & send you a Draught on my Banker for the whole sum. I must desire Brother Berkley will let me have the Medal for yᵉ R. Cumberland Lodge some time next Month that I may take it with me to Bath. I beg you will do me the favour to accquaint Brother Meyler at Bath it is my desire that he will draw on Brother Berkley for £5 & pay it to Brother Way. I shall hope soon to find that you have got No. 2 on yᵉ other side over to us   I am with sincere regard to Sister White & Yourself.

" Your Affect. Brother,
" THOS. DUNCKERLEY.

" Greeting to all *serious* Brethren "
" Wm White, Esq."

" No. 2 on yᵉ other side " was an " Ancient " Lodge which had been for some years in abeyance but was resuscitated in 1784; shortly afterwards it was joined by several " Moderns " which probably gave rise to a hope that it might be brought over to the opposition. Nothing however came of it. The lodge prospered and continued its allegiance to the body from which it emanated. It is now the Lodge of Fidelity No. 3.

"Hampton Court Palace, Sept. 29, 1785

" Dear Sir,

"Indeed I am much concern'd for the loss of our worthy Bro Berkley; as a *truly* sincere friendship had subsisted between us for more than thirty years.   There must be some Mistake respecting the Medals for Bros. Sperling & Tyssen; as those Gentlemen have had their Medals three Months ago.   Bro. Berkley sent them to me at my Lodgings in Piccadilly (on the 3rd of last June), by a young man, to whom I immediately gave a Draught for £50, on Thos. Coutts, Esq., & Co , in yᵉ Strand. I shall be glad to find that it is properly settled.

"The Medal for the R. Cumberland Lodge; I must beg you will send by next Monday's Coach, addressed to Mr. Henry Attwood, Surgeon at Bath : & make me Debtr. for the £25. If it is not too late to be inserted in the Calendar I must desire that yᵉ Meeting of the Lodge at this place may be registered for yᵉ Wednesday *on* or *after* the full Moon in January, February, March, April, Sept., Oct , Nov., & December, at high Noon.   I have the pleasure to acquaint you that I have already made *Nine* Gentlemen in this Lodge ; & *four* are to be made yᵉ 19th of next month when & where I shall be very happy to see you.   We open the Lodge at Noon, do business till 3 ; then go to dinner & at 6, call on to labour ; & close at 7.   Give me a line in return & believe me.

"Your Affect. Friend & Brother,

"THOS. DUNCKERLEY.

" William White, Esq."

"Hampton Court Palace, Oct. 20th, 1785.

" Dear Sir,

"We are greatly obliged to you for the Dispensation & beg to know if any Fees are requir'd for the same.

Only five came to be made ; three being prevented by

business; & I have five to make at our next Meeting should more offer shall avail myself of the Dispensation.

I made James Christopher, who tho' not Nineteen; conducts the Business at the Toy, & maintains 6 Brothers & Sisters, a most worthy Character. We should have been happy if you could conveniently have been with us; hope to see you in the Spring. The *Harmonie Lodge;* Hampton Court have unanimously voted a Loan of £25 to the Hall, I beg you will order a Medal for us and should be glad to have it before the 16th of next Month.*

> "Your Affect. Bro., &c.,
> "Tho?. Dunckerley.

"William White, Esq."

"Hampton Court Palace, Jany. 2nd, 1786.

"Dear Sir,

"I was setting out for Salisbury on the morning that your favour of the 12th ultimo came to hand, with one enclos'd from Bridgwater, to which I paid the proper attention & granted the Dispensation they requested. The same Post brought me a treble letter from Pool. Also a letter from the Lodge at Naples (under a flying Seal, to my care) to the Grand Lodge at London; which I hope to have the happiness of delivering in person at the next Quarterly Communication.

"I beg (if the plate is finish'd), that you will get a Book of Constitutions, bound in rough calf, & letter'd on one of the covers

> LODGE OF HARMONY,
> HAMPTON COURT.

"I wish to know if the Petitions from Bristol met with

---

* The Loan was changed into a Gift in 1787. See p. 81 "No. 474, Harmonie Lodge." H S.

K

the desir'd success : that I may settle Accounts with you for Bro. Lewis & Bro. Meyler of Bath. I have money for the next Qua. Com. from yᵉ Lodge of Science & Apollo Lodge at Salisbury, also 3 subscriptions for Vandyke's Plate —Let me know if you have heard from him. I hope soon to receive from you the accounts of the last Qua. Com. ; but beg you will not be at the trouble to send any more printed notices of the times when the Committee of Charity & Quar. Coms. are to be held as they are of no use to the Lodges under my care ; The Calendars giving them sufficient notice ; and I shall take care to spur them up *annually* for the needful. I was much concern'd at our Bro. Heseltine's Indisposition ; hope you will be able to inform me that he is perfectly recover'd.—My Wife desires to unite with me in sincere regard to him, Yourself & Families ; wishing you all many happy returns of this season.

" I remain (in hopes of hearing from you soon),

" Your Affect. & Zealous Brother,

" THOS. DUNCKERLEY.

" William White, Esq."

THE PRINCE OF WALES'S LODGE, No. 259.

THIS lodge was first held on the 16th of April, 1787, by dispensation from H. R. H. The Duke of Cumberland, then Grand Master, His Royal Highness the Prince of Wales (afterwards George IV.) being one of the founders. A Warrant was subsequently granted, dated the 20th of August, 1787. Membership was at first restricted to those who were either in the service of His Royal Highness, or " firmly attached to his person and interests."

The original plan seems to have been carried out most strictly, even to the extent of making Masons of the household servants of the Prince, four of whom were initiated and passed at the first meeting, many others being afterwards made, although they were not received as members of the lodge. Dunckerley was elected a member February 18th, 1787, in company with one of his friends, Joshua Jones Pritchard, an attorney, whom he had initiated in the London Lodge in 1775. These two signalized their advent by treating the members to "A Lecture in the First degree of Masonry" on the same evening; beyond this, Dunckerley's name seldom appears in the records. He was not in robust health, and resided chiefly in the country, and as the lodge was generally in good hands, there was no occasion for his taking an active part in its affairs.

Several of the most distinguished Masons of the day were warm supporters of the lodge, among whom may be mentioned the Chevalier Ruspini, Dentist to the Prince of Wales. He was the principal founder and many years Treasurer of the Royal Masonic Institution for Girls.

The first Secretary was the Rev William Peters, LL.B., more celebrated as an artist than as a preacher. He was a Royal Academician, and his name should ever be held in affectionate remembrance by the members of the Grand Lodge of England, by reason of his having painted the first four portraits that adorned their Hall in Great Queen Street, viz, Lord Petre, the Dukes of Manchester and Cumberland, and H.R.H. George Prince of Wales. The two former he presented, and for the two latter he consented to accept a comparatively small sum, at the earnest request of the Hall Committee. In 1785, on the recommendation of the Duke of Manchester, Past Grand Master, he received the appointment of Grand Portrait Painter, he being the only person ever appointed to that office.

His first list of members of the Prince of Wales's Lodge, returned to the Grand Secretary, is in his own handwriting and is dated 10th of May 1788. It is complete to the smallest detail giving the name, age, profession, &c., of every member, together with a characteristic note applicable to each individual in the " Remarks " column.

For instance, Francis Broderip, 37, musical instrument maker, Haymarket, is " a good jolly fellow."

William Dickinson, 34, engraver, Bond Street, " a well-looking dark man."

John Hickey, 30, sculptor, Brooke Street, " a very genteel young man."

George Saunders, 26, carpenter, Oxford Road, " a smart dapper lad."

Henry Holland, 36, architect, Hertford Street, " a comely man."

Thos. Ogle, 40, Surgeon to the Prince of Wales, " very well—not too tall."

Thos. Hammersley, 41, banker, Pall Mall, " much the gentleman, but go not near him with forged drafts."

Wm. Addington, 50, Justice of the Peace, Clarges Street, " visit him not in Bow-Street."*

Arthur Robinson, 45, gentleman, Pall Mall, is merely " very well."

Thos. Dunckerley, 63, gentleman, Hampton Court, " something royal about him "

J. J. Prichard, 40, attorney-at-law, Doctors' Commons, " Beware of the Law."

Probably by an oversight on the part of the clerk who entered the names, these quaint remarks are all omitted from the Grand Lodge Register.

As Dunckerley was not identified with the history of this lodge, I shall conclude my brief notice of it by stating that ever since its formation it has occupied a most distinguished position in the craft, having been presided over by

H.R.H. George Prince of Wales, from 1787 to 1820.

---

* Many years Chief Magistrate at Bow Street.   H.S.

H.R.H. The Duke of York, 1820 to 1827.

H.R.H. The Duke of Clarence, 1827 to 1830.

H.R.H. The Duke of Sussex, 1830 to 1843.

H.R.H. Albert Edward Prince of Wales (our M.W.G.M.), from 1874 to the present time.

Among the members enrolled at different periods of its career may be found many whose names are recorded in the pages of history, while a glance at our charity lists will suffice to show that the lodge has not been unmindful of the grand principles of our Order.

MASONIC EMBLEM PRINTED ON DUNCKERLEY'S LETTER-PAPER.

MEMORIALS OF FREEMASONRY IN HANTS
AND THE ISLE OF WIGHT.

HAMPSHIRE was the first Province placed under Dunckerley's care, and he was its first Provincial Grand Master. His Patent, or Warrant of appointment, was dated the 28th of February 1767. From the fact of his having delivered and published a lecture on Masonry about three years after his initiation, we may fairly assume that he had evinced a warm interest in the Craft from the moment of his becoming a member of it.

It is probable that when not on active service his leisure hours were chiefly devoted to Masonry; and judging from his subsequent conduct, he is not likely to have neglected any opportunity for urging upon the brethren the claims of the "General Charity."

In 1758, the only lodge in Hampshire on the "Modern" list was the old lodge in which Dunckerley was initiated, but by the end of 1764, ten new lodges, including the two on board Dunckerley's ships, had been constituted in Portsmouth and its vicinity.

At this time the fee for a Constitution or Warrant was only two guineas; other payments to the Fund of Charity being practically optional. During the period mentioned, a total of £36. 15s. was received by the Grand Treasurer from the lodges in Hampshire—a very handsome amount in those days from so few lodges—a large proportion of which I have no doubt was paid in by Dunckerley himself, either in the shape of Constitution fees or in donations to the Charity given at his instigation. Being well known to several of the Grand Officers, he was probably looked upon by them as the leading Mason in Hampshire long before he was formally appointed to the office of Provincial Grand Master. This seems a reasonable explanation of the unusual appointment of a retired warrant-officer to so distinguished a position.

Many of these newly-created lodges had but a brief existence, and although we have no evidence that Dunckerley was connected with them, it is not unlikely that his masonic enthusiasm and constant endeavours to increase the Fund of Charity had some relation to their being constituted.

However that may be, he evidently lost no time in getting to work after he was appointed, for at a meeting of the Grand Lodge on the 27th of January, 1768; " Bro. Dunckerley, P.G.M. for Hampshire, reported that the Bear Lodge at Havant had, in open contempt, disobeyed his Orders, he therefore desired that for such their disobedience they be crazed out of the List of Lodges, which passed in the affirmative."*

At this meeting Dunckerley sat as Senior Grand Warden.

Probably the first lodge constituted by Dunckerley as Provincial Grand Master was No. 405, at the "New Inn, Christ Church, Hants;" the Warrant being dated 23rd of November, 1770. On this day a Quarterly Communication was held in London, Dunckerley being present at the meeting. This lodge is still flourishing under the name of the Lodge of Hengist, No 195, held at Bournemouth. Unfortunately, its earliest records are lost, but in this respect it is much more happily situated than many other lodges of the same period, only one minute book containing about four years of its proceedings, being missing. From a very readable and concise history of the lodge compiled by the Rev. P. H. Newnham during his Mastership (1870) we learn that the earliest minute book then at his command, begins in

---

* Grand L.... M....t - H. S.

November, 1774, and that it contains a statement that the lodge met for the first time, and was formally constituted, on the 26th of November, 1770. The officers named in the Warrant are Henry Dagge (Master); Edmund Perkins (Sen. Warden); and Thomas Jeans (Jun. Warden).

The first named appears to have been a person of considerable repute, and a Mason after Dunckerley's own heart. He served the office of Grand Steward in 1770-1, J.G.W. in 1774-5 (in which capacity he assisted in laying the foundation stone of Freemasons' Hall), and S.G.W. in 1778-9. He was one of the original subscribers (of £50) to the Freemasons' Tontine in 1775, and was also one of eleven eminent Masons nominated as Trustees on behalf of the other subscribers. With equal readiness he contributed £25 to the "Hall Loan" in 1779. For several years he filled the office of Deputy Provincial Grand Master of Hampshire, but was virtually the head of the Province, his Chief, Lord Charles Montagu being frequently abroad.

Edmund Perkins, Esq., the first Senior Warden, was, probably, a local magnate. According to the Grand Lodge Register he was made a Mason on the 26th of November, 1770, so that he must have been initiated at the first meeting of the lodge; a not uncommon practice in those days. Thomas Jeans, the first Junior Warden appears to have been the mainstay of the lodge during the first half century of its existence. For at least fifteen years he served the office of Master; his last appearance in that capacity being in 1810. In concluding my brief notice of him I cannot do better than to quote the words of the Historian of the lodge; who says, "The Lodge was resuscitated from its torpor on May 23rd, 1822; on which day there was held a meeting of four Brethren, presided over by the venerable patriarch Thomas Jeans; fifty-two years after his name had been prefixed to the Warrant of the Lodge for which he had worked so well. All honour to the grey-headed veteran who had gallantly fought the

Battle of Masonry for half a Century ; who had twice saved a dying Lodge from extinction, and who seems to have died at his post; for his name henceforward disappears from the Lodge Records," His son (Thomas Jeans, junior), was initiated in the lodge on the 13th of August, 1771 ; he is described as a Clerk, and against his name is written "abroad," denoting that when the list of members was returned to Grand Lodge he was out of the country. The absence of the prefix " Reverend " would seem to imply that he was not a clergyman but an office clerk, and if so he was probably

> " Seeking the bubble Reputation even in the Cannon's mouth."

Judging from this list, which contains fifty-five names, and is supposed to include all who had joined or been initiated down to the year 1776, the lodge did a fair amount of good work at the outset of its career. In a subsequent list appears the name of Alexander Mouat, Lieutenant in the Navy. This brother was a midshipman with Captain Cook during his voyages of discovery, and died from fever while in command of the Rattlesnake sloop, in the West Indies in 1793. He was a nephew of Lieutenant Mouat of the Canceaux previously mentioned.*

By the favour of an esteemed Past Master of the Lodge (Bro. J. B. Atkinson), who kindly undertook the task of searching the records for references to Dunckerley I am enabled to present the following extracts which may be found useful to a future historian of Hampshire Masonry.

29th of May, 1776. "This Night the Lodge was Honoured with our Brother Rt. Worshipfull Provincial Grand Master, Thomas Dunkerley, Esq., who took the Chair and opened a Grand Lodge, when the Honble. Ld. Charles Montague was Install'd Provincial Grand Master for the County of Hants, our Rt. Worshipfull Brother Dunkerley,

---

* See page 71.

having resigned. At the same time Brother Ld. Charles Montague appointed and Installed Bro. Henry Dagge, Esq., Deputy Grand Master for the County of Hants, who appointed William Mitchell, Charles Branden, John Rickman, & Edmund Bott, Esq , P. Grand Stewards of this Lodge, who are to wear red aprons,—Brother James Telman P. Gd. Senr. Warden and Joseph Jarvis Clerke, Esq , Grand P. Junr. Warden, who are to wear Blue aprons ; and John Oake P. Gd. Secy., who is to wear a Blue apron." *

The whole of the brethren named were members of the lodge.

26th of Dec., 1778. " This day the Lodge was Honour'd with Bro. Dunkerley, Bro. Sadler, and Brother Staronood.

22nd of June, 1780. " This Lodge convened by order of the Rt. W.M. on account of a Letter Rec'd from Poole Lodge desiring the attendance of the Brethren there on June 24th to Provincial Grand Lodge held by Bro. Dunckerley."

No further reference to Dunckerley occurs in the Minutes of this lodge. The following letters may probably be of some little interest :—

" To the Grand Lodge of Free and Accepted Masons of England in Quarterly Communication Assembled.

" Right Worshipful and Brethren,

" Ever since I had the honour of being appointed Provincial Grand Master for Hampshire, nothing has been wanting in my power to Excite the Lodges in that

---

* At this period the Masters and Wardens of private lodges had plain white aprons, and wore their jewels suspended from white ribbons, the Grand Officers and Provincial Grand Officers only being allowed to have their aprons lined with blue silk, with a narrow edging or border of the same material. From the fact of these colours being so particularly mentioned in the records of Dunckerley's Provincial meetings, I think it not unlikely that he was instrumental in extending the privilege of wearing them to Provincial Grand Officers generally, this privilege being first mentioned in the Book of Constitutions published in 1767. H. S

County to contribute as much as they conveniently could spare to the Grand Charity; and I have, as I thought it my Duty, constantly Exhorted them to comply with the Laws and Regulations of the Grand Lodge ; and to transmit to me, previous to each Quarterly Communication, a list of their Members, particularly of such as had been lately made Masons. I am sorry to acquaint you that the Lodge held at the Nagg's head Lymington, in Hampshire, has paid no regard to any of my letters for two years past. I found myself under the Disagreeable necessity of acquainting them (last March) that if they did not Transmit to me a List of their Members, I would certainly have their Lodge struck off the List. They made no answer to my letter : but sent a Guinea to Bro. Heseltine for the Grand Charity, and acquainted him that they had received an Impertinent Letter from me.

"The Deputy Grand Master advised me to propose the erazement of their Lodge at that time, but I have forbore the application near Eight months longer. But as the aforesaid Lodge still remains in contempt of me; I am to request of the Grand Lodge to support my Authority, by giving direction for the aforesaid Lodge to be struck off from the List of Lodges for not complying with the Directions and Instructions of their Provincial Grand Master, and that all Lodges may have notice of the same, by a copy of the Order being printed with the Account of the several Contributions to the Grand Charity this Evening.

"I am prevented by a severe Cold, the pleasure of waiting on the Grand Lodge ; to whom I beg leave to subscribe myself

"Your Most faithful & Affect^e Brother,

"THOS. DUNCKERLEY, P.G M. for H.

"Somerset House,

"Nov. 29, 1771."

The foregoing letter was read by the Grand Secretary

in Grand Lodge the day on which it is dated, when it was ordered :

"That the Lodge at the Nag's Head, Lymington be wrote to by the G.S. and acquainted with Bro. Dunckerley's complaint, and that the Members be directed to prepare their answer to such complaint, or to settle the matter with Bro. Dunckerley by or before the next Q.C."* Judging from the Grand Lodge Register this Lodge was then at rather a low ebb, but the letter sent by the Grand Secretary had the desired effect, for at the next meeting Dunckerley paid a Guinea on behalf of the Lodge. We may therefore fairly assume that the affair had been amicably settled, but the lodge was evidently out of place at Lymington and in 1777 it removed to Ringwood, where at first it does not seem to have done much better, for after the amount last mentioned, no further payment appears to have been made until 1779. On April the 12th, 1780, it was one of eighteen lodges ordered to be erased for not having conformed to the Laws of the Society. It must have been, however, immediately reinstated, as later in the year it is credited with a Guinea to the Charity, since which period its affairs appear to have been conducted with commendable regularity. It is now, The Lodge of Unity No. 132 meeting at the *White Hart*, Ringwood, and enjoys the very uncommon distinction of having been held under the same roof for considerably over a hundred years.

"Hampton Court Palace,

"April 13th, 1776.

" Dear Sir,

" Your Favour of the 21st Ult., I received in due Course ; but the violent pains which my Daughter suffered & the Salt water being advised, I took her to Southampton, where I had also an Opportunity of Constituting the Lodge

---

* Quarterly Communication.

in Person. During my absence the enclos'd Petition in favour of Bro. Gilchrist, came to Hampton Court, therefore it was not possible it could be transmitted to you till my return.

"This poor old Man was senior Warden in a Portsmouth Lodge 22 Years ago when I was made a Mason; therefore I hope, in consideration that his Petition would have been with you in due Time if I had not been absent on Masonic Business, you will be able to bring it on next Friday; when I will attend and speak to it if you will favour me with a line by return of Post. I raised Lord Charles Montague to the Third Degree and His Lordship did me the honour (When a master Mason), to accept the Office of Deputy Provincial for Hampshire. Capt. Robinson was present and resign'd with great Pleasure on the occasion.

"I have not had a line from Bro. Frederick in return to mine which I sent to him on the Receipt of your last fav^r

"I am, Dear Sir,

"Your much Obliged & affectionate Brother,

"THOS. DUNCKERLEY.

"Mr. Heseltine."

The Lodge referred to at the beginning of this letter, was the Lodge of Concord No. 494, Constituted at the *Star Inn*, Southampton, July the 1st, 1775. It appears to have been a very respectable and fairly prosperous lodge for about twenty-five years; but after Dunckerley's death it declined and was erased from the list in 1813. In January, 1792, Thomas Jeans, M.D., joined the lodge; probably the same brother who did such good service in the Lodge of Hengist.

"Hampton Court Palace, Feb. 5th, 1786.

"Dear Sir,

"I am much disappointed at not hearing from you in return to mine of the 31st of last month, & am uneasy lest the Draught (which I enclosed to you at that time) of

£25 as a loan to the Hall from the Lodge of Liberty and
Sincerity at Bridgwater should not have got safe to hand.
I send you a letter, which I have this moment received
from Portsmouth. I struck their Lodge off the list several
years ago, because they were on the decline & had ceased
to meet regularly. Palmer is one of the first *Antient* Masons
in England; but it would be better to have him *again* under
our Constitution, than to let Dermot get hold of him, under
whose Sanction he held a Lodge 25 years ago; then came
under our Constitution. Write to him and put him in the
way to obtain the Constitution

"I beg to have a line from you to-morrow in return, that
I may have Bro. Lewis' Account with you, & may know what
was done at the Committee of Charity relative to the Petitioners from Bristol.

"Your Affect. Brother, &c.,

"Tho^S Dunckerley.

" William White, Esq."

The foregoing shows the estimation in which Dunckerley
was held by the brethren at Portsmouth although he was
not then P.G. Master. His advice to the Grand Secretary
resulted in the granting of a Warrant for the Phœnix
Lodge No. 485 (now 257) of which Lodge Samuel Palmer
was the first Master. He was formerly a member of No.
68 (" Ancients ") constituted in 1758 which perished in its
infancy, *no* names being returned to Grand Lodge after 1761
In 1780 he joined the Lodge of Antiquity No. 18
" Dermott " was at this time Deputy Grand Master of
the rival Grand Lodge.

"Southton., Aug^st 3rd, 1786
"Lodge of Concord.

" Sir,

"It is requested of the R.W.M. & Brethren of the
Lodge of Concord held in this Town, that Thos. Dunckerley,

Esq., be appointed Provincial Grand Master for this County in the Room of Capt. Pascal deceased; which request I was desired to transmit to you some time back, but being busy it escaped my memory; you will therefore much oblige this Society by communicating the Contents of this to the Grand Lodge & (if agreeable to the Members thereof) to forward Business as fast as possible.

    " I am with due regard & Esteem,

        " Sir your faithful Servant,

            " JOHN MARTIN,

                " Secretary.

" Wm. White, Esq."

Several other letters to the above purport were received by the Grand Secretary from the Hampshire Lodges; the result being that Dunckerley was for the second time appointed Provincial Grand Master for that county.

    " Dear Sir,

    " I beg you will present my grateful acknowledgment to Lord Effingham for the honour he has done me by the appointment for Hampshire in compliance with the request of my Brethren in that County.

    " I am greatly oblig'd to you for your attention to my request in making out the Patent & therefore wish it to be thus ' Do hereby constitute & appoint him the said T. D. Provincial Grand Master of and for the Counties of Dorset, Essex, Gloucester, Somerset and Southampton; together with the City and County of Bristol, and the Isle of Wight; with full power, &c., &c.'

    " This will be very pleasing to the Brethren at Bristol and the Isle of Wight; and it will enable me to appoint a greater number of *blue & red* Aprons; which I find of great advantage to the Society, as it attracts the notice of the principal Gentlemen in the several Counties, who seem ambitious to attend me at my Prov. Grand Lodges.

"I go on saturday into Essex ; & am to hold a Grand Lodge at Colchester the 13th of next month.

" Your affect. & faithful Brother,

" THOS. DUNCKERLEY."

This letter bears no date but it was received by the Grand Secretary in August, 1786, so that Dunckerley's re-appointment must have been made in that month.

" Hampton Court Palace, Nov^{er.} 3^{rd,} 1786.

" My dear Friend & Brother,

"I believe you will be of my opinion that (to avoid Accidents) all Draughts should be tendered for payment as soon as possible, which is the reason of my troubling you with the enclosed (which Bro^r Meyler sent to me) before I transmit the state of the Lodges, when I hope to send (at least) *sixty* Pounds on Account to Brother Heseltine for the Charity & Hall Funds, but fear some of the Lodges will defer it till the last day. Four Lodges in Hampshire, & one in the Isle of Wight have not yet sent in their lists, & I am in daily expectation of remittances from Bristol. This Post has brought me the List of the Southampton Lodge ; & I am ashamed to say there are *four* Registers due ; Viz., Sept. 4th & Nov. 3^{rd,} 1782 ; & April 25th & July 4^{th,} 1783. They have sent me no money, & plead Poverty. I shall write and threaten them with annihilation if they do not send to ye Charity & pay the Fees.

"Let me know per return that the Draught gets safe to hand & believe me,

" Yours Affectionately,

" THOS. DUNCKERLEY.

" William White, Esq."

The foregoing needs no comment ; it is printed merely as evidence of the earnest zeal by which the writer was always actuated in furthering the interests of the Society.

" Dear Brother,

"I was favoured with yours in due course; I have this day drawn on you for £5 in favour of Bro. Raggit—& taken his receipt—Please to insert in the next Calendar No. 18, *Lodge of Antiquity*, Three Tuns, Portsmouth.

"The Brethren of this place unite with me in a hearty Greeting with their request that you will get the account of this day's proceedings (on the other side) publish'd in a London Paper—I doubt not that my name as Subscriber & Contributor to the Hall will appear in its proper place.

"Excuse brevity, & believe me,

"Y^r faithful & affect. Brother,

"THOS. DUNCKERLEY

"21 August, 1788,

"William White, Esq."

Dunckerley's mother Lodge had not hitherto been distinguished by a name, but was only known by its number and the sign of the tavern at which it was held. It is not unlikely that the name was suggested by Dunckerley himself, as was probably the case with the Phœnix Lodge, which was founded by brethren who had been members of lodges that had become defunct. The following is the account of the proceedings referred to :—

"Portsmouth, August 21st, 1788.

"This being the birth-day of His Royal Highness Prince William Henry; the Most Antient & Honourable Society of Free and Accepted Masons assembled at the George Tavern in this Town, by Summons from Thos. Dunckerley, Esq., Provincial Grand Master for Hampshire, &c. A Lodge was open'd in honour of the day: and after Dinner the Provincial Grand Master gave the following Toasts.—The King & the Society—the Queen—the Duke of Cumberland Grand Master of England—the Prince of Wales—the Duke of York & the Army—Prince William Henry, & the Wooden

L

Walls of Old England: with a hearty wish that His Royal Highness may live to be an Ornament to the Navy, & a Terror to the Enemies of Great Britain—the Duke of Gloucester & the Royal Family—the Duke of Beaufort; Lord Effingham, Sir Peter Parker, Sir Edmund Affleck, &c. The Bells were rung & the Standard Display'd on the Church Tower. The Meeting was numerous & very respectable: the day was pass'd with that regular & harmonious Hilarity, peculiar to the Royal Craft, it was ' the Feast of Reason and the Flow of Soul.' "

"Hampton Court Palace, Sept. 5th, 1791.

"My Dear Sir,

"I have received your favour of the 3rd Instant, with admonitory Letters for the Lodges, Numbers 33, 205, 314, & 500. I must beg leave to remark, that it is not two years since No. 33 sent £1. 1s. 0d. to the Charity; and it is not *seven months* since No. 205 sent £1. 1s. 0d. to the same Fund, according to the Printed accounts for Nov. 1789 & February, 1791—No. 314 has not contributed for three years past, but No. 500 sent five shillings to the Hall, last November— being their Arrear to the Hall Fund, that Lodge has been reduced by Naval Armaments, and I believe there are only the Master and Wardens remaining at this time, but it is probable they may increase. However, I have sent Your Letters to Cowes, Christchurch, and Gosport; but cannot (with propriety) send *that* which you have addressed to the Lodge at *Harwich.*

"I beg that you will present my best respects to Mrs. White, and that you will believe me, Dear Sir,

"Your Much Obliged Bro. & Servant,

"THOS. DUNCKERLEY.

"William White, Esq."

No. 33 is now the Medina Lodge, Cowes. No. 205 was the St. Nicholas Lodge, Harwich, erased in 1795. No.

314 is now the Lodge of Hengist, Bournemouth; and No. 500 was the Royal Navy Lodge, Gosport; erased in 1794.

It will be observed that when occasion required, Dunckerley could defend his lodges as well as threaten them " with annihilation."

"Salisbury, August 8th, 1792.

" Dear Sir,

"I left Hampton Court yᵉ 22nd ultᵒ from whence your packet (with Doctor Spry's high flown Composition) was forwarded to me in Hampshire.

"At the request of the Corporation of Southampton I laid the first Stone of All Saint's Church in that Town last Friday, for which purpose I had summoned the Lodges of the County to attend.

"I have the pleasure to acquaint you that a Lodge of *Antient* Masons of Southampton, near 60 in number, requested to join yᵉ Procession which I refused, unless they would come under the authority of our Grand Lodge. In two hours time I received their Petition for a Constitution, and immediately granted them a dispensation. I shall (with God's permission), hold a Grand Lodge at Shaftesbury, for the County of Dorset, in honour of the Birth Day of our Royal Grand Master. On the 16th I am to celebrate the Birth Day of the Duke of York in the City of Bristol; and I have desired the Lodges in Somersetshire to meet me at Wells on the 21st in honour of the Duke of Clarence. In the course of 26 years I have worn out 3 setts of Collars—I think (*entre nous*) the Grand Lodge can afford (from the Money I shall receive this summer) to present me with a new sett; which at all events, I must have next Monday tho' it should be at my own expense—I am therefore to request that you will send addressed for me, to the care of the R.W. Master of the Lodge at the Red Lion, Shaftesbury— *Eight* Collars ready made—by the Mail Coach next Saturday Evening.

"I am to desire that Warrants may be Engross'd for:

"The Lodge of Love and Honour to be holden at the Bell Inn, Shepton Mallet, County of Somerset—Bros. Samuel Norman, Master; Richard Collier, Senr. Warden; Thos. Hyatt, Junr. Warden.

"Dispensation dated June 4th, 1792.

"Royal Gloucester Lodge, East Street, Southampton, William Graves, Master; Wm. Baker, Senr. Warden; Wm. Clark, Junr. Warden.

"Dispensation dated August 5th, 1792.

"Let the first be sent to me at Wells—the other to be address'd to me at Southampton, to which place I shall return from Wells. Sincere regard to Bro. Heseltine & all Friends, from your Affect. Bro. &c.

"THOS. DUNCKERLEY.

"Wm. White, Esq."

The "Lodge of Antient Masons," here referred to, was No. 174 of the "Ancients," and was constituted by that body on the 22nd of April, 1772, Its capture could not have been other than highly gratifying to Dunckerley, who, as far back as 1777, had endeavoured to wean it from its allegiance. We must, therefore, make due allowance for some little jubilation on his part, and not imagine that on this occasion he was endowed with the faculty of seeing treble, or even double, especially as the Procession took place *before* dinner. Truth, however, compels me to notice that his estimate of the strength of his prize is not substantiated by its own records, for at an Emergency meeting held on the same day—August the 2nd, 1792, "To consider the propriety of accepting an offer from Bro. Dunckerley of giving us a dispensation to hold a lodge under the disration (*sic*) of his Royal Highness the Prince of Wales, and on ballotting for the purpose, there appeared, for it eleven; against it four." At a subsequent meeting—on the 10th of August—attended by twelve brethren, a majority of whom had agreed to " Petition Br. Dunckerley for a Warrant of Constitution, which request he was pleased to comply with, and the sum of £5. 15s. was paid into his hands for that purpose."

The Warrant having been granted (No. 503), the Lodge was duly Constituted by Dunckerley himself, he holding a Provincial Grand Lodge for that purpose on the 17th of September, the transaction being thus recorded in the minute book.

"Br. Thos. Dunckerley then read the Warrant of Constitution & the Lodge was accordingly constituted under the name of the Royal Gloucester Lodge under the sanction of H.R.H. the Prince of Wales. After which the necessary Charges & regulations were read by order of the Prov. G.M. from the book of Constitutions

"Br. Dunckerley was then pleased to appoint Br. T. Lansdown, Tyler of this Lodge to be Grand Tyler for this County; likewise Br. Wm. Graves, Br. Wm. Baker, & Br. Wm. Clark, Grand Stewards for the County.

" Br. Dunckerley then proposed himself & Br. Grierson to become members of this lodge which was seconded by Br Macklin," Br. Grierson was balloted for and elected at the next meeting (Sept. 26th), but Dunckerley's name is not mentioned; the ballot probably being dispensed with in his case.

On the 10th of October several new members were proposed by Dunckerley who, together with Br. Grierson, was then "entererd" a member. He was evidently determined to make sure of his new acquisition for he frequently attended the meetings of the lodge and doubtless assisted in the ceremonies. On the 28th of November he appointed " Br Macklin a Grand Steward for the County," and on the 13th of February, 1793, he promoted him to the office of Prov. Grand Secretary, and appointed Br. Dusautoy, Provincial Grand Steward. No further mention of Dunckerley is made in the minutes of the lodge ; he was then in his 69th year, and doubtless found his Masonic duties press more heavily than had hitherto been the case.

It is not unlikely that without his aid the brethren found it somewhat difficult to work the lodge in accordance with the " Modern " usages and therefore determined to return to their old love.   On the 24th of June, 1794, it was " Agreed to hold a Lodge under the Antient Constitution, the transactions therefore of this Lodge shall be inserted in this book as before.

" Agreed that the Grand Lodge dues for this Antient Society shall be paid out of the Royal Arch Chest."*

For several years after this resolution was passed, the lodge acted on the principle of having two strings to its bow, by working under both Warrants, a proceeding which, if not without a parallel was certainly most unusual. Judging from the number of members returned to the two Grand Lodges the " Ancients " had the preference, but many of the names are to be found in the Registers of both Societies.

After 1803, the " Moderns " appear to have been much neglected, no names being *returned* until 1810, when six were sent in, but with no information as to the date of making, age, residence, or profession ; they were, however, entered in the Register and a note appended to the foregoing purport. Five out of the six, had already been returned to the " Ancients " and their names, fees &c., duly entered in the Register of that Society. From this time all intercourse with the " Moderns " appears to have ceased, although both numbers were brought forward at the Union in 1813, when No. 174 became No 212. At the closing up of the numbers in 1832, it became No. 152, and in 1863 it was

---

*For the foregoing extracts from the Records of the Royal Gloucester Lodge and others of an equally interesting character which have been unavoidably omitted, I am indebted to the W. Bro. John E. Le Feuvie, P G D. and D.G.M Hants and Isle of Wight. H. S.

allotted the position on the Roll which it now occupies; viz.,
No. 130. No. 503 became No. 538 of the United Grand
Lodge and was retained in the Register until 1822, when
having evinced no sign of vitality during the preceding
twelve years it was removed from the List, the authorities
having probably arrived at the conclusion that it really had
ceased to exist.

CEREMONY OF LAYING THE FOUNDATION STONE OF
ALL SAINT'S CHURCH, SOUTHAMPTON.

From the records of the Medina Lodge, No. 35.

"On the 3rd of August, 1792, in complyance with the
request of Our Right Worshipful Provincial Grand Master,
Thomas Dunckerley, Esquire; made known by public
Advertisment, the following Brethren now, and formerly
belonging to this Lodge, in their proper Provincial
Cloathing and Jewels, attended by the Tyler, joined the
Provincial Grand Lodge of Concord, opened by Our said
Provincial Grand Master at Southampton, and preceded by
a Band of Musick and a number of Operative Masons,
went in procession to the Audit House, where being
graciously received by Sir Yelverton Peyton, Mayor, the
Aldermen and Corporation and Clergy of the Town and
Neighbourhood, an Oration in praise of Masonry was
delivered by Brother Jeans and a suitable Ode sung.

"The Worshipfull Mayor and Corporation, with all the
Lodges assembled, then proceeded to Saint Hollyrood's
Church where an excellent Sermon, applicable to the
purpose of the meeting, was preached by Brother James
Scot, and Sundry select pieces of sacred Musick, with the
Coronation Anthem, performed by a Band of Fifty Vocal
and Instrumental Performers; after which the Procession
proceeded to the Scite of the Church of All Saints,
in order to lay the Foundation Stone of the New Church,

which was Masonickly done by Our Provincial Grand Master, in the presence of the Brethren, Mayor, Corporation, Clergy and many thousand Spectators assembled on this occasion, who decently testified their joy thereat.

"Sundry Coins and Medals in a Box, also an Inscription Plate, together with the History of the Town of South'ton. engrossed on Parchment and inclosed in a Christial Vial, being deposited under the Foundation Stone at the South-West Corner. An Anthem purposely composed was then sung, as was Brittania Rule the Waves; Afterwards the Mayor and Corporation returned to the Audit House and the Brethren to the Grand Lodge, which was closed in due form.

"The Medena Lodge being the oldest Lodge present, in conformity to a resolution of the Grand Lodge, took precedence of all other Lodges in the Procession of this day, the Lodge Concord excepted, in the Order following:—

Wm. Bennet, Tyler, Apron lined with Garter Blue.
John Major and Geo. M. Ross (Stewards) with white Wands
& Aprons lined with crimson.

Aprons lined with Garter Blue.
{ Lancelot Foquet, Treasurer & Everhard
  Stock, Secretary.
  Robert Fabian, S. Warden & Isham
  Chapman, J. Warden.
  Wm. Holloway, Dy. Prov'l. Grand
  Master P Temp.

All in White Gloves.

"The Brethren to the number of One hundred and fifty, together with his Worship the Mayor and several of the Corporation, dined in perfect harmony at the Public Rooms, attended by a Band of Musick.

"After dinner the Operative Masons to be employed in rebuilding the Church of All Saints, bearing their real working Tools, preceded by their Officers with their proper Attributes, entered the Room and received a suitable Charge respecting the Work they had undertaken; and being refreshed and complimented, with great decorum, returned to their Habitations.* The Brethren and Gentlemen assembled, finished the day in the most social manner and parted early in the Evening, having previously obtained permission of Brothers Jeans and Scot to print their Excellent Oration and Sermon delivered at the Audit House and Saint Holyrood's Church." It is supposed that not less than Ten Thousand Persons were assembled on this laudable occasion.

	£	s.	d.
Paid Vessel Hire to & from South'ton . . .	1	1	8
Gloves and Ribbons		16	0
House Bill at South'ton.	2	13	0
	£4	10	8 "

AN ORATION

PRONOUNCED AT THE AUDIT-HOUSE IN SOUTHAMPTON,

August 3, 1792.

ON OCCASION OF LAYING THE CHIEF CORNER-STONE OF A BUILDING

CONSECRATED TO THE WORSHIP OF GOD

[Inscribed to the Mayor and Corporation of Southampton, and to the R W. Provincial Grand Master, THOMAS DUNCKERLEY, Esq. and Brethren of the Society of Free and Accepted Masons, who associated in public Procession, were present when it was spoken†]

I PRESENT myself before this very respectable audience in order to fulfil my duty as a Freemason—of whom *obedience* is a strong *characteristic*.

Obedient, therefore, to the commands which I have

---

* Of *course*! And without making a *single* call on the way   H S

† This oration, though it has been hitherto handed about anonymously, we take the liberty of saying, was composed by our worthy Br T s J s M D. of S

received, it is my intention to diffuse all explanatory light, not strictly *forbidden,* respecting this *ancient* and *mysterious* Society, that such of my hearers as are not Freemasons, and particularly those who form the chief delight of man in every civilized association, may have some idea of the *origin* from whence, and of the *principles* on which, we act.

Freemasonry is a speculative *science* (if I may use the term) issuing from that important practical *science* Geometry; the laws of which were observed in the *creation,* and still are manifest in the *regulation* of the world.

And as the Grand Lodge of the *universe,* this stupendous globe, excels in magnificence of design and stability of foundation demonstrative of its Builder—so, contemplating this mighty scale of perfection and wonder, with a view to useful application, does our Society proceed—conceiving the importance of *order* and *harmony,* and catching the spirit of *beneficence,* from what is observed of *wisdom, regularity,* and *mercy,* in the world of nature.

Nature, indeed, surpasses art in the *boldness, sublimity,* and *immensity* of her works; man can only contemplate, in awful amazement, her mightier operations; but, in her lesser designs, the ingenuity of man advances, with admirable success, from *study* to *imitation*—as is demonstrated in the wonderful *variety* and *beauty* of the works of art—the *imitative* arts particularly, and chiefly in those of *painting* and *sculpture.*

But of all the works of *human art,* Masonry is certainly the *first,* as most useful, and therefore approaching nearer in effect to the beneficent purposes of Providence. Architecture has justly been deemed the favourite *child* of *civilization;* it is the science which has ever discriminated by its progress *refinement* from *rudeness* : by its presence or absence *savage* from *social* life. In countries where *operative* Masonry never laid the *line,* nor spread the *compass;* where Architecture never planned the *dome,* nor projected the *column,* all other

evidences of elegant improvement are sought for in vain—
all is darkness and barbarism.

If we trace our Order by the Science which gave it
birth, without recurring to the *creation*, as has been done,
or to the chief subject of *creation*, man ; we shall find it of
great *antiquity* — but, without contending for an higher
origin, we refer it, with confidence, to the *building* of
Solomon's Temple.

The general history of this *memorable* building is well
known ; Consummate Wisdom delineated the *plan*, and the
Craftsmen atchieved [*sic*] the *design* of the Great Architect
of the Universe. Under this knowledge we cannot be surprised that Science and Morality went hand in hand : we
are taught that the *workmen* were divided into *classes*, under
competent directors ; that the *implements* of *operative*
Masonry were made symbols of moral duties ; and from the
nature and interpretation of those *symbols*, handed by *tradition* down to us, we learn that the purport of them was to
form good men ; to inspire a love of *fidelity, truth*, and
justice ; to promote *friendship* and *social manners* ; to asso-
ciate men under the banners of voluntary *order* and *virtue*.

It is from this high *origin* that we derive our existence
as a Society ; from this source we draw our *line*, our *rule*,
and our *compass* : It is from hence that we adopt the
Measure of Space, used as such by the *operative* Mason, and
apply it to ourselves as a *measure* of *time*, giving us an
orderly *routine* of *duties*.

The Square, which enables the artist to form and fashion
his work, teaches us *symbolically* to form and fashion our
lives. It is an *emblem* of morality, and instructs us in that
most important moral obligation, to do as we would be done
unto—to live upon the *square* with all mankind.

The Level, used in art to make the building plain and
even, morally teaches us the *equality* of our nature. it
serves as a memorial that we are *equally* born to act our

parts on this great theatre of life ; that we are equally subject to diseases—to accidents—to sorrows ; that we are equally
under the care and protection of the Great Parent of all ;
that we are *equally* doomed to die—to be levelled with the
earth—to corrupt—to be forgotten   Art and accident vary
our chances and situations, but, taking life altogether, we
shall find a more *equal* participation of good and evil than is
commonly imagined.

In the *edifice* of Freemasonry *equality** is the great
corner-stone—without it we know that friendships are ill-
cemented amongst men—the high and the low—the rich and
the poor—the proud and the humble—cannot form an intimate bond of union of any considerable duration.   Every
Brother, therefore, at his *initiation*, enters the Lodge, not in
splendour of dress nor pride of heart, but in a garb of
humility, in a *mind* of *lowliness* ; and he finds, when
admitted, that the laws of the Society have abolished, as far
as order will permit, all adventitious distinctions.

So, again, the Plumb-rule—an *instrument* of *art*, by whose
application the *building* is raised in a *perpendicular direction*,
is another of our *symbols*.—It is figurative of a fair and
honourable *plan* of life—and *typically* cautions us against any
deviation from an *upright* conduct in all our intercourses and
transactions, whether private or public.

The Compass is a mathematical instrument used to describe *circles :* this we adopt as an *emblem* of prudence—
it *symbolically* instructs us to put moral restraints on our
appetites†—to *circumscribe*, within rational bounds, our

---

* Not the modern *egalité* of the French, which, in its direction,
having rooted up all the decencies and charities of social life, has left
us a deplorable picture of moral depravity and degradation

† Men are qualified for civil liberty in exact proportion to their disposition to put moral chains upon their appetites—in proportion as their
love of justice is above their capacity. It is ordained in the eternal
constitution of things that men of intemperate minds cannot be *free*—
their *passions forge* their *fetters*.— BURKE.

wants, our pleasures, our expences—warning us that by an opposite *course* we shall endanger our quiet and our health, our reputation and our liberty.

Freemasonry, therefore, we have seen, deals in *hieroglyphics—symbols—allegories—*and to be qualified to reveal their *meaning,* a man must know more than a mere nominal Mason : the full *interpretation* of them, like that of the *mysteries* of *old,** is in select hands—has been committed only to those of tried *fidelity,* who conceal it with suitable care : others, if not deficient in intellect, yet wanting *industry* or *inclination* to explore the *penetralia* of the Temple, are not qualified, if willing, to betray it.—Hence the secrecy which has so long distinguished the *Fraternity.* This secrecy, however, has been urged against our *institution* as a crime; but the wise know that *secrecy,* properly maintained, is one of the best securities of social happiness : there is more private misery arising from an unqualified communication of words and actions than from the anger of the Heavens.

Other objections have been invented against our Society, but such as we do not condescend to combat—deeming it altogether a waste of time to wage war with *surmises,* and trusting to our conduct to repel the coarser shafts of *malice.*

From what has been said it appears that the *doctrine* of Freemasonry embraces all the *natural, moral,* and *political obligations* of Society.—It directs us to fulfil our *duty* to our

---

* The Eleusinian Mysteries, *e g*—The initiation was into *inferior* and *superior* mysteries, the candidates were *prepared, examined,* and *exhorted* to cultivate a purity of mind and circumspect conduct. After waiting some time at the gate before admission, the Hierophant appeared, invested with *symbols* of power. Proclamation was then made, "Far hence be the *profane,* the *impious,* and those whose souls are *polluted* with guilt." Skins of beasts killed in sacrifices were placed under the candidate's feet; hymns sung; thunder, lightning, and terrific scenes followed · these were *symbolical,* and explained by the Hierophant Afterwards they were conducted to the *sanctuary,* and there were entrusted with *secrets not to be revealed*

God—our King—our *neighbours*—and *ourselves*; it inculcates *reverence, resignation,* and *gratitude* to Him who made and preserves us—*Obedience* and *loyalty* to him who in *justice* and *clemency* rules over us—*Courtesy* and *amity* to our neighbour—*Equity* and *compassion* to all mankind. It teaches us to *pity* and *forgive* our enemies, to *love* and *reward* our friends, to relieve the distressed, and cherish the neglected.

Masonry is confined to no form of faith nor sect of religion; and her *charity,* like her *creed,* is universal. So, too, as she rejects all bigotry in matters of faith, she nourishes no blind zeal on the *subject* of *politics,* nor affords any support to *civil discord* or *popular commotion.* Private *benevolence,* in its extensive operations, becomes *patriotism*—which is, in fact, *public benevolence ;* from *liberality* of thinking and acting towards *individuals,* it becomes propitious to general *liberty*—but it is liberty *void* of licentiousness.

The grand *Principles* of our *Order* are those of *peace,* and *patience,* and *good-will ;* they hold out no *encouragement* to *faction*—no *extenuation* of private *defamation* and *slander.* As far as the welfare of the state depends, our wishes, as those of all good members of the community, are for its improvement, but under the guidance of order and wisdom. In the hands of the *vulgar* and the *violent,* attempts at national reforms lead to anarchy and confusion—to every violation of *property, liberty* and *life :*—A momentous *example* of this truth engages at this time the notice of the world—*

> ————————" May no such storm
> Fall on this land, where *ruin* must reform."

Under the *auspices* of Freemasonry, therefore, we are taught to improve the public tranquillity by following a life of *virtue* and *obedience,* and, in *union* with the wise and the good, to seek *peace* and *enjoy* it.

" Freemasons' Magazine," 1794, vol. iii., page 9.

---

* The Revolution in France. H. S.

THE MEDINA LODGE, No. 35.

The above mentioned lodge first appears in the Engraved List of Lodges for 1734, with 17th February, 173⅔, as the date of its Constitution, implying that it was Warranted in what would now be deemed the year 1733. Some doubt, however, appears to have existed in the mind of the engraver, or on the part of the authorities, even at this early stage of its career, for in the 1740 list the year is altered to 1732, and so it continues through all the lists down to 1787, when 1731 is given as the year of its birth. This last change seems to have been satisfactory to all concerned for nearly a hundred years, but the question does not appear to be finally settled ; for in the Masonic Calendars from 1880 down to the last issue 1733 replaces 1731.

The earliest minute-book of the lodge gives the date of its Constitution as "Saturday, the fourteenth day of February, 1732." John Lane, who has paid particular attention to this subject, having spared no efforts, in the compilation of *Masonic Records*, to ascertain the correct date of Constitution of the various lodges mentioned in his invaluable book, assigns the 17th of February, 1733, to the Medina Lodge. The question is, Which is correct ?

It would appear at first sight that the lodge records should be reliable, especially as they extend to the year 1736, only three or four years after the lodge was constituted. I confess, however, that I am somewhat sceptical on this point, and for these reasons. The volume referred to is not the original minute-book, but a transcript, very handsomely engrossed some few years subsequent to the revival of the lodge. It commences with the by-laws headed as follows : —

" Orders, Rules, and Ordinances to be observed and kept by the Lodge of Free and Accepted Masons, held at the House of Brother Philip Huddy, known by the name of the *Theatre Tavern*, in Mansell Street, in Goodman's Fields, Constituted on Saturday, the fourteenth day of February, 1732."

"Discontinued from the 24th June, 1734. Revived on Monday, Nov. 1st, 1736."

The actual records begin with the minutes of a meeting held on the 8th of November, 1736; and from the absence of all reference to any previous transactions, I infer that the brethren who resuscitated the lodge were an entirely new set of men, who had no knowledge of the existence of previous records, or they would probably have had them engrossed as well as their own transactions, and thus completed the history of the lodge.

The fee of two guineas for the constitution was paid between the 21st of November, 1732, and the 29th of May, 1733, no Grand Lodge being held in the interval. Moreover, the 14th of February, 1732, was *not* on a *Saturday*, but the 17th of February, 1733, *was*. I am inclined, therefore, to the opinion that the date last mentioned is correct.

At the risk of extending this volume beyond its prescribed limits I will venture to extract a few quaint items from the early records of this venerable lodge previous to touching upon that portion of its history which relates to Dunckerley's connection with it.

14th of March, 1737. "Brother William Goudge this night made a present to this Lodge of a painted cloath representing the severall forms of Masons' Lodges." This was probably the first substitute for the old custom of "drawing the lodge" on the floor with chalk, &c., and the forerunner of Tracing Boards.

26th of December, 1737. "Resolved by the Lodge that Br. Thomas Singleton do forthwith prepare us a sett of Mahogony Candlesticks of the Three Orders. To wit, the Dorick, Ionick & yᵉ Corinthian, the price of yᵗ whole not to exceed nine pounds."

10th of July, 1738. " A motion was made by Bro. Cock For gloves for some Brethren and all our Sisters."

8th of January, 1739. " The Master informed the Lodge that he had rec'd a Letter from the Grand Master and Grand Wardens with a proposal inclosed for raising yearly £310, for yᵉ carrying on and providing for 20 children of Masons, Binding 4 to Trades every year, &c."

22nd of January, 1739. "This night yᵉ Lodge took into their consideration, concerning the Letter rec'd from the Grand Master, and the Brethren whose names are hereunto subscribed are desirous to assist and encourage so laudable and good an undertaking."

This was the first attempt to establish a school in connection with Freemasonry. The proposal was formally brought before the Grand Lodge on the 31st of January, 1739, by a Br. John Brayman. "But after a long Debate, and several questions put, there being reason to apprehend that it would greatly affect the Fund of Charity already established, the same was rejected."

12th of March, 1739. " Bro. Standerd made the Lodge a present of Table Jewells.

" Bro Carter on his marriage generously treated the Lodge to a Gallon of wine."

1st of November, 1753. " Brother Seymour being Intoxicated with Liquor, Interrupted our R W.M. Bro. Wooller, in the course of his Lectures in Masonry, therefore it was unanimously agreed that he should be fined one Bottle of Wine for such offence."

18th of April, 1754. " Bro. Wright proposed that every Member or Visitor who brings a Dogg into this Lodge shall be fined in the sum of one shilling. A Ballot was demanded and carried by a majority that there should be no Dogg brought."

The lodge continued to hold its meetings at various taverns in the East-end of London until early in the year

1761, when it migrated to West Cowes, Isle of Wight. For several years after this removal it evidently had but a precarious existence. If meetings were held prior to 1767 no minutes were kept nor were any payments made to the Grand Lodge after the 5th of June, 1761, on which date it is credited with a guinea.

Dunckerley paid £2. 2s. to the Grand Treasurer on behalf of the lodge early in 1767, the minutes commencing in September of the same year and continuing till August the 3rd, 1768. There is then a gap until March 19th, 1771, after which date the lodge appears to have ceased meeting until 1779.

On the 23rd of April, 1773, it was erased by Grand Lodge together with several other lodges, " not having contributed anything to the Fund of Charity for some years past."

In 1779 the lodge appears to have been reinstated, but there is no reference to the transaction in the Grand Lodge Records. Hence, I conclude that Dunckerley himself was responsible for the resuscitation ; and this view is in a measure confirmed by the following extract from the minutes of the first meeting held after that event.

29th of October, 1779. " Lieut. Thomas Dunckerley, Esq , of the South Battalion of Hampshire Militia, P.P G.M. for this County, having in the absence of the Right Honorable Lord Charles Montague, the present P.G.M. granted a Dispensation to Bros. Lancelot Foquett, Robert Dixon, William Holloway, James Davies, and George Maynard, for holding a lodge in this Town to make Masons, &c. A Lodge of the first degree was open'd accordingly, £2. 2s. voted to the General Charity and £2. 2s. to the Hall Fund."

Resolved, " That the Grand Master be required to restore this Lodge to the former Number."

Dunckerley presided over this meeting and attended several meetings held during the following month.

20th of December, 1779. " Proposed and unanimously agreed that Gloves be presented to the Wife or Friend of every Member (as is customary on the like occasion) in consequence of the said Lodge being restored to its antient No. 39."

Had the Medina Lodge remained longer in abeyance "its antient No. 39" would have been lost to it beyond even Dunckerley's power of recovery, for the lodges were then in process of being re-numbered, and the vacancies in the list being filled up in conformity with a Resolution of Grand Lodge, passed on the 7th of April, 1779. Doubtless Dunckerley was aware of what was going on; hence his efforts to save the old lodge from extinction, for had its revival been delayed till the end of the year a new Warrant as well as a new number would have been indispensable.

27th of April, 1787. " Three Letters from our R.W. P.G.M., Thomas Dunckerley, were read, one of which said Letters bearing date the 22nd of December last, acquainted our R.W. Master that Edward Rushworth, Esq., is appointed Deputy Provincial Grand Master of the Isle of Wight, which is now a distinct Province, independent of the County of Southampton. Another of said Letters inclosed a Dispensation for holding a Lodge at Newport for 6 months from 12th of February last. The third Letter, bearing date March 7th last, contained an appointment of Provincial Grand Officers for the present year, vizt., Lancelot Foquet, S.W., Wm. Holloway, J.W., Christ^r Ratsey, Treasurer, Wm. Civil, Sec^y, Joseph Starbridge, Sword Bearer, Wm. Bennett, Tyler (Aprons to be lined with Garter blue silk), John Major, T. H. Eggerking, and Alex^r Watson, Provincial Grand Stewards (Aprons to be lined with crimson silk)."

This being the first appointment of Provincial Grand Officers for the Isle of Wight, it may possibly interest the present members of the Medina Lodge to know something more of their Masonic ancestors. I will therefore give their profession and residence.

Lancelot Foquet, Officer of Customs, East Cowes.
Wm. Holloway,   Do.   do.
Christ^r Ratsey, Grocer, West Cowes.
Wm. Civil, Painter,   Do.
Joseph Starbridge, Watchmaker, West Cowes.
Wm. Bennett, Shoemaker,   Do
John Major, Ropemaker, East Cowes.
T. H. Eggerking, Mariner, Norway.
Alex^{r.} Watson,   Do.   Scotland.

At that time the " Medina " was the only lodge on the Island, and with the exception of the Dep. Prov. G.M., the Provincial Grand Officers were all members of it.

The following letters are copied from a Letter-Book still carefully preserved in the archives of the lodge :—

" Cowes, 22nd Jan., 1787.

" Medena Lodge, No. 33.

" Right Worshipfull Provincial Grand Master,

" Your much esteemed favour of the 22nd ulto. I received in course, and should have answered it sooner but that I had not till yesterday the pleasure of seeing the Gentleman you have been pleased to nominate your Deputy for the Isle of Wight. The Medena Lodge, give me leave to assure you, Sir, are much obliged to you for the favor done them in this appointment, as well as to Mr. Rushworth for the Honor he does them in accepting thereof.

" Agreeable to your directions, inclosed I transmit you a list of our Lodge. From the 5th of July, 1780, to the present time I have had the Honor to preside as Master, and have annually remitted £1. 1s. for the Charity, exclusive of Hall Fees, last year excepted (our Finnances then being low, was under the necessity of deferring it). Mr. Rushworth, the first time he has y pleasure of seeing you, will deliver you £1. 11s. 0d. to be apply'd as follows : One Guinea to the Charity and 10s. to the Hall Fund for registering the two last made Brothers, Eggerking and Watson, as by reference to the enclosed List will more fully be seen.

" Mr. Rushworth having signified to me his wish that a meeting of the Masons of the Isle of Wight be held on next St. John's day to hear a Sermon at Newport Church (that being the most central part of the Island, where, of course, a greater number of Bretheren would assemble than at Cowes), and it being my opinion, also, that a thing of this kind would promote the good of Masonry by inclining the Bretheren of Newport, at some future time to solicit a Constitution for themselves, I shall beg leave to submit the following Queries :—

" Can we (with propriety) adjourn our Lodge on such an occasion to Newport, open it there, and go in procession to Church ?

" May we at any time open our Lodge at Newport, at the request of Candidates desirous of becoming Masons, if it be more convenient at that place than at Cowes ?

" Would not the adjourning or removing our Lodge to Newport for one or more days be deemed by the Grand Lodge an actual removal of the Lodge, there to remain, though our intentions are nothing more than to accommodate the Bretheren in other parts of the Island untill such times as they may apply for a Constitution to hold a Lodge in Newport ?

" If a Dispensation from you for the foregoing purpose should be necessary, we have to beg the favor you will grant it us. As Master of this Lodge, I could wish to do everything to meet your approbation ; therefore take the liberty to crave your assistance, and as I should be at a loss how to regulate a procession to Church, shall be much obliged to you for a List of the Order in which we should proceed, or anything relative thereto you may think proper to communicate. In the meantime, I remain, with the utmost Respect,

> "Right Worshipfull Provincial Grand Master,
>> "Your faithfull & most obed't. Servant,
>>> "WM. HOLLOWAY,
>>>> "Master of No. 33.

"To Thos. Dunckerley, Esq.,
> "Hampton Court Palace,
>> "Middlesex."

> "Cowes, March 2nd, 1787.

"Right Worshipfull P.G.M.,

"Your much esteemed Favor, inclosing a warrant of Dispensation for holding a Lodge at Newport, came duly to hand, for which, as well as the Instructions therein contained, please accept our warmest Thanks. We are very happy in understanding your Intentions to visit us and go in procession to Church on the 24th of June next.

"Your Instructions with respect to Brother Harrington shall be particularly attended to.

"Agreeable to your desire, Inclosed is a List of our Members. I was not made in this Lodge, but in Jamacia, as said list will more particularly explain. Not having been at Newport since I received your Letter, have not seen Captain Prescot, but believe himself and Family are well.

"I have only to add that I am with the greatest respect,
> "Rt. W. Prov. G. Master,
>> "Your most humble Servant,
>>> "WM. HOLLOWAY,
>>>> "Master of No. 33.

"To Thos. Dunckerley, Esq."

> "Cowes, June 8th, 1792.

"Rt. Worshipfull P.G.M ,

"At the request of the Brethren of the Medina Lodge, I have to beg the Favor you will (prior to the ensuing Festival) appoint new Provincial Grand Officers, to enable you to do which I herewith transmit you a List of the Lodge as it now stands, together with the last list of Provincial Grand Officers by you appointed in your Letter to Brother Holloway, dated March 7th, 1787.

" I must at same time beg leave to observe that Edwd. Rushworth, Esq., who you (5 years since) was pleased to nominate your Deputy, has not hitherto vouchsaved to visit us, though repeatedly sollicited ; and, conceiving that his distance from us makes it inconvenient for him to attend, in the name of the Lodge, I have to beg you will be pleased to appoint some other person, and if you are at a loss who to nominate, with your leave, we will point out to you a Gentleman residing near us who, we make no doubt, will readily accept the Office on proper sollicitation. Hoping to hear from you as soon as convenient,

" I remain, with due respect,

" R.W.P.G.M.,

" Your most obed. Servant,

"To Thos. Dunckerley, Esq.   " HUGH SIME.

" Hampton Court Pallace,

" Middlesex."

The following is copied from the minute-book, and was read in the lodge on the 4th of July, 1794 :—

" Southampton, March 28th, 1794.

" Dear Brother,

" Last night I received from the Master of the Packet your Letter with the List of Fees, Contributions to the Charity Fund, and Donations to the Royal Cumberland Free Masons' School, together with Five Pounds One Shilling for the above purposes, which I have sent to the Grand Secretary by this post.

" While it is agreeable for you to execute the Office of Deputy Provincial Grand Master for the Isle of Wight ; it will give me pleasure to have so worthy and respectable a Brother for my Representative.

"I am, with much regard,

"Your affectionate Brother,

"THOMAS DUNCKERLEY.

"N.B.—I purpose (with God's permission) to set off for Hampton Court on Thursday, the first of May next, where I shall remain till you hear further from me.

"To Wm. Holloway, Esq.

"Cowes, Isle of Wight."

William Holloway seems to have been well worthy of the honour conferred on him by his distinguished chief. He was re-appointed by Dunckerley's successor, and continued in the office of D.P. Grand Master for many years. The members of the Medina Lodge owe him, as well as Dunckerley, a debt of gratitude for having prevented its erasure. In the early part of the present century the lodge again fell into decay, and I learn from a note in the Grand Lodge Register that in 1807 it could only boast of seven members; in 1808–9–10 this number was reduced to two, viz., William Holloway and Richard Pinhorne. Two of the former members appear to have rejoined previous to 1813, since which period the Lodge has enjoyed increasing prosperity, and is now held in a commodious hall devoted exclusively to Masonry, at a short distance from the *Vine Tavern*, where it was originally established at Cowes.

I cannot well close this portion of my undertaking without expressing my gratitude for the uniform courtesy extended to me by the Members of the Medina Lodge, my acknowledgments being especially due to Bros. Barfield, P.G. Treasurer, P.M.; Wheeler, W.M.; Faulkner, P.M.; and Mursell, P.M. and Secretary; for having materially assisted me in the compilation of the foregoing sketch by readily placing at my disposal the valuable and most interesting records of their Lodge.

MEMORIALS OF FREEMASONRY IN ESSEX.

Dunckerley's first appearance in Grand Lodge as Provincial Grand Master for Essex was on the occasion of the Dedication of Freemasons' Hall by Lord Petre, on May the 23rd, 1776. Hampshire and the Isle of Wight being then separate provinces, this was the third province placed under his care. He had only recently been appointed, and the accompanying letter was probably the first received by him in his new capacity. The writer, Benjamin Didier, was an attorney, and was made a Mason in 1734. Hitherto Essex had been under the supervision of the Grand Secretary, and as there were but four lodges in the county in 1776, the authorities doubtless concluded that Dunckerley's energy and enthusiasm might be the means of adding to the number, and thereby increasing the much needed contributions to the funds of the Grand Lodge. Two out of the four lodges appear to have been in abeyance at the time, viz., No. 250 at *The Saracen's Head*, Chelmsford, constituted in 1764, and No. 430 at *The King's Head*, Malden. These lodges made no return of their members to Grand Lodge, and were ultimately erased from the list, the former in 1782, and the latter in 1785.

"Globe Lodge, Harwich, 22nd May, 1776
"R.W. Sir,

"This serves to acknowledge the Favour of your obliging Letter, with the printed Account of the intended Dedication of the Hall, therein inclosed, which Ceremony several of us would have attended; had we had earlier Notice thereof. We are all sensible of your great Abilities, from the Specimen thereof given in the printed excellent Charges preserved in our Lodge, and rejoice that we are now under your care. On the other side you have the required List of our Lodge: the Members are the same I delivered to the Grand Secretary's Clerk, with the Monies required towards the Hall, since which we have had no alteration among us.

"Our Lodge was on the 13th Aug. 1764, constituted at the Sign of the three Crowns in this Town: in the Year 1768 removed to the Sign of the half Moon; and in the Year 1771 to the Globe, our present Station.

"I have made no Columns for Members discharged, or for the Occasion thereof, as the only one expelled was Richard Bennett for great Irregularity, of whom I wrote a particular Account to the Grand Secretary on 24th of January, 1775: whereupon he was soon after by Order of the Grand Lodge, expelled the Society, to which Order I must beg leave to refer you; that it may be observed by the Lodges in your Province, as a Caution; That neither he nor any of his pretended Masons may gain admittance among them.

"Your health has been drank with ✡ and with the most respectful Greetings of the Lodge, I beg leave to sub-scribe myself,

"R.W. Sir,

"Your affectionate Brother
& humble Servant,

"B. DIDIER.

"To Thos. Dunckerley Esq."

The lodge here referred to was afterwards removed to *The Swan,* and was known as the St. Nicholas Lodge No. 174. It fell into abeyance after 1792, and was erased by order of Grand Lodge on the 15th of April, 1795.

"Hampton Court Palace, July 10th, 1776.

"My Dear Friend,

"I set out for Essex the 13th Inst., and as I have not yet rec'd my warr't of Deputation, shall call at your house that Day; but if you should be out of Town, beg you will have the goodness to leave Orders that it may be

Deliver'd to me. At the same time, I beg a Warr't of Constitution may be ready for the Lodge at Colchester, as I intend (with God's Permission) to Constitute that Lodge, on Monday, the 15th Inst. It is to be held at the King's Head Tavern, in that Town.

The Rev'd Wm. Martin Leake, LL.B. ⎫ ⎧ Master.
Collin Hossack, M.D. ⎬ ·· ⎨ Sen. Warden.
Thos. Boggis, Esq. ⎭ ⎩ Jun. Warden.

"Let it be dated at London June 11th, 1776, & blanks left for the names of my Deputy & Secretary.

"My Wife and Daughter unite in sincere regard & am,
"Dear Sir,
"Your obliged Friend & affect. Brother,
"Thos. Dunckerley.
"Jas. Heseltine, Esq."

"Hampton Court Palace, July 15th, 1776.
"Dear Sir,
"I did myself the pleasure of Writing to you the beginning of last week to Desire you would Order a Warr't to be made out for Constituting a Lodge at the King's Head Colchester, that I should call for it at your house, next Saturday the 20th Inst.; & at the same time would take my Warr't of Deputation, both which I hope will be ready.

"I had a letter yesterday from Bro. Martin Leake (who I have appointed a Provincial Grand Secretary) he begs I will take a Book of Constitutions with me, which I think will be best in Sheets as a Supplement is intended, and then they may be bound together.

"You will much oblige me by a line in return to-morrow Night.

"Receive our best Wishes,
"From yr Affect. Bro. & Servant,
"Jas. Heseltine, Esq." "Thos. Dunckerley.

The last two letters refer to the Lodge of Unity No. 402, erased by order of Grand Lodge the 9th of February, 1791. Dunckerley's name as an Honorary Member, heads the list of members in the Grand Lodge Register. It seems to have been rather select for a country lodge, and probably declined on his ceasing to take an active part in its affairs.

"CHELMSFORD CHRONICLE," June 25th, 1784.

"Yesterday a provincial Grand Lodge of the most antient and honourable fraternity of free and accepted Masons was held at the Black Boy Inn, in this town; at eleven o'clock in the forenoon the brethren went in procession to church, and heard divine service. A sermon was preached 1 Thess., chap. iv., part of the 9th verse, by the Rev. Brother Firebrace. During divine service a hymn composed by the Prov. Grand Master, was performed on the Organ by the Rev. Mr. Nare, accompanied by the voices of the brethren and the rest of the congregation."

Ibid, May 13th, 1785.

"To the Most Antient and Honourable Society of Free and Accepted Masons. Notice is hereby given, That a Grand Lodge for the County of Essex will be held at the Red Lion Inn, Colchester, on Thursday, the 19th inst., by Thomas Dunckerley, Esq, Provincial Grand Master, in honour of her Majesty's Birth-day. The Lodge to be opened at Twelve, and the dinner to be on table exactly at Three o'clock.

"The present and Past Grand officers and Stewards for this county are requested to attend with their proper clothing, and the Officers and Brethren of the respective Lodges with their Jewels, &c. By command of the Provincial Grand Master.

"Colchester, May 11th, 1785.

"RICHARD WHITE,

"Prov. Grand Secretary.

"Tickets for the feast at 5/- each to be had at the bar, at the Red Lion."

"Colchester, Sept. 14th, 1786.

"Dear Sir,

"Yesterday morning I was favour'd with yours of the 5th forwarded from Hampton Court, but as I met the Brethren (in Grand Lodge) at eleven in the forenoon; I did not leave them before this morning, tho' the Lodge was clos'd at 8 in the evening. We pass'd a very happy day and I appointed Bros. Sperling and Tyssen (Gentlemen of large fortunes in this County) to be my Wardens. I thank you for the Account of the Lodges in Hampshire, that have shewn their regard for me; but I did not know that there was a Lodge at the George Inn, Portsmouth.*

"I am ambitious to have Sir P. Parker's signature to my Patent, therefore beg you will defer it till his nomination is confirm'd.†

"In conformity to my new Patent, it will be proper that the Lodges under my care, be inserted in the next Calendar according to the following alphabetical arrangement.

B. City & County of Bristol. 155; 253; 296; 359; 445; 472.

D. Dorsetshire: 219; 382; with the two *new* Lodges.

E. Essex: 30; 51, 205; 270; 402; 411.

G. Gloucestershire: 462 City of Gloucester.

H. Hampshire: 18; 206; 314; 400; 485.

S. Somersetshire: 39; 212; 230; 294; 369; 473.

W. Isle of Wight: 33.

"The above will give great pleasure to the Brethren of Bristol & the Isle of Wight and I hope will meet with your approbation.

---

* The Hampshire lodges had petitioned the Grand Master to appoint Dunckerley Provincial Grand Master in succession to Captain Pascal, deceased. H. S.

† Sir Peter Parker had recently been appointed D.G.M. of England. H S.

"Next Monday Evening I am to visit the Lodge at Ilford on my return home.

"Believe me most sincerely y^r· Affect. Brother,

"THOS. DUNCKERLEY."

"Hampton Court Palace, March 30th, 1787.

"Dear Sir,

"I have this morning receiv'd a letter from Braintree in Essex, requesting me to grant a Warrant of Constitution to confirm the Dispensation which I gave them to hold a Lodge at a *Private* Room in that Town, Dated Nov 3, 1786, of which I inform'd you and receiv'd for answer that the Number would be 491. I must now desire you will do me the favour to get the Warrant made out with the above date, for the Lodge of Good Will, to be held at a private room, Braintree in Essex. Bro. William Low, Master, Bro. Richard Biss, Sen. Warden ; and Bro. Thos. Osborne, Jun. Warden. If it can be engross'd by next Wednesday I can sign and send it the next day to Colchester, for my Deputy & Secretary to witness it.

"Your faithful and Zealous Brother,

"THOS. DUNCKERLEY.

"William White Esq."

William Low was a Baker at Bocking ; Richard Biss, a Hairdresser at Braintree ; and Thomas Osborne, a Brickmaker at Hedingham Sible. The Lodge was erased in 1823.

"Hampton Court Palace, May 10th, 1787.

"Dear Brother,

"I send this blank Form for a list of your *present* Members, to be delivered to me in the Grand Lodge at Bocking the 19th of this Month ; when I shall be happy to see as many from your Lodge as can make it convenient to attend ; and I propose, (with God's permission) to hold the Grand Lodge for your County *next year* at Harwich. I must desire you will send a line to the Master of the White Hart Inn, Bocking & acquaint him what number of your Brethren will dine there. You will see the Grand Lodge advertised in the General Evening Post of last Saturday, & it will also be in your County Paper.

"I must desire the Brethren to wear *Cock'd* Hats in the Procession to Church.

"Present my affectionate regard to the Brethren & believe me

"Your affect. Brother,

"THOS. DUNCKERLEY.

"The Master of No. 205

"At the Swan, Harwich."

"CHELMSFORD CHRONICLE," 25th of May, 1787.

"Extract of a letter from Braintree, May 20th.

"Yesterday being the Anniversary of her Majesty's Birth-Day, the brethren of the most ancient and honourable Society of Free and Accepted Masons assembled at the White Hart Inn, where a Grand Lodge was held in honour of the day, by Thomas Dunckerley, Esq., Provincial Grand Master for this County. A Grand Procession was formed to the church, and an excellent sermon given by the Rev. Brother Milbourne Peter Carter. A liberal collection was made for the poor, and an elegant dinner provided for the fraternity. The healths of our most gracious Sovereign; our much beloved Queen; the Duke of Cumberland (our Grand Master); the Prince of Wales; Prince William Henry &c. &c. were drank with all Masonic honours. The genuine spirit of loyalty appeared in the town, and the festival was conducted with that cheerfulness and harmony peculiar to the Society."

MASONIC FESTIVITIES AT CHELMSFORD.

From " The Freemasons' Magazine," 1793.

Chelmsford, *August* 16th.

On Monday last being the Anniversary of the Birth-Day of His Royal Highness.

THE PRINCE OF WALES,

GRAND MASTER OF FREE AND ACCEPTED MASONS,

Upwards of one hundred Brethren of that ancient and honourable Society assembled in this town, for the purpose of holding

A PROVINCIAL GRAND LODGE

In honour of the Day, to regulate the Masonic Business of the County, and to constitute the LODGE OF GOOD FELLOWSHIP, at the Saracen's Head ; the Right Worshipful Provincial Grand Master,

THOMAS DUNCKERLEY, Esq.,

Did not arrive till past eleven o'clock, having been previously detained on Masonic Business, by his Royal Highness the Grand Master, and the Right Honourable Brethren Lord PETRE, Past Grand Master, and the Marquis of TOWNSHEND.   Immediately on his arrival The Grand Lodge was opened in ample form, and the following Gentlemen were appointed Grand Officers for the County, viz. :

Brother COOK, Deputy Grand Master.

Brother LAMBERT, and T. WHITE, Grand Wardens.

Brother DICKIE, Grand Treasurer.

Brother CUPPAGE, Grand Secretary.

Rev. Brother LLOYD, Grand Chaplain.

Brother COOK, Grand Architect.

Brother BARTON, Grand Sword Bearer.

After the investment, the procession took place to Church in the following order, viz.

Band of Martial Music.

Two Tylers with drawn Swords.

Masters, Officers, and Brethren of the different visiting
Lodges, viz. :
Melford, Ipswich, Bury, Cambridge, London, &c.
Two Tylers.
Brother Cook, Deputy Grand Master, the Master of the
Lodge of Good Fellowship, Chelmsford, No. 462,
carrying the first great wax light, in an elegant inlaid
candlestick near three feet high.
The Wardens of that Lodge.
Secretary and Treasurer.
Other Officers and Brethren two and two.
The Master of the Lodge of Good-Will, Braintree, No. 401,
carrying the second great light, in a more elegant
candlestick than the former.
His Officers and Brethren of his Lodge, two and two.
The Master of the Lodge of Friendship, Ilford, No. 227,
carrying the third and last great light, in a most
magnificent superb candlestick, curiously inlaid with
different Masonic Hieroglyphics.
His Officers and the Brethren of his Lodge, two and two.
The Master of the Colchester Lodge, No. 47, carrying the
book of Constitutions, superbly bound, on a velvet
cushion, covered with royal blue silk.
His Officers and the Brethren of his Lodge, two and two.
The Master of the Well-Disposed Lodge, Waltham Abbey,
No. 28, carrying the Holy Bible, magnificently
bound and gilt, on a rich crimson velvet
cushion covered with royal blue silk, with gold fringe
and tassels.
The Officers and Brethren of his Lodge, two and two.
A Janitor.
Royal Arch Masons with Sashes and Medals, two and two.
An Equerry, K.T.
The Grand Registrar of the Order of Masonic Knights
Templar, in Uniform.

N

The Companions of that sublime Order, in Uniform, with black silk sashes, ornamented with a silver star of five points, a cross of gold, and an appendage of white satin.

' The Grand Lodge of Essex, in the following Order :

Grand Tyler.

Past Grand Officers, two and two.

Grand Stewards.

Grand Chaplain, and Grand Architect.

Grand Secretary, and Grand Treasurer.

The Two Grand Wardens.

The Grand Master, preceded by the Grand Sword Bearer, and supported on the right by the Deputy Provincial Grand Master,* and on the left by

Capt. Sir W. HANNAM,

Acting Grand Master for England, of K.T.

On their arrival at the Church the procession halted, and opening to the right and left, the Grand Master, with his Officers, preceded by the sword of state, entered first, and was followed by the procession inversed ; the three lights being placed in the middle aisle before the pulpit. During divine service, a Masonic Hymn, composed by the Provincial Grand Master, was sung, and a handsome collection made, which was given to the church-wardens and overseers to distribute to the poor of this parish. A most excellent and truly Masonic Sermon was preached by the Rev. Grand Chaplain, from this text, St. John, chap. viii. verse 32, "And ye shall know the *Truth*, and the *Truth* shall make you *Free.*"

The procession, in the order in which it first set off, returned to the Saracen's Head, where an elegant dinner

---

* This brother had evidently succeeded in solving the supposed difficult problem of how to be in two places at one and the same time, for it will be observed that he is said to have carried " an elegant inlaid candlestick," in another part of the procession. H. S.

was provided that did honour to the purveying abilities of Brother CASWELL.

After dinner the Lodge of *Good Fellowship*, which for more than three years had been acting under dispensation from his late Royal Highness the Duke of Cumberland, was constituted in DUE FORM; A short but most excellent address was delivered by Brother DUNCKERLEY, who, after recommending the cultivating the several moral and social virtues which so eminently distinguish the principles and ground-work of Masonry, recommended to the consideration of the Brethren that most excellent *Charity* the ROYAL CUMBERLAND FREEMASONS' SCHOOL, for clothing, boarding, and educating the daughters of poor Freemasons, and in order that that precept might be enforced by example, and that the Grand Lodge of Essex might be distinguished as well-wishers to the institution, he began a subscription by TWENTY GUINEAS from his own purse; this was followed by every member's contributing what suited his convenience; to which was added a benefaction from the newly-constituted Lodge, the whole amounting to a very considerable sum.

At an early hour the Provincial Grand Master took a most affectionate leave of the Brethren, who, with hearts full of fraternal esteem and cordial regard, accompanied him, preceded by the band of music, to the Black Boy, and after giving him three hearty and heart-felt cheers, parted with this amiable Veteran, who has been justly styled " the great luminary of Masonry." The company returned in form to the Lodge, where the business of Masonry was resumed under the able government of Brother COOK, Deputy Provincial Grand Master . . . but here we must draw the veil. . . . Our readers must excuse our saying anything more than that everything was conducted in that truly harmonic style that should ever accompany the assembly of a society whose tenets and principles have stood the test of revolving ages, and were never more *freely* investigated, more *fervently* embraced, or *zealously* supported, than under the auspices of the present Royal Family of Great Britain.

INSTALLATION OF DUNCKERLEY'S SUCCESSOR IN ESSEX.

From "THE FREEMASONS' REPOSITORY" for June, 1797.

Chelmsford, May 15th, 1797.

His Royal Highness the Prince of Wales, Grand Master of the Ancient and Honourable Society of Free and Accepted Masons, having been pleased to nominate and appoint *George Downing*, Esq , of Lincoln's Inn, and Ovington, in this County, to succeed the late *Thomas Dunckerley*, Esq., as Provincial Grand Master, this day was fixed for his Installation ; upon which occasion a most numerous and respectable assemblage of the Brethren attended.

The morning was ushered in with ringing of bells, &c. At nine o'clock near 100 Brethren assembled at the Black Boy, where a public Breakfast was provided. At ten the Lodge was opened by Brother Cook, of Barking, the Deputy Provincial Grand Master ; Brother Lambert, of Barking, and Brother White, of Colchester, Provincial Grand Wardens ; Brother Cuppage, Provincial Grand Secretary ; and Brother Brooke, Grand Treasurer ; in the presence of upwards of 160 Brethren. Brother Cook then addressed the Brethren in the following manner :—

" *Brethren*, The last time we had the pleasure of meeting each other in the Provincial Grand Lodge; it was under the guidance and protection of our late worthy Past Grand Master, Brother Thomas Dunckerley, a gentleman most justly esteemed by all who had the pleasure of knowing him. Since that period, it has pleased the Supreme Architect of the Universe (whose wonderful works he has so often explored, and so repeatedly explained for our in-

struction and advantage) to take him from the exalted and
honourable situation he held among our Fraternity to a
mansion not made with hands, but eternal in the Heavens.
I can assure you, Brethren that no one has more reason to
deplore his loss and assistance than myself; and I trust,
my worthy Brethren, that you, who were well acquainted
with his excellent character, will readily join with me in
pronouncing that 'take him for all in all, we scarce shall
see his like again.' But, Brethren, as it is contrary to the
true principles of Christianity and Masonry for the honest
and upright mind to despair, even under the greatest afflic-
tions, I have therefore no doubt but we shall meet with
some consolation and return for the loss we have sustained
by the appointment of a worthy Brother, whom I shall have
the honour and satisfaction to introduce to you this day,
and, with your approbation instal in this Chair, to succeed
our late departed friend as Provincial Grand Master for
this respectable and extensive county—a Brother and a
Gentleman who, I believe, is well known to several of the
Brethren present—I mean *George Downing*, Esq., of Lincoln's
Inn, and of Ovington in this County, who is as much
esteemed in private life as he is publicly honoured as a
Mason.

"I take this opportunity of observing that shortly after
the demise of our Brother Dunckerley, the different Lodges
in this County, being made acquainted with our Brother
Downing's character, connection, and situation in life, and
his having expressed a wish to succeed to the honour of
presiding over this respectable county, unanimously petitioned his Royal Highness the Prince of Wales our present
Most Worshipful Grand Master, to nominate and appoint
Mr. Downing to fill up the vacancy that was so great a loss
to Masonry in this county. I can assure you, Brethren,
that when you have the happiness of being acquainted and
connected with him as a Man, who is to preside over you

in future, you will not repent permitting me the great
honour of placing him in the Provincial Chair, and in-
vesting him in due form with the insignia of his office, to
preside over this truly respectable and numerous assemblage
of Brethren, to renovate our knowledge, guide us in the
true path between the Square and Compass, and amply
console us for the great loss we have sustained—And may
the three Grand Masonic Principles, Brotherly Love, Relief,
and Truth, aided and assisted by the three Masonic virtues,
Faith, Hope, and Charity, be a guide to our conviviality
this day."

Mr. Downing was then introduced into the Lodge by
his Friends, Adam Gordon, Esq., Provincial Grand Master
for Hereford, and William Forsteen, Esq., Provincial Grand
Master for Hertford, preceded by the Stewards, consisting
of Brothers Aaron Hurrill, Thomas Holmsted, William
Cuppage, William Low, Nathaniel Hayward, J. Goulding,
A. Brown, D. Wood, J. R. Rowland, and Thomas Wood;
and being conducted to the Chair, he delivered his patent
of appointment, which being read by the Grand Secretary,
and Brother Cook having quitted the Chair, Mr. Downing
was invested and installed by him, in due form, as Provincial Grand Master for the County of Essex, and was
accordingly saluted by all the Brethren with every token
of applause: after which the grand honours were given.

These ceremonies having taken place, Mr. Downing
delivered an oration, of which the following is the substance,
as near as could be collected:

" *Brethren,*

" The pleasure I derive from taking this Chair receives
a melancholy alloy from the consideration, that it is occasioned by the death of our late excellent Brother Dunckerley;
a man who, for conviviality of disposition, correctness of
principles, extent of Masonic knowledge, and readiness of
communication, stood, perhaps unrivalled; and who by the

happy application of these enviable endowments, not only conciliated the affection, but insured the improvement of the Craft over whom he had the honour to preside. He loved Masonry from his soul : and as his attachment was not the effect of a hasty impression upon a lively imagination, but the result of a long and well directed scrutiny into the nature and utility of the institution, he seldom failed to communicate a portion of his zeal to those with whom he conversed.

"In this county he may be considered to have been the Father of the Craft; and his death has been accordingly felt with a degree of filial regret—a regret which I am sorry to think will be increased by a comparison between him and his successor. I confess, Brethren, that when I contrast my own inexperience with his knowledge, and consider that I am going to build on foundations laid by so able an architect, I feel dispirited at what I have undertaken ; and find nothing to console me but the reflection, that with the foundation he has left a design of the superstructure, and a number of well-instructed craftsmen to assist in carrying it on.

"From my first initiation into the mysteries of our venerable Order, they have been subjects of my continual admiration, not so much on account of their *antiquity* as their *moral tendency :*—for though the former may attract the enquiry and gratify the research of the antiquarian, it is the latter which invites the cultivation, gives energy to the exertion, and ensures the final perseverance of the genuine *Freemason*. Let us not, however, affect to think lightly of the venerable sanction which our mysteries have acquired by the adoption of successive ages. Of their antiquity there is a sort of evidence which eclipses tradition. The method adopted by the craft for communicating instructions to their disciples, was in use before the invention of letters

"All the learning of the ancient world was conveyed in symbols, and intrenched in mysteries : and surely that is not only the most ancient, but the most impressive vehicle of knowledge, which, by applying sensible objects to a figurative use, affords amusement as well as instruction, and renders even the playfulness of the *imagination*, that most ungovernable of all the human faculties, instrumental to moral improvement.

"Those who have made enquiries into the rise and progress of science, have found that in the early ages all speculative knowledge was confined to a few, and by them carefully concealed from vulgar curiosity under the veil of mysteries, into which none were initiated, till not only their intellectual capacities, but the firmness of their characters, had been put to a severe test ; the result of which determined the degree of probability that they would resist the stratagems of curiosity and the imperious demands of authority.   The most famous mysteries on record are those in Persia, which were celebrated in honour of the God Mythra, and those at Eleusis, in Greece, in honour of the Goddess Ceres.

"Many arguments might be adduced to prove that both these were corruptions of Freemasonry, and hereafter I shall not want the inclination, if I do not want the opportunity to discuss them.   At present, however, I shall content myself with pointing out the similarity which subsists between the initiatory rites practised by the professors of those mysteries and by our Brethren, both antient and modern ; more especially in the allegorical part of their ceremonials."

Here followed an historical detail of the ceremonies attending initiations into the Mythraic and Eleusinian mysteries, and a comparative examination of them with Freemasonry, all of which we are induced to omit, for reasons that will readily occur to the Masonic part of our readers; and at the conclusion of this account the Provincial Grand Master took an opportunity of making some remarks on the practices of different Lodges in England and France, in what is termed making Masons, and then proceeded as follows:

" I conceive it to the credit of the English Masons in general, that they are content to make a solemn impression without doing violence to the feelings of the candidate, to *awe* without *intimidating ;* and we may be bold to affirm, that by how much soever the terror of an initiation into either of the Heathen mysteries above alluded to exceeded the terror of a Masonic examination, by so much, and more, do the moral and social advantages of the latter institution exceed those of the former. . . . .

" For proofs of the moral tendency of Freemasonry we need only appeal to our lectures, a due attention to which cannot fail of proving highly auxiliary to the practice of religious and social duties. In them will be found a summary of moral conduct, which in soundness of principle and facility of application, may justly vie with the most celebrated systems of ethics ; the whole rendered familiar to our conceptions, amusing to our fancies, and impressive on our memories, by easy and apposite symbols. By them we learn the analogy between physical and moral good ; to judge of the wisdom of the Creator by the works of the creation ; and hence we infer that our wise Master builder, who has planned and completed a habitation so suitable to our wants, so convenient to our enjoyments, during our temporary residence here, has exercised still more *wisdom* in *contriving*, more *strength* in *supporting*, and more *beauty* in *adorning* those eternal mansions where he has promised to receive and reward all faithful Masons hereafter.

" Thus are our *faith* and *hope* exercised by Masonic studies ; but there is a virtue which Divine authority has pronounced greater than *faith* and *hope*, and to this excellent

virtue of Charity are our Masonic labours more especially
directed.   For this is the student reminded '*to consider
the whole race of mankind as one family, inhabitants of one
planet, descended from one common pair of ancestors, and sent
into the world for the mutual aid, support and protection of
each other;*' and that as the pale of our society incloses
persons of every nation, rank, and opinion, no religious,
national, or party prejudices should discover themselves at
our meetings; but that, as our Brother Preston very feel-
ingly expresses it, '*both hearts and tongues should join in
promoting each other's welfare, and rejoicing in each other's
prosperity.*' In a word, that we should not only profess,
but practise the three grand principles of *Brotherly Love,
Relief* and *Truth.*

"There are some, I well know, who are so little
acquainted with our principles and our practices, as to
contend, that the whole of Freemasonry consists in conviviality. To these we are not afraid to declare, that in this
respect we boast only this superiority, that our meetings
are not infested with strife and debate; and were this the
only distinguishing characteristic of the Brotherhood the
candle of Masonry might be pronounced to sink fast into
the socket. But to the honour of modern Masons be it
spoken, that an institution has been lately established
among ourselves, which, though the latest, is perhaps the
brightest jewel in the Masonic diadem. You will easily
perceive that I allude to our infant Charity in St. George's
Fields; an institution which resembles the universality of
our order, being confined to no parish, county, or climate;
it is enough that the objects are the female issue of deceased
or distressed Brethren. They are capable of election
between the age of five and nine, and remain under the
roof of this Asylum till fifteen. And when they are obliged
to make way for others, and sent out into the world to
practise the duties and give examples of the virtues they

have been taught, they are not abandoned by their generous benefactors, but cautiously placed out either as apprentices or domestic servants, with persons whose characters and situations have been scrupulously examined; a sum of money is given to fit them out; and a further sum, if, after a period of probation, they are found worthy of the patronage they have received. It will reflect infinitely more credit on this infant institution than any eulogium I can bestow on it, to state, that although it has not been established ten years, there are several Life Governors on the list, who have become so from having been witnesses of the good conduct of servants educated in this school. And nothing can afford a better proof of the economical use made of the subscribers' money, than the accounts lately published, which shew, that the whole expences of clothing, maintenance, and education, did not in the last year exceed £7. 9s. per child. On the whole, I cannot omit to observe, that a charity, in its design more benevolent, in its selection more judicious, in event more successful, was never established; and when I reflect on the obstacles it has surmounted, the expences that have been incurred, and the present increased and increasing state of the funds, I feel at a loss which most to admire, the liberality of the contributors, the wisdom and enterprize of the conductors, or the excellent management and disinterested frugality of the Treasurer.

"Brethren, I am ashamed to consider how much of your time I have taken up. One word more and I have done. I repose on your candour, of which I have already had an agreeable earnest, to overlook my defects. I request the regularity of your attendance at our Provincial Meetings. I rely on your regular contributions to the Grand Lodge; and your attention to charity in general, and to that I have recommended to you in particular; that the inhabitants of this wealthy and respectable county may support the same rank as Masons, which they justly hold as Men. In the Grand Lodge I shall consider myself as your Representative, and faithfully attend to whatever affects your interests. Finally, I hope you will consider and accept my unwearied attention to your concerns, as the best return I can make you for your recommendation to our Grand Master."

"The oration being finished, certain rites and ceremonies were duly performed. The Lodge was closed, and a polite message was received from Mr. Judd, a Magistrate of the County, with an offer of the Shire-hall for the use of the Brethren, which was very gratefully accepted. This was immediately followed by information, that General Egerton, the Commanding Officer of his Majesty's troops in the Barracks, had given orders for the whole line, consisting of four regiments, to be under arms, in order to grace the procession to church."

Here follows the order of the procession which, being similar to the one already described, may well be omitted.

"Before the procession began, the several Military Brethren belonging to different regiments in the county, consisting of Field Officers, Captains, and Subalterns, took their places, next before the Stewards of the Grand Lodge of England.

"In this manner the whole body, consisting of nearly 180 Brethren, proceeded in the most exact order to the Church. On their arrival at the church porch, the Brethren, dividing to the right and left, halted, making a passage for the Provincial Grand Master, who entered the church first, the rest of the Officers and Brethren following in inverted order.* Prayers were next read by Brother Wix ; and a discourse from the following text ' The Builder of all

---

* How funny they must have looked! H. S.

things is God,' was delivered by the Grand Chaplain*; after which a collection was made for the poor of the parish of Chelmsford, amounting to upwards of £12 and the procession returned to the Black Boy, in the same order as to church. The Grand Lodge was then adjourned to the Shire-hall, which was nearly filled with the Brethren, placed in the most exact order, by the excellent management of the Provincial Grand Stewards. The Grand Lodge of Essex was then opened in the Grand Jury-room, and consisted of the Provincial Grand Master, his Deputy, the Provincial Grand Wardens, and other Provincial Grand Officers, accompanied by the Grand Officers of England, and preceded by the Band of Music. The Provincial Grand Tyler, and the ten Provincial Grand Stewards, entered the Hall; the Brethren all rose, and with plaudits loud, reiterated, and continued, welcomed their Master and his Officers. After parading three times round the room, the Master was placed in the Chair with such demonstrations of joy, as plainly evinced the impression his conduct had made on every Brother. . . . . After dinner a great number of loyal and masonic toasts were drank. The Royal Cumberland Freemasons' School for supporting the Children and Orphans of poor Freemasons having been recommended to the society by the Provincial Grand Master, a subscription was immediately set on foot for its support, and one hundred and seven guineas were subscribed for that purpose.

"The case of a brother in want, who had seen better days, was likewise represented to the society. A handsome collection was made for him, and an application to the Grand Fund of Charity for his further support, was agreed on, which concluded the business of a day—never exceeded, if equalled, in the annals of Masonry."

---

* The Rev. William Brook Jones. The Sermon was published in "The Freemasons' Repository," for April, 1798. H. S.

MEMORIALS OF FREEMASONRY IN
DORSETSHIRE.

It is difficult to fix the exact date of Dunckerley's connection with Dorsetshire, but from its contiguity to his first Province (Hampshire) he was probably well known to the fraternity in that county' for a considerable period before his appearance in the official records as its Masonic chief.

A printed list of subscriptions to the Hall Fund received at a Quarterly Communication, held November the 12th, 1777, contains the earliest mention of him in that capacity which I have been able to find ; it is as follows :—

"Thomas Dunckerley, Esq., Provincial G.M. for Essex, and Superintendant of the Lodges in Wilts and Dorset, £5. 5s." It is evident, therefore, that the County had been placed under his care prior to the 12th of November, 1777, although he was not formally appointed Provincial Grand Master until a few years later. That he did not allow the grass to grow under his feet will be seen from the following :—

G.L. Minutes, February the 4th, 1778.

"The Grand Secretary informed the Grand Lodge that he had received a Letter from Brother Dunckerley, Superintendant of the Lodges in Wilts, Dorset, &c., complaining that the Royal Edwin Lodge at Lyme Regis in Dorsetshire had in a contemptuous manner neglected to answer any of the several Letters he had written to the Master, and that he could not procure any account of the situation of such Lodge, and therefore requesting the Grand Lodge to direct a Letter to be written to the Master of the said Lodge, and acquaint him that unless the Lodge gave an immediate & satisfactory answer to Brother Dunckerley's Letters it would probably be erased from the List at the next Quarterly Communication.

"A Motion to this effect was then made and seconded, and on putting the Question it passed in the affirmative."

Ibid., April the 8th, 1778.

"The Grand Secretary informed the Grand Lodge that he had received a letter from Brother Dunckerley whereby it appeared that the Lodges at Devizes and Lyme Regis still remained in contempt. Whereupon a motion was made that the Lodge at Devizes for such contemptuous behaviour be struck off the List of Lodges, which motion was seconded, and on putting the Question, it passed in the affirmative.

"Brother Hayward then informed the G.L. that the Lodge at Lyme Regis above mentioned had for some time past been in a declining state; and that the few remaining Members were about to remove it, and endeavour to restore it thereby.

"Whereupon the Grand Lodge declined passing any censure at present."

Copy of a letter from the Grand Secretary.

"Drs. Commons,

"14th Dec., 1779.

"To the R.W. Master of the Lodge at Lyme Regis.

"R.W. Master & Brethren.

"Bro. Dunckerley P.G.M. for Dorset has repeatedly complained to the G.L. that your Lodge had not taken any notice of the various Letters written by him, nor corresponded with him in any manner whatever. At the G.L. held on the 4th Day of November last, Bro. Dunckerley's Complaints were taken into Consideration, when it was Unanimously resolved, That a Letter should be written to your Lodge informing you That unless you renew your Correspondence with Bro. Dunckerley and acquaint him with the situation of your Lodge in order to be reported at the next Q.C. to be held on the 2nd day of February next, the Constitution of your Lodge will be withdrawn.

"I am,

" R. W. Master & Brethren,

" Your most Obedient Servant & Brother,

"J. H."

This was apparently a case of " flogging a dead horse," no response being made to these appeals, and as no new members were registered after 1774, the lodge was probably defunct when the foregoing was written. It was erased on the 12th of April, 1780.

"Salisbury, Nov. 9, 1783.

" My Dear Friend Bro. & Compⁿ

"I have now the pleasure of enclosing the lists of the Lodges at Pool, Dorchester, and Weymouth, with the above Draught for £7. 3s., payable to our worthy Treasurer, who I hope has not sustain'd any loss by the late dreadful Fire. I beg to submit to your consideration that in the future forms of the lists to be return'd, a column may be appropriated to enter the Places (for the Lodges) where persons have been made, who afterwards become Members of other Lodges: & remarks, &c., may be enter'd at the bottom, or on the other side. I refer you to the list from Weymouth & hope it will meet with your approbation. I am to request you will do me the honour to acquaint our Royal Grand Master that I held a Provincial Grand Lodge (for Dorsetshire) at Weymouth the 24th of last June—A Procession was made *to* and *from* the Church, by a very respectable number of Brethren in that County, as will appear by the Lists. I also held a Provincial Grand Lodge at Pool, on the 12th of August, in honour of the Prince of Wales compleating His twenty-first year. We embark'd in three Sloops, preceded by the Dorsetshire Band, & din'd by the Castle belonging to Mr. Sturt (Member for the County), where the flag was display'd, and a royal salute was made from the Battery, which we return'd with three times three. In the Evening grand fire-works were exhibited on our return to Pool.

"N.B.—The Mariners in the several Lists are Captains of Merchant Ships.

"The Lodge of Science in this City have, with much reluctance, consented to my application for an acceptance of my resignation of the superintendancy of the County, in hopes no person will be appointed to succeed me, on the recommendation of the Sarum Lodge *only*.

"I am therefore to desire you will make my request to the Duke of Cumberland that he will be pleas'd to accept my resignation of the Superintendancy of Dorsetshire and Wiltshire; and that His Royal Highness will honour me with the appointment of Provincial Grand Master for Dorsetshire, Somersetshire, and Gloucestershire : being already the Grand Superintendent of Royal Arch Masonry in those Counties I shall be very willing to resign Essex, when a proper Person can be found to succeed me. It will give me much pleasure to hear from you, & that the Draught gets safe to hand. My Wife unites with me in sincere regard to Mrs. H—— yourself & family.

"Your Affectionate & obliged Bro. &c.,

"THOS. DUNCKERLEY."

The Brethren whose names are appended hereto having been good enough to search the records of the Lodge and Chapter of Amity for references to Dunckerley, I have much pleasure in recording the result of their investigations.

"Poole, June 24, 1780.

"Provincial Grand Lodge for Dorsetshire.

"Present —

Thomas Dunckerly, Esq. ...	...	P.G.M.
Alexander Campbell, M.D. ...	...	D.P.G.M.

o

John Leer	...	...	...	S.G.W.
John Colbourn	...	...	...	J.G.W.
James Starke	...	...	...	P.G.T.
Bravell Friend	...	...	...	P.G.S.
Rev. George Marsh	...	...	...	P.G.C.
James Hamilton	...	..	...	P.G.A.
Joseph Rule	...	...		P.G. Sword B.

John Fricker ... ... ⎫
Wm. Walker ... ... ⎪
John Lester ... ... ⎪
Wm. Lodder ... ... ⎪
Michael Festing ... ... ⎪
James Buckland ... ... ⎬ P G Stewards
Thos. Mercer . ... ⎪
John Pitt ... ... ⎪
George Oakley ... ... ⎪
Rich. Gibbs ... ... ⎪
Br. Adams ... ... ⎪
Br. Blanchard ... ... ⎭

Thomas Jeans, M.D. ...P.G.W. of Hampshire.*

To Charity	...	...	...	1	1	0
To the Hall	...	...	...	1	1	0
To the P.G.L.	...	...	...	2	12	6

"The Dinner was held in the Town Hall, where Mirth, Good Humour, Jollity, & a Number of Excellent Good Songs Sung by Brother Thomas Dunckerley concluded the P.G.L.

Memo.—Att Dinner Fifty-six att 5s. each Tickett.

Paid Musick	...	...	...	2	12	6
Paid the Singers	...	...	...	1	1	0
Parish Clerk	...	...	...	0	2	6

Relieved Mary Pottle with £1 13s. 0d. by voluntary subscription.

"The Warrant of the Chapter of Amity, dated the 26th

---

* Afterwards D P.G M. of Hampshire   H. S.

June, 1780, was signed by Thomas Dunckerley, Esq., who was present at a Chapter held on that day, and also at a Chapter held on the following day, at each of which there were three Exaltees.

"August 12th, 1783. Lodge of Emergency. This Night The Right Worshipful Provincial Grand Master Bro. Dunkerly visited this Lodge, the day having been spent in grand order and decorum by the Brethren on the Water wth Bro. Dunckerly in honour of the Prince of Wales's Birthday, who came of age this day, & the ev^g was concluded wth grand Fire Works by Bro. Ford.

Visitor   ...   Bro. Van Dyke * . . . .

"August 13th. Lodge of Emergency. . . . Bro. Rich'd. Allen & Bro. John Ackerman were Ballotted for and admitted, and were made E. Apprentices by the Rt. Worshipful Provincial Gd. Master, Bro. Dunkerley.

Visitor   ...   .   Bro. Van Dyke.

"1783, Sept. 3. This night it was ordered that Bro. Garland be Repaid the money he has paid for the Rt. Worshipful Provincial Grand Master's Picture to Bro. Van Dyke ; also that a frame be provided for the picture & paid both by the Treasurer.

"1783, September 5. By Cash paid Br. Jos. Garland for the Deputy (*sic*) Grand Provincial, Br. Dunkerley's Picture £5 5 0

"Dec. 3. By a new case for the Picture   0 3 6."

We certify that the foregoing are true extracts from the Lodge of Amity Minute Book, and Treasurer's Cash Book, and the Chapter Minute Book.

JOHN PAINTER, P.M 749,
Secretary Lodge Amity, 137.
ALBERT TAYLOR,
Scribe E Chapter of Amity, 137.

Poole, 4th October, 1889.

---

* Philip Van Dyke, Limner, was initiated in the Caledonian Lodge, London, ... D ... 177.., and ... Salten in the Dunkerly an Chapter, Dorchester, ... 1788. H. S

The picture referred to has been carefully preserved by the Lodge of Amity, and now adorns the new Masonic Hall at Poole. Notwithstanding the very small amount of his remuneration, the artist appears to have taken considerable pains with his work; and, speaking merely as an amateur, I should say the portrait possesses considerable merit It represents the upper half of a gentlemanly-looking personage of a somewhat florid countenance, cleanly shaven and rather expressive features, with very light brown eyes, which have a humorous twinkle. He is wearing a white Court wig of the period, and the dark blue collar and emblem of a Provincial Grand Master, over a bright red coat and light waistcoat. A Royal Arch jewel is suspended on his left breast. On the whole, he has the appearance of quite a gay young spark of certainly not *more* than sixty years. At first I was puzzled to account for the red coat, which seems a little out of place on a retired naval officer, and I cannot help thinking that the picture would have been all the better had the garment in question been less conspicuous; it may, however, have been a portion of the wearer's uniform, as an officer in the Hampshire Militia. It is the only original portrait of Dunckerley of which I have any knowledge.*

This portrait was engraved by C. West, and published in 1786. Dunckerley refers to it in one of his letters to the Grand Secretary, and says "it is considered a good likeness." At present I know of the existence of only two copies of this engraving; one belonging to the Lodge of Unity at Ringwood, and the other at the Freemasons' Hall, Bristol.

The portrait which forms the frontispiece of this volume

---

* I have since learnt that there is a similar portrait in oil at the Freemasons' Hall, Bristol, probably painted by the same artist and at about the same period H S

was painted some years later, and published as an engraving in 1789. During the interval Dunckerley appears to have aged considerably, having had several attacks of illness, in consequence of which he looks much less robust than he does in his earlier portrait.

"Hampton Court Palace, April 21st, 1785.
" Dear Brother,

"Cavil & Dissipation prevented my talking to you at the Quarterly Communication on *real* Masonry. You may remember I jockey'd Dermot out of Newfoundland by obtaining a Warrant for a Lodge at Placentia, it has produced another petition for a Lodge at Harbour Grace on the Island, I rec'd it this morning under cover of a letter from my very worthy Deputy, Doctor Campbell of Pool. I beg you will get it executed (in the same *neat* manner as that for Gloucester) as soon as possible & send it (by the Pool Coach) to Alex. Campbell Esq., at that place, as the Ship that is to convey it is under sailing orders. Favour me with a line, when it is sent, & I will be Accountable to you for the £5. 15. 6. which will be paid to me when I visit Pool this Summer. The Certificate came safe to hand, for which you will also give me Credit 6s. 8d.

"I had no opportunity when I saw you last of enquiring if you heard of the Captain concerning the letter sent to me from Bro. Webb for a Lodge on the Island of Dominica. I shall be glad to have a line from you in return that I may acquaint Bro. Campbell with the success of the Petition from Newfoundland.

"Make my sincere regard Acceptable to Bro. Heseltine, serious Bro. Berkeley, &c. &c.

"From y^r faithful & Affec. Brother.
"THOS. DUNCKERLEY.

"N.B.—I have paid 6s. for postage since ye last Accounts for Letters from Bristol, Essex, Bath, Pool,

Bridgewater & Dorchester. If the Accounts, of the last Quarterley Communication are printed before the 6th of next month, do me the favor to leave those for the Counties, under my care & also for Newfoundland with Bro. Berkeley as I propose (with God's permission) to attend the Grand Committee of Royal Arch Masons that day at his house.

"William White, Esq."

At this period the principal trade of the "Town and County of Poole" was with Newfoundland. This will account for Dunckerley's frequent visits to the port, and his success in propagating Masonry in North America, while his jovial disposition and nautical experience will readily explain his personal popularity in the neighbourhood, the residents being all more or less interested in seafaring matters.

He continued in the offices of Prov. Grand Master and Grand Superintendent of the Royal Arch for Dorset until his decease in 1795.*

MEMORIALS OF FREEMASONRY IN GLOUCESTERSHIRE.

Although Dunckerley was not the first Grand Master for Gloucestershire, as was the case in most of his other provinces, he was the second appointed to that office. His predecessor seems to have been one of the "more-ornamental-than-useful" sort, a merely nominal head of the Craft in the county, selected probably from motives of friendship, rather than for any special qualifications for the post In 1753, Lord Carysfort, then Grand Master, appointed Sir Robert de Cornwall, "Provincial Grand Master for the counties of Worcester, Gloucester, Salop, Monmouth, and Hereford"

---

* Further references to Freemasonry in Dorset, will be found in "Miscellaneous Letters, etc." See Index. H. S.

With the exception of having attended a meeting of the Grand Lodge when his patron was present, the records throw no light on whatever services he may have rendered to the Craft to merit this great distinction   The Book of Constitutions, published in 1767, contains a list of all the Provincial Grand Masters that had been appointed since the office was created (1726).

This list was revised in 1769 with a view of printing the names of such as were still in existence, with the List of Lodges for 1770.

Those who had not already been superseded were accordingly written to by the Grand Secretary, to ascertain whether they were dead or alive. He apparently acted under instructions, for against the name of Sir Robert de Cornwall is written "Take no notice of him."

It is not therefore a matter of surprise that the name of this highly favoured brother should not be found in "A List of the present acting Provincial Grand Masters" for 1770; nor does it appear in any subsequent list. His successor, Dunckerley, was appointed by the Duke of Cumberland on the 3rd of May, 1784, and doubtless soon made his presence felt in the province, for at the first meeting of Grand Lodge after his appointment, he paid in on behalf of his new constituents the following contributions, viz., No. 253, Union Lodge, *Rising Sun*, Bristol, £2 2s. No. 359, Lodge of Jehosaphat, *White Hart*, Bristol, £2 2s. No. 445, Sea Captains' Lodge, *Three Tuns*, Bristol, £3 12s. The first named lodge had been erased on the previous 7th of April, but was reinstated at this meeting, probably at Dunckerley's request; it was finally erased in 1838 No. 359 was erased in 1809; No. 445 united with No 296 in 1788, now the Royal Sussex Lodge of Hospitality No. 187. At the same meeting the Temple Lodge No 395 at the *Bath Chair*, on the Quay, Bristol, was erased, having "ceased to meet for a considerable time."

Having commenced operations in his usual manner by clearing away the dead, and reanimating the languid, his next step was to infuse new blood into the Order. His first efforts in this direction were eminently successful, resulting in the formation of a highly respectable lodge which remained on the list until 1851. A second lodge was constituted by him a few months later which had but a brief existence (the Temple Lodge No. 472), being erased in 1791. The following letter refers to the first of the two lodges last mentioned :—

"Hampton Court Palace, Feb. 1st, 1785.
"Dear Brother,

"I must beg you will get a Warrant engross'd for the Royal Gloucester Lodge, to be held at the Bell Inn, in the city of Gloucester—Bro. John Phillpotts Master—Thos Woore, Sen. Warden—and Charles Elmes, Jun. Warden. To be dated Hampton Court Palace, Jan. 10th, 1785 (the date of the Dispensation which I have granted them for holding the said Lodge. I hope it will be well wrote, & a proper margin left for frame & glass. You will let me have it as soon as convenient, to be sign'd & forwarded to my Deputy & Secretary at Bristol. It should not be folded, but roll'd on a small roller. Be assur'd of my sincere regard & present my most respectful Greeting to the Grand Lodge assembled in Quarterly Communication. It gives me much pleasure that I have constituted two Lodges in honour of the Dukes of Gloucester and Cumberland.*

"I beg to have the printed Accounts of your Proceedings to-morrow (as early as convenient) for *all* the Lodges under my care, in a parcel by the Hampton Court Coach.

"Your Affect. Brother & faithful Servant,
"THOS. DUNCKERLEY.
"William White, Esq."

---

* The Royal Cumberland Lodge No. 458, Bath. H. S.

From " The History of the Royal Gloucester Lodge By Thos. Taynton, P.M., 839 P.P.S.G.W," we learn that this lodge was duly constituted by Dunckerley in person on the 20th of June 1785, and that a few months later he brought to the notice of the members the subject of the " Hall Fund." After mature deliberation the lodge voted the usual £25, to be repaid by instalments, the amount being paid in by Dunckerley and duly acknowledged in the Grand Lodge proceedings of November 23rd, 1785. The adage " A Mason's Charity should know no bounds save those of Prudence " seems to have been fully exemplified in this lodge. Several very liberal donations were given to the Gloucester Infirmary, and in 1788 it was resolved that the lodge should subscribe three guineas annually to that Institution.

The line, however appears to have been 'drawn at Lunatic Asylums, for in 1793 the governors of the Infirmary appealed to the lodge for " subscriptions towards the erection of a Lunatic Asylum, but the application was, on a ballot at a subsequent meeting, rejected."* In 1786, at the request of Dunckerley, Bristol was made a Masonic Province, independent of Gloucestershire, thus enabling him to appoint all the Provincial Grand Officers for the latter county from the Royal Gloucester Lodge, there being no other lodge in the new province at this period.

In 1798 the members evinced their loyalty and patriotism by voting " 10 Guineas to the present Exigencies of the Government," the said government being then in very straitened circumstances. A fierce rebellion was in active operation in Ireland, and a French invasion being considered imminent, a public subscription had been set on foot for the purpose of aiding in the defence of the Country.

---

* Surely nothing personal could have been meant by the applicants? Some people are so *sensitive.* H. S.

"Hampton Court Palace,
"Oct. 9th, 1785.

"Dear Brother,

"I have this Moment received a Draught at one Month Date from the Royal Gloucester Lodge, No. 462, as a Loan to the Hall; I must beg you will send them a Medal addressed to Mr. Ware, Hatter & Hosier, Gloucester. I hope it will not be too late to be inserted in the Calendar.

"On the 29th Ultimo I wrote in return to your Melancholly letter of the 27th, & desir'd you would send the Bath Medal to Bro. Attwood of that Place.

"If I recollect right a general Dispensation may be had for 10s. 6d. pr. Annum to the Hall Fund for making a Mason under age (in case of necessity), or more than 5 at one time. I beg to hear from you in return (with the said Dispensation) as I have 8 to make the 19th Inst. (when I hope to see you) & one is not *quite* of Age.*

"Your Affec. & Zealous Brother,

"THOS. DUNCKERLEY.

"Are Registering Fees expected for Tylers, or Servants who are made Gratis? Mrs. D—— desires me to tell you that we have a bed at your Service, & desires you will bring Sister White with you.

"William White, Esq"

Bristol Gazette, June 29th, 1786.

THEATRE ROYAL BRISTOL.

At the particular request of Thomas Dunckerley Esq., Prov. G.M. and by the particular desire of the City and County, and of the several Lodges in this City of the most ancient and honourable Society of Free and Accepted Masons.

---

* This refers to the Lodge of Harmony, Hampton Court, see page 128.

For the Benefit of Brother Floor, *Prompter ;*

On Friday next the 30th of June, 1786, will be delivered a Masonic Oration. By Brother Murray. To conclude with an Ode, the Music composed by Mr. Boyton. The different lodges will be on the Stage in their proper Cloathing, while the Oration and Ode are performing.

After which will be performed, a Comedy called

" The School for Wives."

(Here follow the names of the performers).

To which will be added a Musical Entertainment of two Acts, called, *" The Son in Law."*

To begin precisely at half past Six o'clock.

Ceremony of Laying the Foundation Stone of St. Paul's Church, Bristol.

From " The Freemasons' Magazine," August, 1794.

"On Monday, August 17, 1789, being the birthday of his Royal Highness the Duke of York, the Most Ancient and Honourable Society of Free and Accepted Masons resident in Bristol, with a great number of visiting brethren, met Thomas Dunckerley, Esq., their P.G. Master, at the Merchant Taylors' Hall; from whence they went in procession (preceded by a band of music) to Portland Square, in order to lay the North-east corner-stone of St. Paul's Church. The stone being raised up by means of an engine for that purpose, the P.G. Master placed under it a plate with a suitable inscription, and various sorts of coins and medals, the stone was then let down into its place and properly fixed, and the P.G. Master gave three strokes with his Hiram upon which the G. Chaplain implored a blessing upon such a pious and laudable undertaking. The P.G. Master then delivered over to the architect the various implements of architecture, with instructions and directions how to proceed in the work with which he is entrusted.

After which the following lines were sung to the tune of " Rule Britannia."

> To Heaven's high Architect all praise,
> All praise and gratitude be giv'n,
> Who deign'd the human soul to raise,
> By mystic secrets sprung from Heav'n
> Sound! sound aloud! the Great Jehovah's praise,
> To him the dome, the temple raise

" The innumerable spectators testified their approbation by loud and repeated joyful acclamations. This sacred and solemn ceremony ended with a blessing from the G Chaplain. The Brethren then proceeded to St. James's Church, where the service was read by the Rev. D. Horndon A.M., and a sermon from the 13th Chap. of I. Cor. 2 & 3 ver., was preached by the G. Chaplain, the Rev. Brother Joseph Atwell Small, D.D. minister of the Church. During the service a Masonic hymn and an hymn upon his Majesty's happy recovery (written by the P.G. Master), were sung by the choir. The Fraternity then returned to the Merchant Taylors' Hall, where a sumptuous and elegant dinner was provided by Brother Weeks of the Bush Tavern.* The greatest harmony, good humour, and brotherly love prevailed, and the Brethren departed at an early hour, not without uniting in the grand design of being happy themselves, and of communicating happiness to others."†

MEMORIALS OF FREEMASONRY IN SOMERSET.

Dunckerley is first mentioned in connection with Somerset in the Grand Lodge Minutes, the 17th of November, 1784; when "The Grand Secretary having read some Letters and Accounts which he had received from Thomas Dunckerley Esq., Provincial Grand Master for Dorsetshire, Essex,

---

* From which place a donation of 20 Guineas was sent to a widow in great distress.

† For further references to Gloucestershire, see Index. H. S.

Gloucestershire & Somersetshire, whereby it appeared that owing to his Zeal and Assiduity among the Lodges under his care he had collected and remitted large sums of money for the Charity and Hall Funds. Upon which a Motion was made by Brother J. Heseltine, Esq. That the thanks of this Grand Lodge be given to Thomas Dunckerley, Esq. . . . . for his great attention to, and active endeavours in promoting the prosperity and good Order of the Lodges under his immediate inspection and in general for his long and zealous services on all occasions exerted for the Interest of the Society, which being duly seconded, passed Unanimously in the Affirmative."

At this meeting various sums of money were received from Dunckerley, on behalf of ten different lodges, three out of the number being held in Bath, viz., No. 39, *Private Room*, Queen Square, £2 17s. 6d No. 230, Lodge of Perfect Friendship, *White Hart* £4. 16s. and No 458, Royal Cumberland Lodge, *Bear* Inn, £4. 4s. One of the letters read by the Grand Secretary furnishes the date of Dunckerley's appointment for Somerset. This letter is dated the 3rd of November, 1784, and in it he says, "It is six months this day since I had the honour of being appointed Prov. G. Master for ye counties of Dorset, Essex, Gloucester & Somerset." It would thus appear that his formal appointment as head of the Province of Somerset was made on the 3rd of May, 1784. The following letter will show that this new honour was not of his own seeking, but was, in a measure thrust upon him.

"Lodge of Virtue, No. 294.

"Bath, 6th Feb., 1783.

"Hon^d Brother,

"Last Monday being our regular Lodge Night. I laid the Letter of the proceedings of the Grand Lodge of Emergency, 8th Jan. 1783, before the brethren when a

Subscription of Twenty-five pounds was agreed on towards the hall debt (if the Subscription is not yet full of which we beg the favour of your Immediate answer) to make the remittance directly and the fees for our Members made since our Letter of the 6th of Feb. 1782.

"We beg leave to inform the Grand Lodge we should be happy in having a provincial Grand Master appointed for this County; we have petitioned our most worthy Bro. Thos. Dunckerley, Esq. to accept that office; he informs us the Grand Lodge will not permit him to preside over any more provinces than what he already holds. We should esteem it a particular favour of the Grand Lodge to nominate a Gentleman for us who lives in or near this County. And beg humbly to submit to the Grand Lodge the following proposal: That a Plate for Certificates be engraved under the direction of the Grand Lodge to be used by all Lodges, with proper blanks for what may be necessary, and rendred to the Lodges at what price the Grand Lodge think proper and to make a Law that none but the above Certificates be used in future as we think it will be an advantage to the Grand Lodge and prevent Counterfeits.

"I am Sir, with due respect your most affectionate Brother.

"HENRY YOUNGLASS, M."

Extract from a letter written by the Grand Secretary in reply to the foregoing.

"28th Feb 1783.

.　.　.　.　.　"In consequence of the desire intimated of having Bro. Dunckerley appointed Prov. G.M for your County our worthy Bro. Heseltine has wrote to him to know if he will accept of it (in which case another Gentleman will be appointed for Wiltshire) and as soon as we have an answer you shall be informed of it. You certainly could not have thought of a more worthy or better Mason than

Bro. Dunckerley nor of one that is more zealous to promote the interest of the Craft.

"The idea you mention of having a General form for Certificates to be used by all the Lodges has a great deal of Merit in it & you may depend shall be brought forward for consideration."

Dunckerley's character and qualifications were probably well known to the fraternity in Bath at this period, and I infer from certain indications of activity among the Somerset brethren in 1783 that with his usual energy, he had made a tour of inspection of the various lodges immediately after he was asked to take charge of the Province. First we have the £25 to the "Hall Loan" from the Lodge of Virtue, doubtless voted at his suggestion, on the 9th of April the St. George's Lodge, Taunton, was erased, "having ceased to meet, or conform to the Laws." No. 212 Bridgewater met with a similar fate on the 19th of November, but was reinstated on the 11th of February 1784, on a promise of better behaviour, and on the 7th of April following, No. 357 Taunton was struck off the List.

From "Revelations of a Square," by Dr. Oliver.

"At a Lodge of Free and Accepted Masons called the Royal Cumberland Lodge, held at the Bear Inn, in the city of Bath, on Wednesday the 11th day of August, 1784, pursuant to a Warrant of Dispensation for that purpose, under the hand and seal of Thomas Dunckerley, Esq, Provincial Grand Master for the counties of Essex, Gloucester, Dorset and Somerset, bearing date the 7th day of August, 1784. The following brethren were assembled :—

Brother Thomas Dunckerley, P G.M., M. pro tem.

    ,,   William Street, S.W., pro tem.

    ,,   Milborne West, J.W., pro tem

    ,,   Thomas West, T., pro tem.

    ,,   Harry Atwood, ⎫

    ,,   Philip George, ⎭ Members of the said Lodge.

Brother John Smith, P.G. Secretary,
    ,,   Thomas Woolley, P.G. Steward,
    ,,   Peter Appleby, P.G. Steward,   } Visitors.
    ,,   William Birchall,

"A Lodge of the first degree was opened in due form, and it was proposed and unanimously agreed that Charles Phillott, of the said city of Bath, Banker, be made a Mason, He was called in; received the first degree, and *the Lodge was then closed.* After which a Lodge of the second degree was opened, when our Brother Charles Phillott was passed, and the Lodge closed."

Extract from the " Bath Chronicle," August 18th, 1784.

"Thursday (in honour of the birthday of His Royal Highness the Prince of Wales), Thos. Dunckerley, Esq. held at the White Hart in this City, a Provincial Grand Lodge for Somersetshire, of the most antient & honourable Society of Free & Accepted Masons. And on Monday, in honour of the birthday of His Royal Highness the Bishop of Osnaburgh, he also held at the Bush Tavern in Bristol, a Provincial Grand Lodge for that City and the County of Gloucester. The appearance of the Fraternity in compliment to the heir apparent and his royal Brother was very numerous and respectable, and the Entertainment truly elegant. Each day was spent with that social harmony and convivial happiness which has ever characterised the Brotherhood, and was indeed ' the feast of reason and the flow of soul.' "

I am indebted to Bro. John Gard, P.P.J.G.W., Bristol for the following :

"In an old minute book of the ' Sea Captains' Lodge,' No. 445, under date August 19th, 1784, is the following entry. " Thomas Dunckerley, Esq., Prov. G. Master for the Counties of Somerset, Dorset, Gloucester & Essex by virtue of his authority did hold a Provincial Grand Lodge at the White

Hart Inn, State Street, Bath for the county of Somerset, at which agreeably to invitation sent the R.W. Master and major part of the Lodge were present, and on Monday 16th Aug , a P.G. Lodge was held at the Bush Tavern by the aforesaid Thomas Dunckerley. Bro Hopkins R.W. Master of the Beaufort Lodge held at the Shakespeare, Prince Street, in the City of Bristol P.G. Treasurer, Bro. Hawkins R.W. Master of this Lodge P.G. Sec., but Bro. Hawkins intending to go to sea Bro Lewis was appointed in his place; Bro. Springer P.G. Senior Warden; Bro. Maddick R.W. Master of Jehoshaphat Lodge held at the White Hart, Broad Street in the City of Bristol, Bro. Vaughan . . . (erasures) . . . Bro. McCarthy, Bro. Wasborough, Bro. Maillard, Bro. Walters & Bro. Shortbridge of the Beaufort & Bro. Trotman of the Jehoshaphat Lodge P.G. Stewards, &c."

Under date December 12th, 1784, "At a meeting of the under-mentioned Lodges held here this evening it was agreed that the Brethren of the said Lodges meet at the Bush Tavern on Monday morning next at half-past 7 o'clock in order to proceed in procession to Bath, there to attend Divine Service and dine with Thomas Dunckerley, Esq. to celebrate the Festival of St. John the Evangelist." Then follow the names of " Beaufort " members (3); " Jehoshaphat " (3); " Temple " (3); " Union " (1) ; " Hospitality " (1); " Sea Captains " (9).

" N.B.—On Monday morning the 27th inst. as before mentioned, set off in chaises for Bath where the day was spent in perfect harmony."

" Bath, August 21st, 1784.

" Dear Brother,

" I have the pleasure to send you another Draught for *Twenty-five* Pounds lent to the Hall Fund by the Reverend Edmund Gardiner of Charles Street in this City, & I hope it will be with you in time to be inserted in the Calendar

P

for 1785. You will send Bro. Gardiner's medal to the above address. I go to Dorchester to-morrow, where a line from you (acknowledging the receipt of draught) will find me. Pray acquaint Bro. White that *every* Lodge in Bristol is in Gloucestershire, & I beg it may be so inserted in the new Calendar.

"I shall be able (according to the promises I have received) to give him the correct state of all the Lodges under my care in October & hope in addition to what is already done to send near £30 for the Charity & Hall Funds from yᵉ several Lodges.

"Yours *seriously* & sincerely,

"THOS. DUNCKERLEY.

"Rowland Berkley, Esq.

"Very bad pen & ink."

"Bath, August 22nd, 1784.

"Dear Brother,

"Yesterday I address'd a Letter to you covering a Draught of £25 for the Rev. Edmund Gardiner, lent to the Hall Fund. I have now the additional pleasure to send you another Draught for £25 from Charles Phillot, Esq., Banker in this City, for the like purpose. The receipt of said Draughts you will acknowledge in a line to me at Dorchester.

The Three Medals may make one parcel and be sent to Br. West in Trim Street, Bath.

"Yours most sincerely & seriously,

"THOS. DUNCKERLEY.

"Rowland Berkley, Esq."

"October 21st, 1784.

"My Dear Friend & Brother,

"William Street, Esq., Banker, at Bath (my Worshipful Deputy for Somersetshire) desires to assist the Hall Fund, with a Loan of £25, for which I send you his Draught, the receipt of which you will do me the favour to acknowledge by return of Post.

"Bros. West, Phillot, & Gardiner ; urge me to desire you will send their Medals : and as there is nothing more to do than engraving their Names, I must beg that Bro. Street's may be sent with them, addressed to Bro. West, Trim Street, Bath. I was favoured with Bro. White's last letter, pray tell him that if any gentleman offers to be Provincial Grand Master for Kent, I shall hope (for the good of the Hall Fund) he will be appointed : but if no such application is made I am very ready to comply with the request of the Brethren & take the County under my care 'til such an Offer is made. My hearty Greeting to all my *serious* Brethren (among whom place yourself) & believe me Your Zealous Bro. & Affect. Friend,

"Thos. Dunckerley.

" Rowland Berkley, Esq."

" Grand Lodge Report, 7th April, 1802.

" Charles Phillot, of Bath, Esq., and Thomas West, of Bath, Esq., having declared their intention of giving up the remainder of their Subscription to the Hall-Loan, and requested the Society to accept the same, it was thereupon " Resolved unanimously,

" That the Thanks of the Grand Lodge be given to Charles Phillot, Esq., and Thomas West, Esq., for their liberal and generous Present."

Newspaper cutting enclosed with a letter from Dunckerley to the Grand Secretary.

"Bath, *Dec.* 30 [1784]. Monday last the Antient and Honourable Society of Free-Masons of this County met their Provincial Grand Master, Thomas Dunkerley, Esq. at the Bear Inn, to celebrate the Anniversary of their Patron St. John the Evangelist ; from whence they proceeded, accompanied by a band of music, to attend divine service at the Abbey church ; where an excellent sermon was delivered by the Rev. Brother Dart, from Micah vi. 8 , in which he convinced a most numerous congregation, that Free-Masonry was founded on the divine principle of " acting justly, loving " mercy, and walking humbly with our God." A Masonic Hymn, the production of the Provincial Grand Master, was delightfully sung by the Choir of St. James's. From church they as they returned came in regular procession to the Bear, where an elegant entertainment was provided, and where the remaining part of the day was spent with that festivity, harmony, and fraternal affection, which has ever peculiarly characterised this Society. Nor was that benign guest Charity absent; several petitions from distressed Brethren being read, their claims were attended to, and their wants amply relieved.

"Redbridge, January 3rd, 1785.

" Dear Sir,

"On my return from Bath I have receiv'd your favour respecting the Provincialship for Kent—I cannot prevail with myself to attend to a meeting of the Lodges at Maidstone; having but just finish'd a journey of 120 miles over Ice & Snow, to discharge my duty in Somersetshire. If the Kentish Lodges apply to the G. Master for me to be appointed for that County, I am ready to oblige them, but cannot canvass for their Votes & Interest. I hope (with God's permission) to be at Hampton Court next Saturday, where I shall be glad to hear from you. I have receiv'd the Accounts of the last Quarterly Communication, & am sorry you did not receive my letter from this place, desiring they might be addressed to me at the White Hart, Bath.

" I was met at that place by 120 Brethren.

" Your Affect. Bro. & Servant,

" THOS. DUNCKERLEY.

" I shall be obliged to you, if you will write to Mr. Gillman, as you propos'd—let him call a meeting. Send him my letter, but tell him there is no necessity for my attendance.

"William White, Esq." "T. D.

"Hampton Court Palace, Nov. 26th, 1785.

" Dear Sir,

"I most sincerely thank you for your favour of yesterday. Not a man in the Society can have a more *grateful* regard for Bro Heseltine nor honour him more for his continual service & the zeal he has shown, at a *critical time,* by accepting the Office of Grand Treasurer. I have at the request of the Lodges No. 39 & 458 permitted them to consolidate & take the Name of the latter & remove to the Bear Inn: by the Members of the R. Cumberland Lodge becoming Members of No. 39 in the same Manner as the Somerset House Lodge united with No. 2. I am therefore to desire the Loan to the Hall may be thus inserted, ' No. 39 Bear Inn, Bath, Royal Cumberland Lodge £25 : ' & of course they may eraze No. 458 from the Medal & engrave 39. It will be a satisfaction to the Lodges under my care to see *Asterisks* put to the respective sums I have paid to the Charity & Hall, & I shall be obliged to Bro. Heseltine to cause to be inserted. ' On all business respecting Masonry write to your Provincial Grand Master (*post paid*) ' &c. &c.

" I have acquainted Bro. Vandyke with your kind offer, & directed him to send you Proposals immediately, shall be obliged to Bro. Heseltine if he will insert a Note in the Accounts of the Quarterly Communication respecting the said proposal. I should have sent this letter last Saturday, but that I expected the Calendars. When you send them, favour me with a line expressing your intention to insert— ' R. Cumberland Lodge Bear Inn, Bath No. 39 (not 458) £25, Loan to the Hall Charity, £1. 1s. 0d., registering Fee, £0. 5s. 0d.' That I may acquaint them it will be done : & of course they may alter the Number of the Medal to 39. If the Calendars should be sent before you receive this, favour me with a line by the Post. Mrs. Dunckerley desires to unite with me in sincere regard, & am,

" Y^r Affect. Brother,

" William White, Esq."   "Thos. Dunckerley.

The proposal of Bro. Vandyke referred to in the foregoing related to the engraving of Dunckerley's portrait which he had recently painted.

"An Abridged History of The Royal Cumberland Lodge, No. 41," by Thomas Payne Ashley, P.P.J.G. Warden of Somerset, contains the intelligence that as far back as 1767, Dunckerley was a frequent visitor at the old lodge, No. 39, and that he was elected an Honorary Member of it. It was probably at his suggestion that the two lodges amalgamated.

The history referred to contains much valuable information relating to this justly celebrated lodge, one of the very few old lodges now remaining that works under its original Charter, and having records reaching back into the early part of the last century—certainly to the year 1732; and in all probability it was in existence prior to its constitution as a *regular* lodge.

What a boon it would be to the Students of Masonic history if the whole of these interesting records could be printed and put in circulation! In this instance the compiler has given us only sufficient to make us wish for more. We must, however, be grateful even for small favours.

Bristol Gazette, June 15th, 1786.

"Bath, June 7. On Monday last, in honour of his Majesty's birthday, Thomas Dunkerley, Esq., held a Provincial Grand Lodge for this county at the Assembly Room in Wells. The appearance of the fraternity on this occasion was most numerous and respectable indeed.

"The procession to St. Cuthbert's Church, preceded by a band of wind music, was regular and splendid. Prayers were read by the Rev. Brother Foster, and a masonic sermon preached by the Rev. Brother Gardiner from 1st Cor. 1, 8. The choir from the Cathedral attended, and sung the Provincial Grand Master's hymn. The procession returned to the Assembly Room, where the Masonic Ode was performed, and an excellent charge given by Brother Dunkerley. An excellent dinner in every respect was provided by Brother Bacon; many masonic and loyal toasts were given, and the day concluded in harmony; it was indeed so well and so chearfully conducted through the whole that all were happy in the lodge, and many poor and infirm brothers out of it, rendered so by donations."

"Hampton Court Palace,

"Nov. 16th, 1786.

"Dear Brother,

"I have this morning receiv'd the enclosed from Bro Meyler; and as it is my duty to pay every attention to applications from the several Lodges under my care, I beg the following notice may be given in the next printed Accounts of the Quarterly Communication. 'That a Person travelling by the name of Clark, who some time since kept a Tavern in London, having fraudulently obtained money from the Lodge at Wells; Notice of the same is given to prevent farther imposition: and whereas several Persons disguised like Turks, who pretend they were made Prisoners in attempting to relieve Gibraltar, have imposed on Lodges at Bristol & Bath; notice of the same is hereby given that such itinerant Mendicants may be detected.' Please to make the above motion (in my name) to the Committee of Charity, to whom I beg you will present my most respectful Greeting.

"I sent you a Bank Post Bill (for £60) yesterday, which I hope got safe to hand. I beg your Assistant Clerk may not send any more letters to the Lodges in the Counties I have the honour to Superintend It will save him the trouble of writing 90 letters in a year.

"If you can favour me with a line by Saturday's Post, it would give me pleasure to know that the motion on the other side meets with their approbation.

"At the same time, you will return me the enclosed from the Provincial Grand Secretary for Somersetshire.

"Madam unites with me in sincere regard to Sister White & yourself, & am

"Your faithful Brother, &c.,

" William White, Esq."　　　　　" THOS. DUNCKERLEY.

"Hampton Court Palace,

" Dear Sir,　　　　　　　　　" Feb. 1st, 1792.

"I have received from the Lodge No. 212 at Bridgwater a list of their Members, which, with list from Hampton Court, shall be left at Free Masons' Tavern next Friday, address'd to you. I rec'd a Draught from No. 212, value £3. 18s. 6d., which I did intend to have sent by the same Conveyance, but think it safer to send you a Draught on Mr. Coutts for the balance due to the Grand Lodge; the receipt of which you will do me the favour to acknowledge.

" Your Affect. Brother,

" THOS. DUNCKERLEY.

"P.S.—When the accounts of Quarterly Communications are publish'd, I am to request that six or eight may be sent to me, that I may be able to inform my Deputies of the state of the Society: at the same time, if you find any of the Lodges remiss in their Contributions which may have escap'd my notice; give me the hint, and I will admonish them. But by the Cash, &c., being sent to you, a considerable Expense of Postage will be sav'd to the Grand Lodge; and as it is probable that I may very soon leave this World, my Widow will not be Embarrassed with the Accounts of the Grand Lodge, to whom I beg you will present my affect. regard.

" William White, Esq."　　　　　" THOS. DUNCKERLEY.

Probably this was Dunckerley's last remittance to the Grand Secretary on behalf of his constituents in Somerset. The handwriting of the letter evinces considerable shakiness.

"Frome, Oct. 28th, 1795.

"Dear Sir,

"Inclos'd I have sent you a list of the persons I have made in the Royal Clarence Lodge since my last return to you; the amount of the Regestering fees is £2. 10s. 0d. One Guinea we have also sent towards the general Charity, and one shilling to have the night of our meeting inserted in the Free Masons' Calendar, which is *Monday nearest the Full Moon;* the whole inclos'd is £3. 12s. 0d., which I hope you'll receive safe. I have given an order on the Postmaster of Portsmouth, who will pay it to your order on demand.

"I hope your health is better then it ware, when I had the honor to hear from you last; I hope soon to make the R. C Lodge the most respectful in the West of England, as I have hints given me that I shall shortly have many respectful caracters and even Noblemen to Make; it is my greatest pleasure to see Masonry flourish, but more particularly the Lodge to which I have the honor to be the Master, under that P.G. Master for which I have the greatest Affection & most profound respect, and the honor to subscribe myself his truly and most Faithful Brother and very Humble Servant, "T. Jones."

The writer of the foregoing was the first Junior Warden of the Royal Clarence Lodge, which was constituted by Dunckerley in 1790 as No. 560, at the George Inn, Frome. It was erased from the list in 1838. Doubtless this was the last communication made to Dunckerley from the Province of Somerset. The writer seems to have been of a somewhat sanguine temperament. The Grand Lodge Register shows that his hopes as to the "many respectful caracters" joining the lodge were in a measure realised, but the expected "Noblemen" do not appear to have "turned up."

" Sir & Brother,

    " It having been intimated to me that several respect-
able persons in this town and neighbourhood are desirous of
becoming Masons, if they can be made in a provincial Grand
Lodge, I beg leave to address you on the subject.

    " Before the Death of Brother Dunckerley (whose loss
we much lament, and whose memory we revere) it was
proposed to him to appoint our right Worshipful Master
Bro. Jones (who has already served the Office of Provincial Grand Warden) Deputy Prov. Grand Master for this
County, to enable him to hold a Grand Lodge; which he
was pleased to approve, & would have accomplished if he
had not died so soon.   If this can be now done, I doubt not
but it would add many very respectable Members to ye Society
at large, & to our Lodge in particular; & I need say no
more of Bro. Jones than that his Character as a Man, and
a Mason, & his peculiar zeal for the Cause, raises him high
in the Estimation of all Brothers & entitles him to general
esteem.

    " As I have not yet learnt who is to succeed Bro.
Dunckerley I shall be obliged to you to inform me; & also
to say if it is possible to obtain a Deputation to accomplish
our design.

    " If any other plan should occur to you will you favour
me with your sentiments thereon by a line at your first
leisure?

            " I am, Sir, Your affectionate Brother

                                " (in Masonry)

    " Pilly Hill, near Frome,   " CHAS. BAYLY.
        " Dec. 24th, 1795.
" To Wm. White, Esq."

Dunckerley's successor in Somerset was John Smith,
Esq., M.P., who had filled the office of Provincial Grand
Master for the County prior to Dunckerley's appointment.

MEMORIALS OF FREEMASONRY IN WILTSHIRE.

It would seem from the following that Dunckerley had taken an active part in masonic affairs in Wiltshire several years before he was appointed to preside over the province.

"Marlborough, 24th Sept., 1768.

"Dear Sir,

"Last night while the Lodge was open I received your very polite, friendly and obliging Letter, which I read to the Brethren; they unanimously ordered Two Guineas for the General Fund of Charity; which (if I should not be in town by the twenty-eighth of next month) I beg you will pay on my account.

"To Mr. Dillon, the Grand Officers, and the board of Stewards, be pleased to make my sincere Respects, and to all who do me the honour of an enquiry.

"I am, Dear Sir, Your Faithfull friend

"And affect. Brother,

"THOS. DUNCKERLEY.

"To Brother French, G.S."

A CHARGE.

Delivered to the Members of the Lodge *of* Free *and* Accepted Masons, *held at the* Castle Inn, Marlborough, *at a Meeting for the Distribution of* CHARITY *to twenty-four poor People, at which most of the* Ladies *in* Marlborough *were present, Sept.* 11, A.L. 5769.

BY THOMAS DUNCKERLEY, Esq.

BLESSED IS HE THAT CONSIDERETH THE POOR. *Psal.* xli. v. 1.

"BRETHREN,

"It is with the greatest satisfaction I meet you here in the cause of *charity: Charity* is the basis of *our* Order; it is for this purpose we have a Grand Lodge at *London,* another at *Edinburgh,* and a third at *Dublin.* Lodges are now held on every part of this globe, and charities are collected and sent to the respective *Grand* Lodge of each Kingdom or state : *there* the distress'd brethren apply and find relief : nor is any exception made to difference of country or religion.

"For, as in the sight of God we are all equally his children, having the same common parent and preserver— so we, in like manner, look on *every* Free-Mason as our brother; nor regard where he was born or educated, provided he is a good man, an honest man, which is 'the noblest work of God.'

"A laudable custom prevailed among our ancient brethren; after they had sent their donations to the *general* charities, they considered the distresses of those in *particular* that resided in their respective neighbourhoods, and assisted them with such a sum as could be conveniently spared from the *lodge.* In humble imitation of this masonic principle, I recommend the present charity to your consideration; to which you readily and unanimously consented. The sum is, indeed, but small : yet when it is considered that this lodge is in its infant state; having been constituted but little more than three months : I hope, as the widow's mite was acceptable, *this* act of ours will be considered, not with respect to the sum, but the principles by which we are influenced.

"I have told you in the *lodge,* and I repeat it now, that *brotherly-love, relief,* and *truth,* are the grand principles of Masonry, and as the principal part of the company are unacquainted with the original intention of this society, it may be proper for their information, and your instruction, that I explain those principles, by which it is our duty in particular to be actuated.

"By *Brotherly-love,* we are to understand that generous principle of the soul, which respects the human species as one family, created by an All-wise Being, and placed on this globe for the mutual assistance of each other. It is this attractive *principle*, or power that draws men together and unites them in bodies politic, families, societies, and the various orders and denominations among men. But as most of these are partial, contracted or confined to a particular country, religion, or opinion ; *our* Order, on the contrary, is calculated to unite mankind as one family : High and low, rich and poor, one with another ; to adore the same God, and observe his law. All worthy members of this society are free to visit every lodge in the world; and though he knows not the language of the country, yet by a silent universal language of our own, he will gain admittance, and find that *true* friendship, which flows from the brotherly-ove I am now describing.

" At that peaceable and harmonious meeting he will hear no *disputes* concerning religion or politics; no *swearing ;* no *obscene*, *immortal** or *ludicrous* discourse ; no other contention but *who can work best, who can agree best.*

" To subdue our passions, and improve in useful scientific knowledge ; to instruct the younger brethren, and initiate the unenlightened, are principal duties in the lodge ; which, when done, and the word of God is closed, we indulge with the song and cheerful glass, still observing the same decency and regularity, with strict attention to the golden mean—believing with the poet, that—

'God is paid when man receives,
T' enjoy is to obey.'

" Let me travel from *east* to *west*, or between *north* and *south*, when I meet a *true* brother I shall find a friend, who will do all in his power to serve me, without having the least view of self-interest : and if I am poor and in distress, he will relieve me to the utmost of his power, interest, and capacity This is the second grand principle ; for, *relief* will follow where there is brotherly-love.

---

* Probably a misprint for *immoral* H S.

"I have already mentioned our general charities as they are at present conducted, it remains now that I consider particular donations given from private lodges, either to those who are not masons or to a brother in distress. And first, with respect to a Charity like this before us, perhaps it is better to be distributed in small sums, that more may receive the benefit, than to give it in larger sums, which would confine it to few.

"With regard to a brother in distress, who should happen to apply to this *lodge*, or any *particular* member for relief, it is necessary that I inform you in what manner you are to receive *him*. And here I cannot help regretting, that such is the depravity of the human heart, there is no religion or society free from bad professors, or unworthy members, for as it is impossible for us to read the heart of man, the best regulated societies may be imposed on, by the insinuations of the artful and hypocrisy of the abandoned. It should therefore by no means lessen the dignity and excellency of the *royal craft*, because it is our misfortune to have bad men among us, any more than the purity and holiness of the *Christian* religion should be doubted, because too many of the wicked and profligate approach the holy altar.

"Since, therefore, these things are so : be careful whenever a brother applies for relief, to examine strictly whether he is worthy of acceptance: enquire the *cause* of his misfortunes, and if you are satisfied they are not the result of *vice* or *extravagance*, relieve him with such a sum as the lodge shall think proper, and assist him with your interest and recommendation, that he may be employed according to his capacity, and not *eat the bread of idleness*. This will be acting consistent with TRUTH, which is the *third* grand principle of Masonry.

"TRUTH is a divine attribute, and the foundation of all masonic virtues · to be *good men* and *true*, is part of the first great lesson we are taught; and at the commencement of

our freedom, we are exhorted to be fervent and zealous in
the practice of *truth* and *goodness.* It is not sufficient that
we walk in the light, unless we do the *truth.* All hypocrisy
and deceit must be banished from us. Sincerity and plain
dealing compleat the harmony of the brethren, within and
without the lodge; and will render us acceptable in the
sight of that great Being, *unto whom all hearts are open, all
desires known, and from whom no secrets are hid.*

"There is a charm in *truth* that draws and attracts the
mind continually towards it: the more we discover, the more
we desire, and the great reward is, *wisdom, virtue,* and
happiness.

"This is an edifice founded upon a rock, which malice
cannot shake, or time destroy. What a secret satisfaction
do we enjoy, when in searching for truth, we find the *first
principles* of useful science, still preserved among us, as we
received them, by *oral* tradition from the earliest ages; and
we also find this truth corroborated by the testimonies of the
best and greatest men the world has produced. But this is
not all; the *sacred* writings confirm what I assert; the
sublime part of our ancient mystery being there to be found;
nor can any *Christian* brother be a *good* Mason that does not
make the word of God his first and principal study.

"I sincerely congratulate you on the happy establishment of this lodge, and the prospect you have of its utility
and permanency, by the choice you have made of members
capable to conduct it. Let Wisdom direct you to contrive
for the best. Strengthen the cause of Masonry, by mutual
Friendship, which is the companion and support of fraternal
love, and which will never suffer any misunderstanding to
inflame a brother, or cause him to behave unbecoming a
member of our peaceable and harmonious society. Let us
then resolve to beautify and adorn our Order, by discharging
the duties of our respective stations, as good subjects, good
parents, good husbands, good masters, and dutiful children,

for by so doing we shall put to silence the reproaches of foolish men. As you know these things, brethren, happy are ye if ye do them; and thrice happy shall I esteem it to be looked on as the founder of a society in *Marlborough* whose grand principles are, brotherly-love, relief, and truth.

" Let us consider these poor persons as our brothers and sisters, and be thankful to Almighty God, that he has been pleased to make us his instruments of affording them this small relief; most humbly supplicating the GRAND ARCHI-TECT OF THE UNIVERSE, from *whom all holy desires, all good counsels, and all just works do proceed*, to bless our under-taking, and grant that we may *continue* to add some little comfort to the *poor* of this town.

" Next to the Deity, whom can I so properly address myself to as the most beautiful part of the creation ?

" You have heard, *Ladies*, our grand principles explained, with the instructions given to the brethren ; and I doubt not but at other times you have heard many dis-respectful things said of this society. Envy, malice, and all uncharitableness will never be at a loss to decry, find fault, and raise objections to what they do not know. How great then are the obligations *you* lay on this lodge ! with what superior esteem, respect, and regard, are we to look on every lady present, that has done us the honour of her company this evening. To have the sanction of the *fair* is our highest ambition, as our greatest care will be to pre-serve it. The virtues of humanity are peculiar to your sex; and we flatter ourselves the most splendid ball could not afford *you* greater pleasure, than to see the human heart made happy, and the *poor* and *distrest* obtain present relief."—" The Freemasons' Magazine " *September*, 1793.

It is not unlikely that the publication of this and other Charges, &c., by the same author originated the tradition that Dunckerley revised or remodelled the Craft Lectures; but to me it seems more than probable that the compiler of the lectures made a very free use of Dunckerley's brains in the work of compilation.

From the "History of Freemasonry in Wiltshire" by Frederick Hastings Goldney, P.G.D.

"CITY OF SALISBURY, *September* 22*nd*, 1777.

"A Provincial Grand Lodge for Wiltshire was opened in ample form.

Present:

The Most Worshipful Thomas Dunckerley, Esq., P.G.M.

„	Worshipful Hugh Skeats,	D.P.G.M.
„	Worshipful Jos. Hodgson,	P.G.S.W.
„	Worshipful J. Edgar, Jun.,	P.G.J.W.
„	Worshipful Jas. Wilkinson,	P.G.T.
„	Worshipful Michael Burrough,	P.G.S.
„	Worshipful T. Shuttleworth,	P.G.S.B.

P. G. Stewards:

John Norton.	Wm. Weeks.
Wm. Chubb.	Geo. Scandover.
Alex. Minty.	D. N. Keele.

P. G. Tyler, G. Brown.

"The Master, Officers, and Brethren of Salisbury Lodge, No. 47.

"The Lodge at (the) Crown, Devizes, was called, and no one appeared.

Visiting Brethren.

"Right Hon. Lord Charles Montague, P.G.M. for Hants, with six of his officers.

"Six brethren from No —— at Ringwood. Four brethren from No. —— at Blandford, and three from lodges in London, being in all No. —— on the occasion.

"The Salisbury Lodge paid two guineas for the Hall, and one for the fund of Charity.

"The P.G.M. recommended that no Mason be made in future for less than three guineas in this county.

"The brethren dined in open lodge, and in the evening the lodge was closed in due form and time.

"The Most Worshipful took occasion to observe that an assembly had lately been formed in S. of persons who call themselves Antient Masons, and pretended to derive an authority from D. Athol. He informed the lodge that the D. had disclaimed any knowledge of or connection with persons acting under that sanction, and that the meetings of such are so inconsistent with the principles of Freemasonry, that they had been publicly reprobated by the Grand Lodge, and that it was his wish that the Wiltshire brethren would by no means countenance their proceedings, but rather that they should give a public denial of what that assembly had asserted relative to the patronage of the D. Athol."

It will be observed that Dunckerley is here described as Provincial Grand Master for Wiltshire, this, however, is not strictly correct, he having only been appointed to superintend temporarily, as in more recent times the Grand Registrar was usually placed in charge of a province wherein a vacancy had occurred in the office of Provincial Grand Master, until a new appointment was made.

The first Provincial Grand Master for Wiltshire was Thomas Fowke, Esq., of Clarges Street, Piccadilly, who was appointed late in 1775 or early in 1776. I cannot find that he ever did anything in discharge of the duties of his office, but he had family connections at Salisbury and was Groom of the Bedchamber to the Duke of Cumberland. His name was removed from the list of Provincial Grand Masters in 1777; Dunckerley may therefore fairly be deemed the first *real* head of the province. In his endeavours to exemplify the proverbial qualities of a new broom his Masonic zeal appears to have far exceeded his usual discretion, as will be shown by the following extracts from the Grand Lodge Minutes of the "Ancients."

"Dec. 3rd, 1777.

"Heard a letter from No. 200 at Salisbury setting forth that a Mr. Dunckerley, P.G.M. under the Moderns, had taken upon him to doubt the legallity of their Warrant, &c., also the Deputy Grand Master's answer thereto, Heard the D G.M's letter to his Grace of Atholl enclosing the original letter from No. 200, with the Right Worshipful Grand Master's answer also a letter enclosing the proceedings of Lodge 200 as published in the Salisbury Journal.

"Resolved Unanimously, That the thanks of this Grand Lodge be returned to the Most Noble Prince John Duke of Atholl, &c., &c., &c., our Right Worshipful Grand Master, for His Grace's great Condecension & goodness in so clearly and firmly avowing his Intentions of supporting the Ancient Craft, by so nobly and generously acknowledging that Patronage which this Grand Lodge have so long happily flourished under, and that they will by every means in their power endeavour to convince His Grace that the Sanction of the Noble Family of Atholl has been extended to the Ancient and Universal practice of the Royal Craft and on a People not altogether undeserving his Lordship's protection.

"Heard a letter from No. 174, Southampton, similar to that from No. 200 at Salisbury. Resolved Unanimously, that the thanks of this Grand Lodge be returned to the Deputy Grand Master for his attention relative to the Lodge No. 200 Salisbury and to assure him of the readiness of the Grand Lodge to concur in every step to rescue his Character from the false and Malicious insinuations propagated by Mr. Dunkerley as set forth in the letter from No. 174 or by any other person or persons whatever, for so far from thinking the said Lau. Dermott capable of committing the allegations made by Mr. Dunkerly, that the Fraternity have repeatedly experienced singular advantages from the Integrity and abilities of the said D.G. Master during a

q 2

series of Twenty-Six Years, that Justly entitles him to the favour and esteem of all real well wishers to the Ancient Craft as more fully appears by the Grand Lodge Transactions from the year 1751 to this time.

"Resolved. That it is the opinion of this Grand Lodge, that the steps taken by Lodge 200 at Salisbury were proper on the present occasion."

Probably Dunckerley carried too many guns for the enemy; at all events this lodge made but little headway under the "Ancients" only 21 members being registered down to January, 1782. In 1783 the members transferred their allegiance to the "Moderns" and Dunckerley granted them a Warrant for the Apollo Lodge, No. 454, which prospered for many years, but was struck off the list in 1828. The "Ancient" Warrant was returned and the number declared vacant in 1792. In 1801, No. 200 was granted to certain brethren for a lodge at Carisbrooke, Isle of Wight; which lodge is now the Albany Lodge, No. 151, Newport.

A storm was at this time brewing among Dunckerley's own flock which eventually occasioned him much trouble and annoyance. The only lodge in Salisbury in 1776, was the Sarum Lodge No. 47, the members of which had refused compliance with the regulations made for the purpose of raising funds wherewith to build a Hall in London, alleging that as they had recently built and furnished " a new room from their own stock only " Grand Lodge ought to do likewise.

Bro. Goldney, in his excellent history, has printed the proceedings of this lodge from its opening to its extinction, with the exception of those contained in a missing minute book, from 1777 to 1794, and as the accompanying extracts and letters will throw some little light on the condition of the lodge during part of that period I now offer them in the hope that they may assist in the completion of this most interesting portion of the history of Masonry in Wiltshire.

G.L. Minutes, Nov. 12th, 1777.

"The Grand Secretary read a Letter from the late Master, and other late Members of a Lodge heretofore held in the City of Salisbury, No. 47 and known by the Name of the Sarum Lodge which was erased from the list of Lodges in February last for not conforming to the regulations of the Grand Lodge. And the said Brethren having in such Letter expressed their concern for their past errors, and promised due obedience to the Laws in future, a Motion was made that the said Lodge should be reinstated, which was duly seconded, and on putting the question it passed unanimously in the affirmative.

" Brother Dunckerley superintendent of the Lodges in the County of Wilts complained that the Lodge No. 47* held at the———Inn in the Town of Devizes in the said County, had in a refractory manner refused to correspond with him or give him any account of the situation of such Lodge. He therefore moved that the Grand Secretary might be desired to write to the said Lodge and acquaint the Brethren that unless they acquiesced and attended to their duty in future, the Lodge would at the next Quarterly Communication, be erased from the list. This motion was seconded and on putting the Question it passed in the affirmative.

" The thanks of the Grand Lodge were then given to Brother Dunckerley for his unwearied zeal in the service of the Society."

The four following letters are copied from the Grand Secretary's letter book :—

"To the Right W. Master of the Old Sarum Lodge, Salisbury,

" Sir & Brother,

"I am sorry to perceive by a Letter from Bro. Wm.

---

* Obviously a clerical error, as the only Lodge then held in Devizes was The Lodge of True Friendship, No. 39s, at the ℂ ⸱ ⸱ *I* ⸱ H. S.

Burbridge addressed to our worthy Brother Jas. Heseltine, Esq., that any doubt should exist in the minds of the Brethren of the Old Sarum Lodge relative to the appointment of Thos. Dunckerley Esq., to the superintendance of the fraternity in Wiltshire, an appointment which he regularly received from the Grand Master for his known zeal for the Society and his ability in the Craft.

"The reason why it was never notified to you in a formal manner or noticed in the publications of the Society is its being only a temporary office untill the appointment of a Prov. G.M. for the County, and I am authorized to acquaint you that any Nobleman or Gentleman whom you may think proper to recommend will be appointed to that Honourable rank by our Most Noble Grand Master, whose desire I am well convinced it is, as well as that of the Grand Lodge, to act in all things so as to give satisfaction to the Brethren and of course promote the interest of the Society.

"That peace and concord may ever subsist in your Ancient Lodge is the sincere wish of him who has the honor to subscribe himself with fraternal regard and esteem, &c.

" W. W."*

"To the Master of the Sarum Lodge, Salisbury.

" Dec. 31st, 1781.

"I am sorry my absence from town for about a fortnight prevented my answering sooner Bro. Burbridge's Letter which I hope you will excuse. The appointment of a Merchant or Tradesman to be Prov. G. Master of your County, would hardly be consistent with so exalted a rank in the society unless it was a Merchant of the very first eminence and one who possessed that respect and weight in the County as to induce the Brethren of Rank and fortune to attend his general meetings, and by that means perhaps

---

* William White.

increase the fraternity and add to the Lodges. The most eligible Characters for this dignity (and such as in general possess it) are either Noblemen, Members of Parliament, or Gentlemen of large Estates, who at the same time that they receive an Honour from the Society, by their Name and Rank reflect it back. These hints added to your own desire of having a person of Consequence at the head of your County will (I doubt not) cause you to nominate such a one as our most Worshipful G. Master will have no objection to delegate his authority to. The expence attending this appointment is 10 Guineas to the fund of the Society and one Guinea and a half for making out the Patent or 5 Guineas if elegantly written on Vellum and emblematically ornamented.

    .   .   .   .

" I remain with great regard and Esteem R. W. Master.
    " Your most Obedient Servant,
        " W. W., G.S."

" R.W.M. & Brethren of the Sarum Lodge.

        " 19th March, 1782.

    " Annexed I transmit to you a Copy of the minutes of the Committee of Charity which was unanimously confirmed by the Grand Lodge, and in consequence of which our most Worshipful Grand Master, His Grace the Duke of Manchester has been pleased to grant by Instrument under the Great Seal of the Society, an Authority to his Junior Grand Warden, James Galloway, Esq to hear and decide the unhappy misunderstanding subsisting between Thomas Dunckerley, Esq. Superintendant for Wilts and your Lodge. The appointment of so worthy a Brother who is not higher in Rank than Esteem in the Society cannot fail I apprehend of being satisfactory to you and I doubt not but you [will] second the good intentions of the G. Lodge & his endeavours, by every means in your power, & not suffer any

pique or trivial cavil to prevent the return of Concord among
the fraternity in Wiltshire, but by chearfull acquiesence in
his decision prevent any further interposition of the G.
Master's authority. I had the honour of seeing the Junior
G. Warden yesterday who informed me that he intends
going into Wiltshire in about 10 days or a fortnight & that
he will give you timely notice for the summonsing of your
Lodge.

" It will give me great pleasure to hear of an amicable
termination being put to this affair, being with sincere
wishes for the prosperity of the Sarum Lodge.

" Yours, &c.,
" W. W., G.S."

" Thos. Dunckerley, Esq.,
　　　" Salisbury.

" Annexed I have the honour of transmitting to you
a Copy of the Minutes of the Committee of Charity relative
to the differences between you and the Sarum Lodge. To
you Sir it will be needless for me to enlarge on the subject,
I shall only beg leave to assure you it is the wish of the
Brethren here to have everything made as agreeable to you
as your endeavours for the prosperity of the Society so justly
merits. I had the pleasure of seeing Mr. Galloway yesterday
who desired me to present his Compliments to you and to
acquaint you that he expected to be in Wiltshire in about
10 Days or a fortnight.

" I am with the greatest respect, &c., &c.,
" W. W."

" Salisbury, January 19th, 1783.

" My Dear Friend & Brother,

" It is with much reluctance that I give you this
additional trouble respecting the Sarum Lodge: they would
not attend my summons to the Provincial Grand Lodge
(which I held in this City the 27th Ultimo) nor will they

send me a list of their Members & Masons made ; denying my having any Authority for that purpose.

"It is a constant rule with me (in conformity to a former resolution of the Grand Lodge) to have lists (at least once a year) from the several Lodges under my direction ; in order to know what Fees are due to the Hall Fund ; which I must confess I have ever been anxious to advance.

" As I would not (if it can be avoided), complain against them to the Grand Lodge ; it is my request that you will be so obliging, or Brother White by your direction, to desire of them (by a letter enclosed to me) to make out & give me the said list in order to prevent any complaints against them in future. And I hope & trust that if they send the List to you or Brother Berkley, it will be returned to them, with advice to deliver it to me.

" I beg to know in return, when the next Quarterly Communication will be held ; having registering Fees to remit for the Hall Fund.

" Make my grateful regard acceptable to Bros. Atkinson, Brooks, Allen, &c.

" Mrs. D—— my Daughter & her Husband unite with me in sincere Wishes for y_e health and happiness of your Self, Sister Heseltine & little folks & am your affect. & much obliged Brother.

" Thos. Dunckerley.

" James Heseltine, Esq."

Dunckerley's Seal.
Actual size.

*"Thomas Dunckerley, Esq.,
" Drs. Commons,　　　　　　　　　　　　" Salisbury.
　" 20th March, 1783.
　　　　　　　　　　　　　　" Substance of Letter.
" Dr. Sir & Brother,

　" I will now trouble you with a few Lines in respect of the Sarum Lodge. The List of Members was sent up by the Secretary of that Lodge to Mr. White; your Letter to me arrived about the same time, desiring if the List was received that it might be returned to them, with advice to deliver it to you. I advised with the Grand Officers on the subject; and they all thought the most proper step would be to mention the matter in Committee of Charity, and to pursue such directions as might be given rather than take any step of my own accord where former misunderstandings had prevailed. The substance of your Letter was accordingly mentioned to the Committee and fully considered but no decisive Orders were given thereon, it appearing to be the wish of every Brother present to endeavour to adopt some expedient of a mild and healing nature, and not to proceed to extremities.

　" The sincerest respect and attention to you was manifested by every Brother in the Assembly, but at the same time it was observed by many Gentlemen that the sending back the List to the Lodge, with orders to deliver it to you would most likely be productive of a refusal on the part of the Lodge and would compel the Grand Lodge to withdraw its Constitution, an event that ought in prudence to be avoided if possible.

　" I was, therefore, desired to write to you and to request it as a favour that you would (for the sake of harmony and peace, and as a farther proof of your forbearance and uniform inclination to promote every wish of the Fraternity) volun-

---

* From the Grand Secretary's Letter Book. H. S.

tarily and without any kind of notice to the Sarum Lodge, resign the Superintendancy of the County of Wilts, which step would most likely be productive of future good humour in that Lodge, and could not, it is presumed, derogate from the honour or respectability of your situation in the Society, inasmuch as it would be a voluntary act on your part and not in consequence of any decision of the Grand Lodge approving or countenancing the refractory behaviour of the Brethren of the Sarum Lodge. At the same Committee a Letter was read from the Lodge of Virtue at Bath, in which, among others, it was said the Brethren would be happy in having a Prov. Grand Master, and that they had petitioned you to accept that Office, but that you had returned for answer that the Grand Lodge would not permit you to preside over more Provinces than you already held. I apprehend it would not be irregular for one Gentleman to have different Counties as P.G.M., for instance, Sir Herbert Mackworth P.G.M. for all South Wales, and other instances might be adduced to prove this position.

"I have mentioned the Contents of the Letter from the Bath Lodge, and the Committee intimated that if it was the desire of the Lodges in Somersetshire to have you appointed their P.G.M. and you would take the trouble to represent them, it might be recommended to the Grand Master in the name of the Committee to appoint you to that Office, upon resigning the Superintendancy of Wilts, which would certainly convey the highest degree of Masonic Respectability to you, and be an indirect rebuke to the Sarum Lodge, without any absolute Censure that might give offence, and thus universal peace and fraternal goodwill might be restored.

The Grand Officers have also since the Committee reconsidered this plan, which they still approve, and flatter themselves with the hopes of your concurrence.

"J. H."

"Salisbury, March 25th, 1783.

"My Dear Friend & Brother,

"Mrs. Dunckerley and Mr. Edgar desire to unite with me in sincere thanks for your kind concern and condolence on our much lamented loss. At the request of my son-in-law, I have promis'd to remain with him, and in all probability shall pass the remainder of my days in *this* County; except a little time in each summer, at Hampton Court. I have the greatest respect for the Grand Officers; and am very sensible that some of my sincerest Friends are among them : it is therefore my request that they would take into consideration my zealous services for the Society during *thirty* years, and my earnest endeavours to promote the authority of the Grand Lodge for the *seventeen* years that I have been a Grand Officer : and not desire me to resign Wiltshire because the Sarum Lodge (which was struck off the List for contumacious behaviour to the Grand Lodge, but restored at my request) with the blackest Ingratitude deny my Authority. If it is the will of the Grand Lodge that the Sarum Lodge should continue on the List with the same contumacious disposition towards me; Be it so ! I shall never trouble the Grand Lodge any more concerning them.

"I am much oblig'd to the Brethren at Bath for the regard they express for me, and should be happy to render them any service, but cannot prevail with myself to take Somersetshire & resign the County where I now reside, & (with God's permission) propose to remain; and it would be ingratitude to the Lodge of Science in this City who have been at the expense of a Warrant of Constitution to be under my Authority & Instruction.

If the Grand Master for the Counties of Dorset, Somerset, & Wilts; I shall esteem it a pleasing Employment for the very little time I may remain in this life.

Accept our sincerest regard to yourself and family and believe me,

"Your Affect. & much Obliged C. & B.,*

"THOS. DUNCKERLEY.

"Jas. Heseltine, Esq."

†"10th Sept. 1783.

"Thomas Dunckerley, Esq.,

"Salisbury.

"I am directed to acquaint you that our Royal Grand Master anxious to preserve the peace and unanimity of the Society in every part has thought proper to determine for the present not to appoint a P.G.M. for the County of Wilts, apprehending such a measure might have a contrary effect as the Lodges in the County do not agree in their application for the person they wish to hold that Honourable Rank. At the same time he has been pleased to direct that as the Sarum Lodge has not behaved with that degree of attention to you that could be wished, that in future on all business of the Society they shall correspond immediately with one of the Grand Secretaries and that you will not interfere in the affairs of that Lodge which will be relieving you from the trouble of having anything to do with those who do not seem disposed to act cordially with you and at the same time will prevent the possibility of any fresh differences arising.

"I am, &c.,

"W. W."

The apparently misplaced leniency of the authorities may be explained by the fact that "the foe was at the gate," and to have adopted coercive measures with the members of the Sarum Lodge would in all probability have resulted in the return of the Warrant and the acceptance of a Consti-

---

* Companion & Brother. H. S
† From the Grand Secretary's Letter Book H. S.

tution from the opposition Grand Lodge. It is easy to conceive that with such an old lodge in the case, this would have been a heavy blow to the prestige of the "Moderns," and a most important acquisition to their rivals.

"Salisbury, Sept. 16th, 1783.

"Dear Brother,

"In return to your favour of the 10th I shall at all times most obediently attend to the determinations and Commands of our Royal Grand Master.

"I shall not in future interfere with the affairs of the Sarum Lodge; and to prevent the possibility of any fresh disputes I shall not permit any Members of that Lodge to be present at any Provincial Grand Lodge that I may occasionally hold in future for this County.

"I have the honour to be,

"With the greatest respect and esteem,

"Your affectionate Brother,

"THOS. DUNCKERLEY."

Whether Dunckerley and the Sarum Lodge were ever reconciled I know not, but there appears to have been a fractious spirit among its members, for, in 1800, fresh complications arose with the authorities which led to the final erasure of the lodge on the 25th of November, 1801

"Salisbury, Dec. 21st, 1783.

"Dear Sir,

"I was Duly favour'd with yours of the 11th instant, together with 6 Calendars, & the Acc'ts. of the last Quarterly Communication; & beg you will oblige me with 12 more, by the same conveyance, that I may Distribute them in the Prov'l. Grand Lodge next Saturday. At the same time, please to inform me whether Bro. Heseltine had an opportunity of laying my request before the Grand Master. I have the pleasure to inform you that a Lodge of Antient Masons, constituted 7 years ago, by Mr. Dermot, by authority from the Duke of Athol; have apply'd to me for my Instruction & Patronage. I have granted them a Dispensation for holding a Lodge, & gave them the several obligations, in an extra Prov. G. Lodge, the 11th inst. Their Warr't. of Constitution will be Deliver'd in Prov. G. Lodge on St. John's Day, and I would put the impression of the Grand Lodge Seal to it if you can send it on a piece of paper. Previous to the next Qua. Com. I shall send you a Draught for the Fees of yᵉ said Constitution.* If the new Book of Constitutions is printed, I am to Desire you will send it to me this week, or as soon as it is pub-lish'd. Present my sincere regard to Bro. Heseltine & such Brethren as do me the honour of an enquiry & believe me.

"Your affect. & obliged Brother,

"THOS. DUNCKERLEY.

"William White, Esq."

"Hampton Court Palace, May 31st, 1789.

"Dear Sir,

"By desire of the Lodge No. 443, held at the Parade Coffee House, Salisbury, I wrote to you *last Thursday*, requesting (as soon as possible), a Dispensation for the Master of that Lodge to make Mr. Charles Burrell Blount, a Mason; he is not quite of age, but is going abroad im-mediately. Yesterday I receiv'd a Parcel with the Accounts of yᵉ last Quarterly Communication, &c. but no letter from you. The Parcel was not seal'd nor any pack thread, or cord put round it. I beg to hear from you by the Post to morrow, as I shall write to Salisbury on Tuesday morning

"Your faithful & Affect Brother,

"THOS. DUNCKERLEY.

"William White, Esq."

In November, 1791, Dunckerley paid to the Grand Treasurer £1. 16s on behalf of the above mentioned lodge it is therefore probable that he continued to superintend

* See page 227 (?)

Masonry in Wiltshire during the rest of his life; at all events the office of Provincial Grand Master for that county was not filled by anyone else during his lifetime, John Dainton is said to have been at the head of the province in 1792, but no trace of his appointment can now be found; for the simple reason, that he was never appointed. Under the "Ancient" *régime* every new lodge was supposed to be constituted by the Grand Master, in a Grand Lodge specially summoned for that purpose. In the Metropolis either the Deputy Grand Master, or the Grand Secretary usually officiated as Grand Master, by virtue of a dispensation to hold a Grand Lodge "for the space of three hours" at the house where the new lodge was to be held.

In this branch of the Order Provincial Grand Masters in England were almost unknown—indeed we have evidence of but one appointment of that character, and this might be described as an experiment, or an attempt in 1781, to form a Provincial Grand Lodge for the Counties of York, Chester, and Lancashire.

In the absence therefore of a definite head, it was usual for the Founders of a new lodge in the country to nominate some brother in the neighbourhood to perform the customary ceremonies.

The following correspondence between the Grand Secretary of the "Ancients" and Stephen Bell of Devizes, relative to the constituting of No, 270, in 1792, will doubtless be considered a sufficient explanation of the origin of the tradition, that John Dainton was Provincial Grand Master for Wiltshire in that year.

" Dear Sir & Brother,

"You have by this day's Coach from Lad Lane, the Warrant & Jewels. You must send me by return of post the Name of a Brother Past Master to receive our Powers to Constitute the New Lodge; and also send the Names and Additions of all the New Members, according to the above mentioned 9th Rule, at the particular request of the R.W. Deputy Grand Master. I have entered the parcel directed for you at Mr. Smith's and hope it will come safe.

"Yours very Affectionately,

" 27th Feb. 1792." "ROBERT LESLIE.

This note was written at the foot of the Grand Lodge Report on which a portion of the Rule referred to was printed. A few days later the following reply was received by the Grand Secretary.

"Devizes, 29th Feb. 1792.

" Right Worshipfull Sir & Brother,

"Yesterday came safe to hand the Warrant, Jewels, &c. which gives great satisfaction, and this morn your further Letter which you will find punctually complied with. We have nominated our worthy Brother John Dainton, Past Master, as Past Master. Our days of Meeting, by having a reference to a former letter, you will find was to be the second and last Monday in the Month during winter, and the second Monday in each Month during summer.

"You have not sent us the No. of our Lodge, and if there are any farther Instructions, should be glad to receive them as soon as possible, for which we wait. We did not know it was necessary for each to sign his name or it could have easily been before done ; it is our earnest wish to act with the greatest propriety.

"We are, Right Worshipfull Sir,

"Your most humble Servants.

" E. F. Williams, Woollen Draper, Master.

John Dainton, Cloath Worker, P M.

Saml. Smith, Victuler & Seeds-man, Sen. Warden.

George Clark, Baker, Jun. Warden.

Stephen Bell, Hair Merchant, Secretary

Andrew Heath, Taylor & Draper, Treasurer.

John Coleman, Yeoman P M.

The following appears to have been written by Dainton himself.

"Devizes, 15th March, 1792,

"R. W G M.

"We transmitt to you the Following Transactions of the Grand Lodge, Held at the Sign of the Saracen's Head Devizes, the 14th Inst. The R.W.G.M. in the Chair, Bro. John Dainton, R.W.D.G.M , Bro. John Carson, R.W.S.G.W., Bro. John Austen, R.W. Jun. G.W., Edward Sweeper, R.W.G.S. Bro. Alexander Leishman. Was open'd at Eleven o'Clock, on the third Step of Masonry, where was Presented to the R.W.G.M. by the R.W.D.G.M. Brother Edward F. Williams, Elected Master of Lodge 270. Certain Ceremonies being past, was placed at the Left Hand of the R.W.G.M. when was Elected the Sen. and Jun. Wardens & the rest of the Officers according to Antient Constitution. The By Laws being read & the Regulations, according to Antient Custom. The Grand was clos'd for ever in due form at 2 o'Clock.

John Dainton.
John Carson.
John Austen.
Edward Sweeper.
Alex^r Leishman."

FREEMASONRY IN HEREFORDSHIRE.

Dunckerley's last appointment was for Herefordshire; his Patent of Provincial Grand Master for that county being dated the 5th of May, 1790. At this period there was only one lodge to occupy his attention, although he is supposed to have had two predecessors; viz., Sir Robert de Cornwall, appointed in 1753, and Charles Duke of Norfolk, in 1789. The good works of the former have not reached to our time*

See Freemasonry in Gloucestershire, page 199.

and I can find no record of the appointment of the latter. Prior to Dunckerley's appearance Masonry in this province seems to have been practically without a head. The only lodge in the whole county was the Palladian Lodge No 187 (now No. 120), which appears to have enjoyed an unbroken existence from its constitution in 1762 to the present time.

On the 25th of January, 1791, Dunckerley constituted the Silurian Lodge No. 576 at the *Sun Inn*, Kington, it was afterwards removed to the *King's Head* in the same town but it does not seem to have been firmly established, for although the members evidently consisted chiefly of the well-to-do residents in the neighbourhood, it appears to have ceased working about the time of Dunckerley's death (1795), and ten years later the Warrant was transferred to Ludlow, the title being changed to that of The Mercian Lodge. Here it passed a lingering existence until it was erased by Grand Lodge at the filling up of the vacant numbers in 1832, having registered no names nor paid Grand Lodge dues during the previous six years. In 1793, Dunckerley added to his list the lodge which is the subject of the following letter, evidently written under difficulties, he being at that period in ill health, or, as he puts it, "In confinement at the suit of Madame La Goutte."

"Southampton, Dec. 3rd, 1793.

"Dear Sir & Brother,

"I am now to desire that you will send to me a Warrant of Constitution for the Royal Edward Lodge to be holden at the *Red Lion Inn* at Leominster, in the County of Hereford on the second Monday in each Month, to bear date the 19th of Nov. 1793. Bro. William Wood, Master; Bro. Samuel Nicholas, Sen. Warden & Bro. Thos Hull, Jun. Warden. It convenient, l g   n v   y   te end of this week, that the Brethren may proceed to business as soon as possible.

> " Affectionate regard to Bro. Heseltine, &c.,
> " From your faithful Brother,
> " Thos Dunckerley."

This lodge was No. 533 when it was constituted, and No. 560 at the Union in 1813. It seems to have done a fair amount of good work up to the year 1814, and then to have suddenly ceased, although it was retained on the list until 1828, when it was erased by the Grand Lodge.

Dunckerley's successor in the province was Adam Gordon, Esq., who was appointed on the 24th of March 1797.

MEMORIALS OF ROYAL ARCH MASONRY.

I shall make no attempt to remove the veil of uncertainty which envelopes the origin of Royal Arch Masonry. Abler hands have tried it, and the result may be found in their works. The subject has recently been dealt with in a masterly and most exhaustive manner by two well-known English writers who have made this branch of the history of Masonry their particular study, and those who may be desirous of benefitting by their researches I would refer to Gould's " History of Freemasonry " and Hughan's " Origin of the English Masonic Rite."

I am persuaded that my immediate object will be best attained by recording as briefly as possible, the part played by Thomas Dunckerley in the Order as he found it, being under the firm conviction that he had nothing whatever to do with its origin, but a very great deal to do with its extension and elevation. The earliest evidence of the existence of Royal Arch Masonry in London is contained in a Minute Book in the archives of the Grand Lodge of England. The first meeting therein recorded was held on the 22nd of March

1765, "at Mr. Inge's." We have no evidence as to who or what Mr. Inge was—where he lived—or how long this Chapter had been in existence. Among the members were Dunckerley's particular friends James Galloway and Thomas French; the former seems to have been particularly active at this time in procuring funds to provide furniture and jewels for the Chapter. On the 12th of June a removal was made to *The Turk's Head* in Gerrard Street, Soho, then a much more fashionable quarter than it is now.

The first Anniversary Feast was held on the 8th of January, 1766; Dunckerley being present, he was proposed to become a member by Galloway, " which was approved Nem. Con." This being election day Bro. Galloway was chosen Z, Bro. Maclean H, and Bro. Dunckerley J. It is scarcely necessary to add that these officers attended to their duties with characteristic punctuality during the remainder of the year. In the course of a few months the Chapter was joined by many of the leading Masons in London including the Grand Master, Lord Blayney, the Grand Treasurer, Rowland Berkeley, and the Grand Secretary, Samuel Spencer. Lord Blayney, shortly afterwards introduced several of his personal friends, and at the next Election meeting he was unanimously elected Z or " Grand Master of the M.E C. [Chapter] or Fourth Degree" . . . " Bro. Dunckerley was elected by ballot unto the office of Z. in the absence of the M.E.G.M. and of M E.D.G.M. in his Lordship's presence, and was Invested & Installed accordingly, making the most solemn promise on that occasion—which done, he received that homage from all the Officers and Companions, which is due to so great an office."

This honour, be it observed, was conferred on Dunckerley about six months previous to his royal descent being acknowledged by George III.

More particular details of the working of this important Chapter are set forth in " Masonic Facts and Fictions," I need now only add that in 1767 it was formed into a Grand Chapter by a Charter of Compact* between Lord Blayney, Galloway, McLean, Dunckerley, French, and several other eminent brethren. The Royal Arch Degree was not, however, then formally acknowledged by the Grand Lodge; it occupied a position similar to that held by the Grand Lodge of Mark Master Masons at the present time.

On the 13th of January, 1769, the first three charters were granted for private chapters, No. 3 being for a chapter at Portsmouth Common, under the title of "The Lodge of Tranquility or Chapter of Friendship" which certain R.A. Masons had "requested by letter to Bro. Dunckerley." This was the beginning of Dunckerley's unexampled career as a propagator of Royal Arch Masonry in the provinces. For several years he seldom attended the meetings of the Grand Chapter, being closely engaged in all parts of the country enlisting recruits and promoting the interests of the Order generally. With the exception of the minutes of the various meetings and the Register of members, scarcely anything of a documentary nature has been preserved relating to the early history of the Grand Chapter. No doubt a large amount of correspondence was carried on between Dunckerley and the London officials, but probably in consequence of the Grand Chapter being separate and distinct from the Grand Lodge, and having no permanent office of its own, letters of this period are not now available; I am therefore compelled to rely on the aforesaid minutes for whatever information I can afford with regard to Dunckerley's labours on behalf of the Royal Arch Degree.

Being under the impression that my readers would prefer the genuine records before any composition of my own, I shall now place before them, word for word, every

---

* This document is printed in Hughan's "Origin of the English Rite."

item contained in the minutes having reference to the subject of these memoirs.

Grand Chapter Minutes.

Dec. the 12th, 1777. "It having 'been represented to the Chapter that Bro Dunckerley had exalted Brethren at Colchester to the sublime degree, Bro. Smith propos'd that a polite letter be wrote by the Secretary to Bro. Dunckerley acquainting him of the disapprobation of this Chapter of Brethren being exalted without a regular dispensation for that purpose. Pass'd Nem. Con.

"Bro. Leake who having been exalted by Bro. Dunckerley at Colchester applying to be admitted, it was resolved that he be admitted, but that such admittance be not taken as a precedent to others exalted in a like manner"

Dunckerley's version of this business will be found in the following letter :—

"Hampton Court Palace,

"My much esteem'd Brother   "Jan. 14th, 1792.

"& Knight Companion,

"Sir Benjamin Craven,

"I do myself the pleasure to appoint you Provincial Senior Grand Warden for the County of Essex, also Deputy Grand Superintendant of Royal Arch Masons, and Eminent Deputy Grand Master of Knights Templar for the said County. I am to inform you that there are two Chapters of Royal Arch Masons—at Bocking and Braintree —that I am to desire you will visit whenever it may be convenient to you. The Chapter at Colchester, No. 12, and the Lodge at the Red Lion in the same Borough, I have struck off the List since the death of my much valued Bro. Thos Boggis, Esq. The Lodge No. 51 have been very irregular and have given me much trouble as our Bro Abell and other Brethren can inform you, & I have been inform'd that they have exalted Royal Arch Masons illegally, (for they never had a Constituted Chapter), and some have asserted that they exalted me. I was Grand Z. of the Grand and Royal Chapter in 1767, and in 1776 when I was Grand Superintendant for Essex I exalted Bros. Boggis, Affleck, Leake, &c. by virtue of my Authority, and some of the Brethren of Lodge 51—being Royal Arch Masons— assisted. This is the simple Truth & I beg it may be mention'd in the Lodges to crush all false reports concerning me. I was exalted at Portsmouth in the year 1754, & at that time had never seen Colchester.

"Bro. Lane at Braintree is a Knight Templar; I believe there are some at Colchester, but do not vouch for any. If you can find a *third* I will send you a Patent for holding a Conclave.

" Yʳ Affect Knt. Compⁿ

" Thos. Dunckerley."

This letter is of great historical value and I am under obligations to Bro. G. F. Lancaster of Gosport for the privilege of printing it. Until it was brought to light the time and place of Dunckerley's exaltation were unknown. It also implies that he was " Superintendent " for Essex as far back as 1776, and therefore the first holder of that title in Royal Arch, as well as in Craft Masonry.

"Bro. Smith," who seems to have been somewhat officious on the occasion mentioned, I need hardly say, was no friend of Dunckerley's—indeed, had he not been a Mason, I should be inclined to the opinion that a feeling of jealousy may have had some little influence on his actions at this particular period.

The following bears no date but it was evidently written by him about the time of the occurrence just referred to, and was apparently the outcome of a visit to the Grand Secretary's office during his absence.

" Dear Sir,

"Mr. Dunckerley having declined his Intention of having the Provincial Grand Mastership of Kent, I beg leave to renew my desire for that Honourable Post, should it meet with your approbation.

" I am, Dr Sir, Your most obedient,
" Humble Servant,
" Free Masons Hall   " G. SMITH.
" 4 o'clock."

Captain George Smith, Inspector of the Royal Military Academy at Woolwich, was appointed Provincial Grand Master of Kent in 1777, but not content with this distinctive honour, in 1780 he appears to have got the right side of the Duke of Manchester, then Grand Master, to make him Junior Grand Warden. This appointment was strongly opposed in the Grand Lodge by Heseltine, the Grand Secretary, on the ground of it being contrary to the "Spirit of the Laws of this Society" for the two offices to be held by the same person. This spirited action on the part of the Grand Secretary naturally led to a very warm discussion, but, being the day of the Grand Festival, the subject was adjourned for consideration at the next meeting of the Grand Lodge. Before that day arrived, however, Captain Smith resigned the office of J. G. Warden on the plea of ' the ill state of his health." In 1783 he published "THE USE AND ABUSE OF FREE-MASONRY," for which he endeavoured to obtain the official sanction of the Grand Lodge, but that body would have nothing to do with his book. In 1784 he was charged with having concocted a begging petition, to which was affixed the seal of the Society, supposed to have been taken from a Certificate or Warrant, and with having forged the signature of the Grand Secretary thereto. Not attending in response to a summons to answer this complaint, he was formally expelled the Order on the 2nd of February, 1785.

Grand Chapter Minutes, 12th of May, 1780.

" A letter was read from Comp" Dunckerley, Gd.

Superintendant for the County of Wilts, &c &c., stating
that in consequence of applications he had granted a
Warrant of Constitution for a Chapter at New Sarum and
also a Dispensation to some Companions of the first Regiment of Dragoons then quartered in that City, for holding
a Chapter for one Year, the said Companions having an
Authority from Perth were exalting many Bros. gratis: the
impropriety whereof being explained to them by said
G. S^t, they requested him to receive them under the
authority of this G. & R. Chapter. . . . The Companions (with the utmost respect for Comp^n Dunckerley
and regard for his great Attention to the Honour as well as
Prosperity of the G. & R. Ch^r) considered these Grants as
exceeding the Bounds of his Office. . . . Sir Herbert
Mackworth moved thereupon. 'That a regular Patent for
Grand Superintendants be made out, as also Instructions
necessary for regulating their Conduct; which motion
receiving the Approbation of the Members, Companion
Brooks obligingly undertook the framing them & also to
write to Companion Dunckerley. Whereupon a motion was
made that an extra Chapter be held on this day fortnight
for adjusting the same, which was agreed to ' "

26th of May 1780. " Companion Brooks produced the
form of a Warrant for authorizing Grand Superintendants,
which, being read, met the unanimous approbation of the
Comp^s He then produced a set of Instructions necessary
to be observed by said Superintendants, which being duly
considered & some small alterations being made therein the
same were ordered to be esteemed binding as those contained
in the printed Book of Bye Laws.

" A polite Letter from Companion Dunckerley explaining
his last in the fullest & most satisfactory manner being read,
a Warrant of Constitution was ordered to be made out for
the Chapter of Harmony at Salisbury, Comp^s Dunckerley,
Maton, & Burbridge: Principals."

As there is nothing else on record expressing, or even implying, disapproval of Dunckerley's conduct in connexion with the Grand Chapter; the statement, that he was "frequently reprimanded" by that body is incorrect and consequently misleading.

October 13th, 1780. "A Letter was received & read from Comp^n Dunckerley acknowledging in the politest terms the Receipt of the Warrant of Constitution for the Chapter of Harmony at Salisbury, requesting that the County of Devon might be added in his Patent, and petitioning that Warrants may be granted as hereunder, viz :—

Pool in Dorsetshire	{	To Alexander Campbell, Esq., John Fricker, William Walker,	}	Chapter of Amity, the 2nd Wednesday.
Dorchester	{	George Andrews, Richard Lacey, Henry Bryer,	}	Durnovarian Chapter.
Plymouth, Devon.	{	George Lewis, Robert Weatherley, John Bidcock,	}	Chapter of Unity, 3rd Thursday, King's Arms Inn.

w'h Chapters being moved for separately, the petitions were unanimously granted & the G. Scribe was desired to make out Warrants for the same, as also a Patent for appointing, in form, our most Ex^t Comp^n Dunckerley, Grand Superintendant for Essex, Hants, Wilts, Dorset & Devon."*

8th of November, 1782. "Several irregularities having crept into the Chapters held in the Counties of Somerset & Gloucester the Scribe was order'd to write to Bro. Dunckerley impowering him to act as Superintendent of the said Counties."

---

* This Patent as well as the Warrants named was duly signed at the next Grand Chapter, and on the 12th of January, 1781, a letter containing a Bill for the Fees of the Chapters at Poole and Plymouth was received from Superintendant Dunckerley. H S.

11th of April, 1783. "M.E. Compⁿ Dunckerley by Letter inform'd the Chapter he had granted a Dispensation for a Chapter to be held at Birmingham by the Name of the Chapter of Fortitude and appointing,

> Richard Jescoate,*   ⎫
> John Lloyd,   ⎬ Esqrs.
> John Hallen,   ⎭

to act as Principals, bearing Date the 6th inst, and requesting a Warrant of Constitution to be made out from the above date ; which was order'd accordingly."

7th of November, 1783. "M E Compⁿ Dunckerley having granted a Dispensation for a Chapter to be held at Weymouth, a Warrant for the same was this evening executed, bearing Date by Dispensation 16th June, 1783, by Constitution 7th Nov. 1783, and appointing as principals

> William Weldon, Z.
> James Stark, H.
> James Hamilton, J.

12th of November, 1784. "Order (upon the application of the M.E. Dunckerley) for a Chapter to be held at Ipswich by the name of 'Prudence,' Bros. Robert Manning, Z. James Garrod, H., Robert Cole, J., to be addressed to Bro. Dixon, Trumpet Major of the 1st Regt. of Dragoon Guards at Ipswich."

6th of May, 1785. "M.E. Dunckerley stood up in his place, and reported that he had wrote to 13 Chapters under his superintendance, the several answers to which he specified, he also reported that he had been applied to, in writing from the various Chapters in the County of Kent, praying to be admitted into his particular care, as Superintendant of the County : but not conceiving he had sufficient power at present for that purpose, he pray'd the G. and R. Chapter to grant him licence

----

* Jescoate " in the R. A Register. H S.

" The question being put, & duly seconded, it passed in the affirmative, unanimously."

11th of November, 1785. " M.E.Z. produced a Letter from M.E. Dunckerley, stating that he had sent him a Bill of £6. 0s. 0d. for registering members of the G. and R.C. at Bristol: and also that he had sent a Letter to M.E. Const above a month before, containing a Bill of £7. 3s. 0d. for registering members of the G. and R. Chapters at Colchester and Bocking."

10th of March, 1786. " M.E. Galloway having informed the Chapter that M.E. Dunckerley had it in prospect to establish a Chapter in the County of Surrey; moved, and it was duly seconded, that Compⁿ Dunckerley's intention merits the thanks and approbation of this G. & R. Chapter, which was unanimously agreed to."

10th of November, 1786. " A motion was made by M.E. Galloway and seconded by M.E. Brooks, that M E Dunckerley should be appointed Superintendant for the County of Suffolk, in the room of M E. Holt, deceased; it was carried unanimously."

9th of February, 1787. " A Letter was read from our M.E. Compⁿ Dunckerley giving an account of two Constitutions and Registering Fees and enclosing a Draft on his Banker for Ten Pounds, viz. Six Guineas for two Constitutions for Kingston & Bridgewater, and Three Pounds 14/- for Registering Fees."

9th of March, 1787. " A Letter was received from our M.E. Companion Dunckerley which was read, and by particular desire of M.E. Brooks was referred to a Committee "

13th of April, 1787. " M E. Galloway acquainted the Companions that our M E. Compⁿ Dunckerley's Letter read at the last Chapter had been considered; and it was *unanimously* agreed, that a Letter should be wrote to acquaint him, that a Plate was preparing for Printing the Constitutions, which w··· l prevent in f ·ture tl·· l··ay···l· l··l· ··p··· ··l· ·· i of."

November 9th, 1787. "M.E. Heseltine moved that our M.E. Companion Dunckerley be permitted to take the Superintendance of the County of Sussex, and to annex the same with the other Counties at present mentioned in his Provincial Warrant; which, being duly seconded, passed unanimously in the affirmative."

January 11th, 1788. "A Letter was received from our M.E. Companion Dunckerley containing a List of Chapters granted Constitutions, and a List of Companions to be Registered, with the sum of £149. 1s. 0d. for Fees, &c."

March 14th, 1788. "Companion Thos. Dunckerley having by letter requested to be appointed Superintendant of the County of Durham, It was unanimously Ordered in the Affirmative.

"Companion Dunckerley having also by his said Letter informed the R.A.C. that he had received a Letter dated 11th January with a Petition from the Chapter of Vigilance to be held at Darlington, in the County of Durham, It was unanimously ordered in the Affirmative, and that a Warrant be made out thereupon."

February 13th, 1789. "A Letter was received from Companion Dunckerley inclosing a Draft for £12. 10s. being the Balance of his Acc^{t,} also requesting a Warrant of Constitution for a Chapter to be held at Bury St. Edmunds, in the County of Suffolk, John Pate, Z., William Norford, H., James Parker, J. A Warrant was accordingly granted."

December 11th. "A letter was received from Comp'n. Dunckerley informing the Grand Chapter, that the Chapter of Unity No. 23, held at Plymouth, had not sent any registering fees for Seven years past, pretending not to have received the Exaltation fees, also that their Companions were now in arrears, on which Compⁿ Dunckerley requested the Grand Chapter would confirm his having struck the said Chapter off the List.

"A Motion was thereupon made & Confirmed that a

Letter be forthwith writ to the said Chapter, informing them if they do not pay up their arrears, that the Grand Chapter will of course accede to the request of Compⁿ Dunckerley."

January 28th, 1790. " A Letter was received & read from Compⁿ Dunckerley, inclosing a Draft for £10. 0. (which was paid to the Treasurer) requesting the Chapter to agree to erase the Chapter No. 23."

This request does not appear to have been complied with for the Chapter remained on the List until 1813 although it registered no members after 1791.

During this year Dunckerley attended several meetings of the Grand Chapter, generally filling one of the Principal Offices. On the 27th of January, 1791, he " was unanimously elected our M E Z. for the current year." He was installed on the 24th of February when it was " Resolved— That the M.E.Z. do now appoint his own Officers which was accordingly done." The officers were usually elected by ballot at the same time as the M.E.Z. Eight meetings of the Grand Chapter were held during the year 1791, at four of which Dunckerley presided. His last attendance was on the 4th of May, 1792.

October 29th, 1795. "The Recorder produced several Letters received since the last Chapter, one of which was from our M.E. Compⁿ Thomas Dunckerley Dated 9th ulto by which he most solemnly declares his surrender of the Office of Superintendant of the several Counties, &c., and every other Office named in the Grand Chapter."

November 26th, 1795. " Present, Allen & Cooper.

" Examined several Accounts.

"M. E Compⁿ Dunckerley died 19th ulto. at Portsea.* It was judg'd proper that an enquiry should be made of his Executors for any Accounts relating to this Order, as he had received from time to time many Sums of Money for Registers, &c , which he had never communicated."

The Grand Chapter appears to have been then at a very low ebb, and was nearer dissolution than at any other period of its history, the attendances being exceedingly small. Only two Companions are mentioned as attending the last two meetings; one of these being Benjamin Cooper, Grand Recorder, or Scribe E., whose pen was made the instrument of as gross a libel as ever was perpetrated.* Had not this contemptible and unfounded statement already appeared in print, I should not have given it a place in this volume, and I am of opinion that in justice to the memory of one who did so much for the Craft in general and Royal Arch Masonry in particular, it should be expunged from the records.

' At this period the Grand Chapter was most unfortunate in the selection of its executive officers, the accounts appear to have been kept in the loosest possible manner, or rather, not kept at all, unless in the interest of one individual. On the 14th of April, 1792, a Committee of Investigation was held, and " the Treasurer attended with his accounts, being obliged to retire, by reason of some particular business before the arrival of Companion Cooper, left the following memorandum : —

"I have left with the Committee an Account of all monies received by me of *any* person on account of the Royal Arch, at *any* time during the time to which this book reaches. " (Signed) Fr^s Const."

" Companion Cooper's account of monies received by him as entered in the Minute Book and List of Members Amounting to the sum of (for the years 1791

and 1792) £208 11	6
The Treasurer's receipts for the above period	
amounting to 182 4	6
Deficient ... 26 7	0

---

* The Lion was dead! H S.

"Order'd that the above variance in the said accounts be adjusted previous to the next meeting of the Chapter."

Whether or no this order was ever complied with is not clearly stated; but the committee made a lengthy report to the Grand Chapter a fortnight later, a portion of which is as follows :—

"Your Committee regret that after the most minute enquiry, they have not been able to discover in whose possession the original Minute Book, Cash Book, and your Treasurer's *late* Accompt Book is, which puts it out of their power to make a particular statement of Receipts and Disbursements. . . . .

"Your Committee recommend that Compⁿ Cooper make out a List of such companions marked in the Book by him as paid : (which *he* says is a mistake) and that he make enquiry & answer for them on the next Chapter night.

"Your Committee recommend that the Cash account be balanced every Chapter night and read with the Minutes for Confirmation."

In 1800 fresh financial complications arose, and strenuous efforts were made to induce the Recorder to produce his accounts with what success will be shown by the following extract.

"FREE MASONS TAVERN, 27th August, 1801. At a Meeting of Principals of Chapters convened for the purpose of receiving Mr. Cooper's Report as to his Receipts and Disbursements for the Grand Chapter.

"RESOLVED, that Mr. Cooper be indulged agreeably to his last request with further Time to produce his Accounts so long and so frequently promised.

"RESOLVED also, that Mr. Allen, the Grand Treasurer be requested to give directions to Mr. Cooper to summon the Grand Officers and Members of the Grand Chapter together with the Principals of the several Chapters within the Bills of Mortality to meet here as a Special Grand Chapter on

Friday, the 16th day of October next, at 7 o'Clock in the Evening—When it is expected that Mr. Cooper will not, on any account, fail to attend such Chapter with his Accounts completely made out, together with the Books and Papers belonging to the Society for General Inspection. And that a Copy of this Resolution be transmitted by the Treasurer to Mr. Cooper."

There is no record of a meeting on the 16th of October, but, on the 17th of December, "The Grand Recorder paid over to the Grand Treasurer £80 on acc't. of the balance of Cash received by him but was not able to state the *exact* sum from having mislaid some of the Papers."

The Grand Chapter had evidently seen almost enough of Cooper, for at the election of Officers on the 16th of December, 1802, he was superseded, and a more competent and trustworthy person appointed, who appears to have experienced considerable difficulty with his predecessor.

At a meeting held on the 22nd of February, 1803.

"It was order'd that Comp" Cooper should be summoned to appear in his place and finally render up his accounts, together with such Articles belonging to the G. Chapter as remain in his possession by virtue of his late office, on or before the General Chapter of Communication in March next." Companion Cooper did not attend in response to this summons nor is he again mentioned in the records. In my opinion Grand Chapter was well rid of him at any price, for, judging from the Minutes, it improved immediately, as if relieved from a dead weight, and soon attained a higher degree of respectability and importance than it had occupied for several years. I think enough has been said to show the true character of Dunckerley's detractor and how utterly unworthy of credence must be the slanderous statement made by him, probably with a hope of covering his own malpractices.

The worst that can be honestly said of Dunckerley is, that his zeal occasionally prompted him to actions which might now be deemed improper, but which doubtless at that period and from his point of view were perfectly justifiable. The alleged offence of having granted a Dispensation for the Chapter of Harmony at Salisbury would in the case of Craft Masonry, have been deemed perfectly legitimate and deserving of the commendation of the Society; it being customary for Provincial Grand Masters to grant Dispensations, and, in some cases Warrants, for lodges in their jurisdictions and then report the circumstances to the Grand Lodge. There can be little, if any, doubt that it was mainly owing to the exertions and influence of Dunckerley and his personal friends that the Grand Chapter was brought into existence and the fact of his having been placed at the head of that Assembly a second time sufficiently evinces the regard in which he was held by the members of it.

The following is a List of the Counties presided over by Dunckerley as Grand Superintendent of Royal Arch Masons, with an approximate period of his service.*

Bristol, 1782-1795.
Cornwall, 1793-1795.
Devonshire, 1780-1795.
Dorsetshire, 1780-1795.
Durham, 1788-1795.
Essex, 1776-1795.
Gloucestershire, 1782-1795.
Hampshire, 1778-1782.
Herefordshire, 1793-1795.
I. of Wight, 1778-1795.
Kent, 1785-1795.
Nottinghamshire, 1793-1795.
Somersetshire, 1782-1795.
Suffolk, 1786-1795.
Surrey, 1789-1795.
Sussex, 1787-1795.
Warwickshire, 1793-1795.
Wiltshire, 1780-1790.

---

* Dunckerley was the first Grand Superintendent of all these Count... ex... t Kent and Suff...

MEMORIALS OF MASONIC TEMPLARISM.

It would afford me great pleasure to be able to introduce the following letters by a brief sketch of the origin of the Order to which they refer, but I feel that by attempting anything of the kind I should run a serious risk of getting out of my depth. I must, therefore, content myself with merely offering them as contributions for the use of possible future historians.

That Dunckerley was the first Grand Master of the Masonic Knights Templar in England, is, I believe, not disputed, but whether he introduced the degree to this country or only consolidated and organised what was previously a comparatively small number of enthusiasts without an acknowledged head are questions which I have no means of determining. As an expression of opinion merely, I should say he had no more to do with the invention of Masonic Templarism than he had to do with the invention of the Royal Arch Degree, and that his first acquaintance with these bodies was of a similar character. Undoubtedly he had a strong affection for both Orders, and had they been his own creations he could not possibly have been more proud of them.

The following correspondence for which I am indebted to Michael C. Peck, Past G. Standard Bearer of England, who has kindly permitted me to publish it, will throw considerable light on Dunckerley's early connection with the Order under notice.

Copy of Draft Letter from York, 1791.

" Dear Brother,

" After our Most Excellent Exalted Bro. Sir Thomas Dixon of the 1st Dragoon Guards left York, we the Companions whose Names are annex'd had met occasionally, & waited with the most fervent anxiety till the time sh⁴· arrive that we were to look up to a Grand Master under whose patronage the Knights Templar sh⁴ again flourish, & the happy moment has now come, in which we most cordially congratulate our Most Excellent & Exalted Bro. Comp^n. Knight, & Grand Master, Sir Thos. Dunckerley as our Head & Chief. And we all most cordially submit ourselves to your care & protection, and to such Bye Laws & Regulations as shall be sent from time to time for the better guidance & government of the Encampment, whose Title is Redemption, & purpose holding our encampment regularly the First Friday in each month at Brother Seller's, the Golden Lion Inn, Thursday Market.

"We shall esteem ourselves most particularly obliged by being favoured with such Laws & Regulations as are now in being for the better order & good govern^t. of the Encampment, with a power to make such other regulations for the better govern^t. of our own private encampment as may not infringe upon the General Laws of the original Institution.

"We shall be happy to hear that the Encamp^ts. in England increase, & make no doubt but they will, under such an able & judicious Grand Master, which God Almighty grant that all the Kingdoms of this world may become the Kingdom of our Blessed Lord & Saviour Jesus Christ.

"P.S.—Should Sir Thos. Dixon be in the Neighbourhood all our best wishes attend him.

"Any Hymns or Sonnets &c. relative to the Order will be considered as an additional obligation."

DUNCKERLEY'S SEAL OF THE KNIGHTS KADOSH.

*"Hampton Court Palace,

"March 22nd, 1791.

"Most Excellent and Exalted Knights Companions of the Encampment of Redemption (being No. 5 of England) held at the Golden Lion Inn in the City of York.

"I accept with gratitude the confidence you place in me as Grand Master by the Will of God, of the Most Noble and Exalted Religious and Military Order of Masonic Knights Templar of St. John of Jerusalem. I must request that as soon as possible you send to me the Names, Ages, Profession & Residence of all the Knights of your Encampment, as I intend to have a regular Register of our Order. Being Grand Superintendent of Royal Arch Masons at Bristol, I was requested by the Knights Templar in that City (who have had an Encampment time immemorial) to accept the Office of Grand Master, which I had no sooner comply'd with than Petitions were sent to me for the same purpose from London 1, Bath 2, the first Regiment of Dragoon Guards 3, Colchester 4, York 5, Dorchester 6, and Biddeford 7. I suppose there are many more Encampments in England, which with God's permission I may have the happiness to revive & assist. It has already been attended with a blessing, for I have been but *two* months Grand Master & have already 8 Encampments under my care. You will see by the List on the other side that the Chapter of Unity of Royal Arch Masons No. 17 is held in the City of York. I beg to know if there are any Knights Templar among them. Is Thursday Market the name of a Street in York? I had the pleasure of a letter from that very worthy Knight Sir Thos. Dixon, dated the 4th

---

* A portion of this letter first appeared in the Appendix to Peck's edition of "Mackey's Lexicon." H. S.

instant from Dorchester, the Regiment is to march for Salısbury the beginning of next Month; he expects soon to pass the Board at London for Superannuation, & has promis'd to pass a day or two with me at this place. I shall form a few Statutes for regulating our Order as soon as I have appointed the Grand Officers of the Grand Encampment of All England, to be held on the 24th of June annually at London.

"The following I submit to your consideration :—

"That every regular Encampment be constituted by Warrant, sign'd by the Grand Master, & witness'd by the Grand Scribe, for which one Guinea is to be paid; 10/6 for furnishing Robes for the Grand Master & 10/6 for engross-ing the Warrant

"That every Knight pay 5/-, for which he will receive a certificate sign'd by the second Grand Scribe of his being register'd in the Gd. Chapter.

"That no Knight be install'd for a less sum than One Guinea for the use of that Encampment, and 5/- for his Certificate from the Grand Chapter.

"I have given No. 5 to y^r Encampment tho' Dorchester & Biddeford petition'd previous to your Application, but as no Dispensations or Warrants are yet made out, I show every preference in my power to the second City in the kingdom.

"If these Regulations meet with your approbation, signify the same to me as soon as convenient, and I will send you a Dispensation, till the Warrant is made out.

"Your Most Affectionate Comp^n, &c,

"THOS. DUNCKERLEY

"I never heard of any Hymns or Odes on the Order of Knights Templar, but will on a future day (with God's assistance) attempt something of the kind. I did some years past write a Hymn to be sung after the opening of a

Royal Arch Chapter. It is published with the Music (price 6d,) by Mr. Fentum at his Music Shop, the corner of Salisbury Street in the Strand, where it may be had by any of your Friends in Town. T. D."*

For copies of the following letters I am under obligations to William James Hughan, Past Grand Deacon of England.

"Redruth, 17th August, A.D. 1791.

"A.L. 5795.

"To Thomas Dunckerley, Esq.,

"Grand Superintendant of the Most

"Exalted Order of Royal Arch Masons, &c., &c.

"Bro. & Companion,

"Your letter of Dispensation of the 15th July, directed to Bro. Companion Harrison of the Peace & Fame Chapter at Plymouth Dock was handed to us by Bro. Companion Tregoning one of the Principals of that Chapter, and agreeable to your directions, The officers have been placed in their proper Chairs & have Exalted three Brethren of the Druids Lodge of Love & Liberality to the sublime Degree of Royal Arch Masons, you may be assured that every attention shall be paid to its Glorious precepts, and particular care taken in the Exaltation of Companions. As soon as the Warrant is ready you will be pleased to forward it to us at this Place, with such instructions as will suit you to send for our assistance & Government. We see on your Letter to Bro. Harrison of the 8th July a Print relative to the Royal & Exalted Religious & Military order of Knights Templars & that you are the Most Eminent & Supreme Grand Master.

"There are some of that Order in this place, & Bro.

---

* See page 301.

John Knight of the Druids' Chapter has formerly presided a Grand Master, we cou'd wish to know the expence of a Warrant or Dispensation & what steps it will be necessary to take for the obtaining the same.

"We beg leave to return you our warmest thanks for your ready compliance with our Petition as also for your condescension in offering to take us under your immediate Patronage, this we assure you we shall accept with the greatest pleasure & that we remain,

"Most exalted & Noble Grand Master of Royal
"Arch Masons, &c., &c ,

" Your affectionate Bros. & Companions.

JOHN KNIGHT, Z.
PETER PENDER, H.
PHILIP TREVENA, J."

" Hampton Court Palace,

" M. E. Comp^n ,   " August 26th, 1791.

" As the Grand & Royal Chapter will not meet till the last Thursday in October, your Warrant cannot be signed before that time, when the Scribe sends it to me I shall forward it immediately to you. The price of a Patent for a Conclave & Chapter of Knights Templars is £1. 6s. with 5/- for each Knight, for which Certificates will be sent. If there are 3 or more Knights among ye I will grant you a Patent, if you can send me the first letter of the Pass word and last letter of sacred word.

" The established Sash to be worn by every Knight in
    Chapter will cost   -   -   -   6/-
" The Gilt Cross   -   -   -   7 6
" The Silver Star   -   -   -   7 6
                                                    21/-

Statutes, 3/- When you write in future I must request you will pay the Postage & charge it to your Chapter.

"Present my affectionate Greeting to all the Companions.

"From your faithful Bro., &c., &c.,

"Thos. Dunckerley."

"Most Excellent Companion,

"It is with great pleasure that I can now send your Patent for the R.A. Chapter with a Book of the Statutes & also those of the order of Knights Templars, with an impression of the Great Seal, I shall (in the next printed list) insert the County of Cornwall under my superintendance & shall at all times take pleasure in doing every service in my power for the Druids' Chapter.

"Please acknowledge the receipt of your Patent by a letter in return (Post paid). Present my affectionate regards to all the Comp^ns & believe me,

"Your faithful Comp^n, &c.,

"26th November, 1791."   "Thos. Dunckerley.

	£	s	d
"To a Patent of Constitution - - -	£1	6	0
3 Certificates at 5/- - - - -		15	0
3 Sashes, 3 Stars & 3 Crosses - -	3	6	0
10 Books of Statutes at 6d. - - -		5	
Box - - - - - -		1	6
Carriage of the Sashes &c. from London			
to Hampton Court - - -			6
	5	14	0

"Hampton Court Palace,

"21st Dec., 1791.

"Dear Bro. & Kn^t. Comp^n,

"According to your request I send the above, the last letter of the principal word is right therefore when I hear from you in return shall forward what you desire; let me have the Title of your Conclave & the names, ages & professions of the other Knights. When the next list is published of R.A. Chapters you will know the number. I believe you have forgot the Pass word, but trust you will find it among your Companions to whom present my affectionate regards.

" Your faithful Bro. & Kn^t. Comp^n.,

" THOS. DUNCKERLEY."

" Hampton Court Palace, December 30th,

"A.L. 5795, A.D., 1791.

" A. O. 673, A. C. 477.

* " My much esteem'd Bro. & K^t. Comp^n.,

" Sir B. Craven,

" It was with much pleasure that I heard, lately, from Miss Hervey of your having a Company for I understood that you was in Ireland. I *thrice* heartily congratulate you on your Marriage and your promotion. If you have not relinquish'd Masonry I do myself the pleasure to appoint you Senior Grand Warden for the County of Essex. I have the honour to be G. Master of the Knights Templars and send to you (by our Bro. White of Colchester, G. Secretary for Essex) the Statutes of the Order and ye impression of the *Great Seal*. I am inform'd there are Knights companions at Malden of which (if convenient) I beg you will enquire, as I should be glad to constitute a Conclave & Field Encampment in Essex of which I would appoint you the *Eminent*.

---

* The original of this letter is in the possession of Mark E. Frost, P.P.S G. Warden of Hants, who kindly placed it at my disposal for the purp se f th s colnm . H. S.

"I shall be happy to hear from you in return. Your Sister D. the Lady Patroness of Knights Templars unites with me in wishing all happiness to Sister Craven & yourself.

"I remain your affect. Bro. & K^t Comp$^n.$

"THOS DUNCKERLEY."

"Hampton Court Palace,

"January 27th, 1792.

*"Dear Bro. & Kn^t Comp$^n.$

"I am concerned that there is so great a distance between us as it would give me much pleasure to communicate to any Conclave that I have constituted, the Masonic knowledge which I have gleaned in Europe, America & Africa for forty years past.

"Although Mrs. Dunckerley (the Lady Patroness of Knight Templars) is near 80 years of age, and I am not far from 70, yet we intend (with God's permission) to visit the West of England next summer, and if we should winter at Plymouth, it is probable that I may have the happiness of conversing with some of the Knights Companions from Exeter, Redruth & Biddeford. I was selected Grand Master to revive the Order in England in February, 1791 and have had the pleasure to constitute the following Conclaves, viz :—

CONCLAVES.	ENCAMPMENTS.
Of Observance of the Seven Degrees.	London Coffee House, Ludgate Hill.
Of Redemption.	York.

---

* A Copy of this letter was sent to George Blizard Abbott, in 1877, by the late John Coombe, of Hayle, with permission to publish it, but as Bro. Abbott did not then use it he has kindly consented to its insertion in this volume. H. S

CONCLAVES.	ENCAMPMENTS.
Royal Cumberland.	Bath. Bear Inn,
Fortitude.	First Regiment of Dragoon Guards.
Trine.	Biddeford. New Ring of Bells.
Naval.	Portsmouth.
Durnovarian.	Dorchester. Royal Oak.
Harmony.	Salisbury. Parade Coffee House.
Royal Edward.	Hereford. Bowling Green.
St. John of Jerusalem.	Redruth. London Inn *

"I have sent a Uniform button and pattern of the Cloth for a Frock to be worn, which I have established to be worn in the several Conclaves. The Coat will take 14 Buttons, ten in front & four for the hips, & shirts with two very small gilt buttons at the opening of each sleeve, and a White Kersymer Waistcoat & White French casket buttons, with black breeches. A cheap suit of Clothes that may be worn by men of all professions, and at any time. I paid the Taylor £4. 4s. 0d. for my Coat & Waistcoat. In all the Chapters Cock'd Hats and Cockades are worn with Swords and black velvet stocks. The Stocks, Cockades & Swords to be kept in a box at each Chapter.

"Most of the Knights (I have more than 120 registred) have already appeared in their uniforms, in compliance with my recommendation and request, and I shall be happy to

---

* Shortly after this list was written another Conclave was established in London, at the Rainbow Coffee House, Cavendish Square, the Charter, bearing Dunckerley's signature and an "impression of the Great Seal" has recently been presented to The Great Priory of England and Wales, by John J. Pakes, P.M. & Secretary of the Royal Oak Lodge No. 871. It is a very neatly engraved document but the written parts are nearly illegible. It appears to have been granted to Sir Knight Thomas Troop Turner, and others, and bears date 9th of February 1792. H S.

hear that you add to yᵉ number, if not attended with inconvenience.

"The sashes &c. &c. are come to hand within this hour & I write hastily that the Box may go from London by yᵉ mail Coach to-morrow evening.

"My Wife unites with me wishing every success to our Order sacred to the memory of Redemption, and you have our hearty Greeting.

"Your faithful & affectionate

"Compⁿ· & Brother,

"THOS. DUNCKERLEY."

"I wish you would amend the 卐 on the Patent, under my name. It is the signature of our Order, *Templum Hierosolyma Eques.* For the Royal Arch it is 卍 *Templum Hierosolyma.*"

LETTERS FROM

HIS ROYAL HIGHNESS PRINCE EDWARD,

DUKE OF KENT, GRAND PATRON

OF THE ORDER OF MASONIC KNIGHTS TEMPLAR.

The following four letters from the pen of the Father of our Most Gracious Majesty Queen Victoria, and the Grandfather of our Most Worshipful Grand Master, will, I make no doubt, be deemed well worthy of perusal, evincing as they do, the warm interest taken by the writer in Freemasonry, but more especially in relation to the branch of the Order under notice.

"Quebeck, 27th Oct., 1792.

"Dear Mr. Dunckerley,

"I have the pleasure of acknowledging the receipt of your 2 kind letters of the 28th May & the 21st July. I request that you express to the Noble Knights my particular thanks for their most acceptable Present of your

Portrait. It is a Masterpiece of execution & extremely like. You may be assured that I value it doubly, as being their Gift & a remembrance of you. I hope you are sufficiently acquainted with my sentiments of regard & esteem for your person, so that I trust my repetitions on that Head will be needless.

" Nothing gives me greater pleasure than to hear of the advancement of that Order, which, in my humble opinion, is of all Masonry the most valuable

" I believe I mentioned to you at Carlton House my great predilections for the lodges of that high Order being decorated with compleat hangings adapted to the Class of the Craft; pray let me have your opinion & that of the Kts. on this subject, for on my return to England, which I hope will be in 1794 or 1795, I should be pleased to find this Idea carried into execution for the Grand Conclave. I have received the different Masonic Papers with which you favoured me. In answer to your kind enquiries after my Health, I have the pleasure of informing you that it continues good, notwithstanding the prodigious variation in this Climate from the month of June to that of October.

" I shall now with sincere wishes for your Health and Happiness, conclude with subscribing myself

  " Your most truly devoted

    " And obedt. Humble Servant & Brother,

      " EDWARD,

    " Col. of the Royal Fuziliers.

" Thomas Dunckerley." *

     "Quebec, Nov. 20, 1793.

" Dear Sir,

  " I had the pleasure of being favoured with your kind letter of the 4th of July about three weeks since.

---

* The original letter is in the archives of the Grand Lodge of England. H. S.

Accept my thanks for your communication of the proceedings of the Grand Chapter. I regret much that from the nature of my situation there is no likelihood of my removing from hence till June or July next year; and even then it is out of my power to say whether my lot will carry me back to England or to another foreign station. I shall think myself particularly fortunate when circumstances will permit my meeting the Knights in Grand Chapter in London: of this I request you will assure them the first time that you assemble, begging them to accept of my most hearty and best wishes for their welfare and prosperity. I shall be flattered with hearing from you from time to time, and particularly so when you are able to inform me of the good state of your health; having nothing further to add, I beg, with the sincerest esteem, to subscribe myself

" Your most devoted and obedient servant,
" EDWARD,
" Colonel of the Royal Fuziliers.
" Thomas Dunckerley, Esq.,
" Hampton Court Palace." *

DUNCKERLEY'S SEAL OF THE GRAND CONCLAVE, K.T.

---

* From " The Freemasons' Magazine." August, 1794. H. S.

For the two following letters I am indebted to Bro. Reuben Williamson, P.M. of No. 521, who carefully copied them, with others, from printed documents in the archives of the Hope Preceptory, No. 4, Huddersfield, and I much regret that want of space precludes my utilising all the interesting extracts, &c., so kindly forwarded.

"Halifax, Aug. 8, 1794.

"Dear Sir,

"By a number of unforeseen circumstances, a Servant of mine into whose Hands my Agents in London gave your Letter of the 9th of May, '93, did not join me until the second of last month, and consequently I did not receive your Favour till that Period. I now beg to take the earliest opportunity that has offered of writing, to return you my best Thanks for the Calendar and Masonic Papers, which came safe to Hand. The very obliging manner in which you mentioned having held a Grand Chapter of Knights Templars at Southampton, to celebrate my Birth-Day, was particularly flattering; and I now beg you will accept of my warmest Thanks for yourself, and at the same Time present them to the Brethren for their Remembrance of me. You will probably have heard of my leaving Canada, in the commencement of last Winter, to join the Army in the West Indies. I returned from thence to this part of the World as soon as the Campaign was over, and am now waiting here for his Majesty's further Commands. I now beg to subscribe myself, with true Regard,

"Your sincere Well-Wisher,

"And most obedient Servant,

"EDWARD,

"Major-General, &c., &c.

"P.S.—Aug. 23. The July Pacquet arrived here a few days since, and with it your kind Letter of the 4th of July, with its Inclosures. I have only Time to return you my Thanks for the Communication of the very respectable Conduct of the Knights on the late Appearance of the French, threatening to invade England ; and I beg you to assure them of the true Pleasure I have received from this Circumstance. His Majesty has decided for the present that I shall remain to command in Nova Scotia.

"Thomas Dunckerley, Esq.,
    "Hampton Court Palace, Middlesex."

"Dear Sir,   "Halifax, July 19th, 179̲5.

    "I was favored on the 30th of last month with your obliging letter of the 17th of April ; for which, and the assurance therein contained of the kind remembrance of the Noble Knights, I beg to return you and them my most hearty thanks. It gives me the truest satisfaction to hear that the Order increases so rapidly ; and I am particularly pleased to learn from you, that the zeal of the Knights has induced those residing in Cumberland, Cornwall and the distant Counties, to enroll themselves in the regiments stationed in those Counties ; I think your own intention of standing forward in the defence of the Kingdom highly meritorious. I was much concerned to hear of your having suffered so much from ill health ; but sincerely hope, as your letter is written in most excellent spirits, that you are thoroughly recovered. It remains for me to return you my thanks for the very polite attention you paid to the celebration of my Birth-Day and to request, that you will assure the Noble Knights of my particular friendly remembrance. Trusting that you will remain assured, that I shall ever be proud to acknowledge myself,

    "Your truly devoted and obedient,
                    Humble Servant,
                        EDWARD.
"Major General, commanding His Majesty's Forces in
    the Province of Nova-Scotia and its Dependencies.
"To Thomas Dunckerley, Esq.
    "Hampton Court Palace, Middlesex."

On the 10th of February, 1790, the Grand Master in the Chair, reported to the Grand Lodge, that "H.R.H. Prince Edward had been initiated into Masonry in the Union Lodge, at Geneva; it was thereupon, RESOLVED UNANIMOUSLY, That, in testimony of the high sense the Grand Lodge entertains of the great Honour conferred on the Society. . . . . his Royal Highness be presented with an Apron lined with blue silk, and, in all future processions, do rank as a Past Grand Master."

By a Patent bearing date the 26th of January, 1790, His Royal Highness was appointed "Provincial Grand Master for the Garrison, Town and Territory of Gibraltar, and the Province of Andalusia in Old Spain."

In 1792 he was appointed Provincial Grand Master for Lower Canada, by the Grand Lodge "According to the old Institutions," and in 1813 he accepted the Grand Mastership of that Society in order the better to facilitate an union of the two rival Grand Lodges. His efforts being happily crowned with success, he nominated his younger brother, the Duke of Sussex, as Grand Master of the United Grand Lodge, and a few months later, in conjunction with the Duke of Athole, he installed his Royal relative into that high office.

"DEAR BROTHER AND KNIGHT COMPANION.

"As the nation is preparing to guard against an invasion from our enemies, if they should have the temerity to make an attempt, it is become my duty, at this important crisis, to request and *require* that such of you as can, without prejudice to your families, do hold yourselves in readiness (as Knights Templars) to unite with and be under the command of the officers of the military corps stationed in your respective counties, as may be most convenient, taking the name of 'Prince Edward's Royal Volunteers.' When the important moment arrives, I shall offer my services in the navy or army; and whenever I have the honour to be received, shall inform you of my address; and although we are prevented, by adverse circumstances, from assembling together where I might have had the honour and happiness of commanding in person, yet our hearts will be united in the glorious cause, in conformity to the sacred obligations we are under. Let our prayers be addressed to the Throne of Grace; that as Christ's faithful soldiers and servants we may be enabled to defend the Christian religion, our gracious Sovereign, our laws, liberties, and properties, against a rapacious enemy. Let the words of the day be *The Will of God:* and let us remember that a day, an hour of virtuous liberty, is worth a whole eternity of bondage.

"The Knights Companions are required to wear the uniform of the corps in which they serve as volunteers, with the *Cross* of the Order of the Knights Templars on a black riband between two button-holes on the breast of the waistcoat.

"Your faithful Brother and Knight Companion,

"THOMAS DUNCKERLEY (G.M.)

"*Southampton, April* 11*th,*

"*A.D.* 1794. *A.O.* 676."

"The following is the COPY of a LETTER from REDRUTH in CORNWALL, in answer to the preceding."

"MOST EMINENT AND SUPREME GRAND MASTER.

"AGREEABLE to your desire, signified to me by your esteemed favour of the 11th ultimo, I held a conclave of the Order of Knights Templars in our field of encampment at this place, on Monday the 28th ultimo; where I laid your letter before the Knights Companions. I have the happiness to inform you that I found them steadfast in their religious principles and unanimous in their loyalty and patriotism to their King and Country. Two of the Knights Companions are officers in the Penryn Volunteers corps, and will follow your directions in wearing the *Cross* of the Order, &c. The rest of the Companions residing at a distance from any established corps, will be ready on any emergant occasion to unite with them ; and they have entered into a subscription (as Knight Templars), to be applied towards the defence of the country ; and as there is a general subscription at Bodmin, for the county, and several volunteer corps on the coast for local defence, we beg your opinion and advice how to apply the money we have subscribed. I am (M.E. & S.G.M.)

      " Your faithful and affectionate

        " Brother and Knight Companion,

                  " J—— K——.

" *Redruth, 3rd May,* 1794.*

" To The Most Eminent Commander, Captains commanding Columns and others The Knight Companions of the Conclave of Hope.†

" I take this early opportunity with great Grief and Concern of announcing to you the Death of our Most Eminent Grand Master Sir Thos. Dunckerley who paid his tribute to Nature on Thursday last at 7 a.m.

" By his decease the Community in General particularly the different Orders in Masonry have Sustained a Signal loss, as well as the Several Conclaves of Kᵗ Templars, especially those in this Kingdom, in its present renovating State.

" Permit me, therefore, to express my Sincerest Condolence on this Solemn occasion. But in the midst of our Sorrow We have the Consolation to believe he is now receiving the Reward of a Life devoted to the Service of the Supreme Architect of the Universe having conducted himself while on Earth with that Benignity, Charity, and Zeal, which distinguishes A Good Man & a Sincere Christian.

---

* These two letters were printed in " The Freemasons' Magazine " for May, 1794. H. S

† Copied by Bro. R. Williamson from a written letter in the Archives of the Hope Preceptory No. 4 Huddersfield. H. S

" After having Paid a decent Attention to the loss of **Our** Grand Master, it behoves us to turn our attention upon who shall be his Successor.

" Permit me to Point out as the Person Most Eligible to do Honour to the Society The R^t Hon'ble. Lord Rancliffe, who is a Member of the Chapter & Conclave of Observance. The more so from his being a Colonel in the Army.

" If my Idea in his Lordship's favour meets your approbation, You will please to signify the same in a line to me in answer as soon as you can get the sence of the Noble Knights Companions of your Chapter on the subject.

" I have the Honour to be,

" Dear Sir Knight,

" Your Bro. & K^t· Comp^n

" W. HANNAM,

"Savoy, London,   "Acting G^d· Master,

" 23rd November, 1795.

" Lord Rancliffe is a Character of the highest Respectability of large Fortune, has lately been created a Peer of Ireland, is Member for Leicester, and better known by the name of Thomas Boothby Parkyns.

" It is hoped on your first Meeting you will request The K^t· Compn^s· of your Chapter to appear in decent Mourning."

KNIGHTS TEMPLAR CERTIFICATES.

Thomas Meyler, P.P.G. Reg. of Somerset kindly sent for my inspection the K.T. Certificate of his grandfather— William Meyler, Prov. G. Sec. and afterwards D.P.G.M of Somerset—whose name is frequently mentioned by Dunckerley in his letters to the Grand Secretary.

This document is of parchment about 10 inches by 9 and is printed from a neatly engraved plate with an elaborate emblematical heading probably designed by Dunckerley himself. It has an impression of Dunckerley's seal in black wax affixed,* and bears the date 24th of June, 1791. It is interesting as being one of the earliest issued.

R. Williamson, P.P. of the Hope Preceptory, No. 4, has another of these certificates issued in 1795.

A SONG.

For the Knights Templars,

Written by Thomas Dunckerley, Esq., Grand Master.

At the bright Temple's awful dome,
  Where Christian Knights in arms are drest;
To that most sacred place we come,
  With Cross and Star upon the breast,
Pilgrims inspir'd with zealous flame,
  Through rugged ways and dangers past;
Our sandals torn, our feet were lame,
  But Faith and Hope o'ercame at last.

Remember, Knights, the noble cause,
  Let Simon's fate prevent your fall,
Be firm and true, obey the laws,
  Nor let the cock unheeded call.
Let none the sacred word profane,
  Nor e'er like Peter, Christ deny,
Your conduct still preserve from blame,
  Nor let the urn be plac'd on high.

Unite your hearts, unite each hand,
  In friendship, harmony, and love;
Connected thus Knights Templars stand,
  Our love and charity to prove.
Until that awful final day,
  When fire shall melt this earthly ball,
Your courage and your faith display,
  Attend to Freedom's sacred call.

True to our God, our Laws, and King
  Devout, obedient, loyal, free
The praise of Royal Edward sing,
  The Patron of our mystery.
In uniform each Knight is drest,
  Distinguished all by *black, red, blue*
The Cross and Star upon the breast,
  Adorn the heart that's just and true.'

" The Freemasons' Magazine," August, 1794

---

* See page 273.

THE LIGHT AND TRUTH OF MASONRY EXPLAINED.

BEING THE SUBSTANCE OF A CHARGE, Delivered at Plymouth, in April, 1757.

By-THOMAS DUNCKERLEY, Esq., P.G.M.*

" Brethren,

"Light and Truth being the great essentials of the *Royal Craft,* I shall begin this discourse (prepared for the opening of this Room) with that awful message which St. John delivered to the world, *That God is Light, and in him is no darkness at all;* and that we are not worthy of the *true Fellowship,* unless we walk in the *Light,* and do the *Truth.* O! sacred *Light!* whose orient beams make manifest that *Truth* which *unites* all good and faithful *Masons* in a heavenly *Fellowship!*

"This sublime part of Masonry is that firm base on which is raised the shaft of Faith, that supports a beautiful entablature of good works: it is the foundation of a superstructure unbounded as the universe, and durable as eternity. To attempt a description of this stupendous fabrick may seem presumptuous in me, who have been so few years a Mason: but as you, my Brethren, were pleased to request something of this kind, give me leave to assure you that I am truly sensible of the honour; and though there are several among you, who by knowledge and long experience are well qualified for such an undertaking, yet as it is my duty to execute your commands, I shall cheerfully begin the work; and humbly hope by *patience* and *industry* to make some amends for the little *time* I have served.

---

* Some years ago a well-known Masonic writer more than insinuated that this Charge was *not* delivered by Dunckerley in the year 1757; the following notice or advertisement which appeared in the *Gentleman's Magazine* for *that year* will perhaps settle the question "*The Light & Truth of Masonry Explained* By T. Dunckerley. 6d., published by Davey & Law." H S.

"The *Light* and *Truth* which St. John takes notice of in his message to the World, being a principal part of sublime Masonry, I have, as I observed before, taken it for the subject of my discourse, on this solemn occasion. I intreat you to hear me with attention; and whatever deficiencies you may discover in this Essay impute it to inexperience, and admonish me with Brotherly Love, that while I am pleading the cause of *Truth* I may be free from *error.*

"*God said let there be Light; and there was Light.* Without it the rude matter of Chaos, *though brought into form,* would still have been to little purpose. *Let your Light so shine before men, that they may see your good works,* was the advice of him that was *a Light to lighten the Gentiles.* Our *Lights* are not hid, but placed on *Candlesticks;* and these are silent monitors continually intimating to us, that as *the ancient and honourable badge* we wear has placed us above the rest of mankind, so all our duties to our Heavenly Master, our fellow creatures, and ourselves, should be *formed* and *contrived* by the *wisdom* of God's word: *strengthened and supported* by Love, Truth, and Charity; and *beautified and adorned* by Honesty, Temperance, and true Politeness. All Masons that are, or ever have been, were *shewn the Light:* and though they cannot forget it, yet alas! how *faintly* does it shine in the hearts of too many! How is its lustre sullied, and splendor diminished, by the folly, stupidity and madness of irreligion and impiety!—These are the persons of whom St. John says, *they went out from us: but they were not of us: for if they had been of us, they would no doubt have continued with us but they went out, that they might be made manifest that they were not all of us.* And thus it is that those who depart from the Light bring an evil report on the *Craft.*

"Truth, as it is a divine attribute, so is it the foundation of all Masonic Virtues. It is one of our grand Principles, for to be *good men and true,* is part of the first great lesson we are taught: and at the commencement of our *Freedom* we are exhorted to be *fervent* and *zealous* in the pursuit of *Truth* and *Goodness*. It is not sufficient that we *walk in the Light*, unless we do the *Truth* also. All hypocrisy and deceit must be banished from among us: they are *sincerity* and *plain-dealing* that complete the harmony of a Lodge, and render us acceptable in the sight of Him unto whom all hearts are open, all desires known, and from whom no *secrets* are hid. There is a charm in Truth that draws and attracts the mind continually toward it. The more we discover, the more we desire; and the great reward is Wisdom, Virtue, and Happiness. This is an edifice founded on a rock, which malice cannot shake or time destroy.

"What a secret satisfaction is it to Masons, when in searching for Truth, they find the rudiments of all useful knowledge still preserved among us, as it has descended by oral tradition from the earliest ages: and to find likewise this Truth corroborated by the testimonies of the best and greatest men the world has produced. But this is not all; the Sacred Writings confirm what I assert, the sublime part of our Antient Mystery being there to be found; nor can any Christian Brother be a perfect Mason that does not make the word of God his study. Indeed we own all Masons as Brothers be they *Christians, Jews* or *Mahometans* (for Masonry is universal, and not strictly confined to any particular faith, sect, or mode of worship): all Masons I say, of whatever religious denomination, who rule their passions and affections, and square their actions accordingly are acknowledged by us as Brothers, but, for *our* parts, the Holy Scripture is to be studied by *us*, and occasionally read and consulted.

"Since without *Light* we cannot perceive the beauty and excellency of *Truth* and since we are certain that no man can be a worthy Brother who is wanting in either; it may not be improper at this Time to draw the character of him *Who walks in Light and does the Truth ;* and who, according to St. John's Account, is worthy of the *true fellowship.*

"As we call any building or piece of architecture *perfect* which hath *all its parts,* and is finished and completed according to the *nicest rules of art ;* a *Brother* is in like manner said to be a good *Mason* who has *studied* and *knows himself,* and has learnt and practises that first and great lesson of *subduing his Passions and Will,* and tries to the utmost of his power to free himself from all vices, errors, and imperfections ; not only those that proceed from the heart, but likewise all other defects of the understanding which are caused by custom, opinion, prejudice, or superstition ; He who asserts the native *freedom* of his *mind,* and stands fast in the *liberty* that makes him *free,* whose soul is (if one may so express it), universal, and well contracted, and who despises no man on account of his *Country* or *Religion,* but is ready at all times to convince the world that *Truth, Brotherly Love,* and *affording relief,* are the grand principles on which he acts.

"His whole life will be conformable and agreeable to that *true light,* the Law of God, which shines clear to his heart, and is the model by which he squares his judgement. In his outward behaviour he will be very careful not to give private or public offence, and (as far as appears to him right) will strictly comply with the laws, the customs, and religious institutions of the country in which he resides To all mankind he will act upon the square ; and do to others as he would have them do unto him. He will be firm and consistent with himself, and continually in expectation and on his guard against all accidents to which this life is exposed, and in particular he will by a *well spent life be daily preparing for death,* that final period of human action, which sooner or later will take us hence, to give a strict account of our stewardship and the improvement of our talents.

"In fine, all good Masons should be pious, prudent, just, and temperate, and resolutely virtuous.

"From what I have advanced, and from these our ancient charges, I hope it is evident to everyone at the present, that it is the duty of every Mason to live soberly, righteously, and godly; or, according to the words of the Evangelist, He should walk in the Light, and do the Truth. Continue, My Brethren, to persevere in principles that are disinterested, and I doubt not but you will find this room, which we have now opened and dedicated to MASONRY constantly resorted to by the wise, the faithful, and the good.

"Let us consider the intention of our Meetings; let submission to your Officers, and Brotherly Love to each other be shown by your diligent attendance in the Lodge and be very careful to enquire into the *characters* and *capacities* of those who are desirous to be admitted among you.

"Study the CONSTITUTIONS and CHARGES, and improve in the FIFTH SCIENCE as far as your abilities and several avocations will permit. Have universal Benevolence and Charity for all mankind, and wherever you meet your necessitous Brethren dispersed, relieve them to the utmost of your ability, remembering, notwithstanding, not to do things that may really prejudice yourselves or families.

"Let us by well-doing put to silence the ignorance of foolish men.

"As free, but not using our liberty for a cloke of Maliciousness, but as the servants of God. Honour all Men, Love the Brotherhood, Fear God, Honour the King."*

LETTERS TO THE EARL OF CHESTERFIELD.

"The Freemasons' Magazine" for July, 1794, contains the following announcement. "We have permission from our R.W. Brother *Dunckerley* to present our Readers with Copies of Letters to the late Earl of Chesterfield, descriptive of

---

* "The Freemasons' Magazine," October, 1793

Gibraltar, Minorca, Leghorn ; Bastia and Florenzo on the Island of Corsica ; Cagliari on the island of Sardinia ; Barcelona, Malaga, Alicant, and Cadiz on the coast of Spain : written by Mr. D. in the years 1748 and 1749, when that Gentleman was an officer on board his Majesty's ship the Crown."

Probably owing to Dunckerley's illness or absence from town, the three letters here reproduced are all that were published out of the number above mentioned.

A DESCRIPTION OF ST. GEORGE'S CAVE AT GIBRALTAR.

" In compliance with your Lordship's desire, I do myself the honour of giving you the following description of St. George's Cave, as related to me by an officer of this garrison.

" A little above the Red Sand, not far from Europa Point, on the S.W. side of the hill, is a large cavity, which is the mouth of St. George's Cave : the entrance is very steep, in some places descending regularly, in others very irregularly, and all the way very dirty and slippery, occasioned by the continual penetration of the water through the top and sides of the rock, which causes a mouldering and decay in the stones, so that one cannot well go down without boots. The descent to the Cave is in some places a man's height, in others you are obliged to crawl on hands and knees. After several turnings and windings, which renders the passage very tiresome, you enter the Cave itself ; the bottom of which is level, and the roof very regularly arched after the antient Gothic manner. There are several tables, with benches round them, the workmanship of which is very curious, all cut out of the solid rock, but the roof and sides surpass all imagination for beauty and magnificence The gentleman from whom I had this account assured me, that all the descriptions invention ever furnished us with are poor and mean in comparison with the glories that strike you on your first entrance into this Cave: adding, that it infinitely exceeded the finest paintings or sculpture he had ever seen, as well for the prodigious lustre and diversity of colours that shine round you on every side, as for the neatness of the carving and other embellishments.

"This Cave, in common with most other extraordinary productions of art or nature, is ascribed to preternatural architects, and various are the stories raised of apparitions, &c. haunting this place. The most probable conjecture that can be raised is, that some priests, or other retired persons, chose this spot to seclude themselves from the world, and employed their leisure hours in beautifying this their retreat. The beauties that are celebrated in this Cave are, in my opinion, the equal productions of Art and Nature. The tables, with their surrounding seats, are doubtless hewn out of the rock, and as the water is continually dropping from all parts, it polishes the sides of the Cave, and renders them as smooth as the finest marble, and the tops of the tables are finer than the smoothest glass.

"Most that visit this Cave are obliged to carry lighted torches with them, to find their way; now the rays proceeding from these lights are thrown upon the polished surface of the internal parts of the Cave, which is entirely composed of convexities and concavities, and again reflected back in all the beautiful diversity of colours, in the same manner as we see a diamond or cut glass reflect the beams of a candle; and this I take to be the natural cause of this wonderful appearance. There was formerly a very good entrance to this Cave, but it is now stopt up by the falling in of the rock, and I don't doubt but the Cave itself will, in process of time, share the same fate.

"I have the honour to be
"Your Lordship's most obedient Servant,
"Thos. Dunckerley.
" *To the* Earl of Chesterfield, London."

The Freemasons' Magazine, June, 1794

A DESCRIPTION OF GIBRALTAR.

" Port Mahon, on the Island of Minorca.

"June 1, 1748.

" I had the honour of sending to your Lordship some account of St. George's Cave at Gibraltar, and now proceed to give you a description of that garrison.

" Gibraltar is a very high and steep hill, of an oblong figure, arising out of a plain almost perpendicular, which adds greatly to its loftiness. This place is the key to the Mediterranean, by reason that no fleet can pass to or from it unobserved or unlicensed by the masters of this important spot, which were formerly the Spaniards, but at present the English. Though the fortifications of this place are universally allowed to be the most regular and strong imaginable, yet is all that art has effected, but a poor superstructure upon the most wonderful production of nature who seems to have played the engineer here with her utmost skill.

" The Eastern, or back part of the hill, is one continued horrid precipice ; the North side, which arises out of a low marshy plain, is extremely rugged and steep : and the South part, or Europa Point, is also very steep, and runs out into the sea. On the North side, towards the Spanish lines (the advanced posts of which are not above a pistol-shot from ours), on the declivity of the hill, is a very strong battery of several brass pieces, called Willis's Battery, which has communication under ground with the lines which run up the side of the hill, and are, as I am informed by connoisseurs, of incredible strength ; all along the side, and up to the top of the hill, appear the vestiges of the old Moorish lines, cast up by them when they were in possession of this place; there are, also, the ruins of an old Moorish castle. At the top of the hill is the Signal-house, which has a most extensive prospect, and from whence, by signals, the garrison is informed of whatever ships are either coming into or going out of the Streights.

"Towards Europa Point, on the South side of the hill, is the New Mole, capable of containing ships of the greatest burthen, where our men of war commonly heave down and refit: a little above this, upon the side of the hill, is the hospital for sick and wounded seamen. This is a very good building on the inside; the wards are very neat and clean; there is a large spacious court-yard in the middle, surrounded by several apartments, which are built upon piazzas, and form an open kind of gallery or balcony all along, much like those we have in some of our stage-inns in London, which is extremely agreeable, as by this means the least breath of air that stirs in the warm season of the year in this hot climate, is brought into the apartments for the benefit of the sick. This hospital is served by a physician, surgeon, and two mates, with proper assistants. Near to this are the barracks for the soldiers, a neat and regular piece of building of free-stone, it is in form a long square with two wings; the apartments are neat and commodious.

"A little further lies a great plain of sand, called, from its colour, the Red Sand, which is the common burying-place of the garrison; at the North end of this sand is the place where ships send their boats for water, called the Ragged Staff, a very convenient place for watering the largest fleet, and affords abundance of most excellent water. About a quarter of a mile from this place is the South-port gate, by which you enter the town which consists of a small number of houses, very low and ill-built, and upon the whole, cuts a very mean figure.

"The governor has indeed, a very handsome house and gardens, which were formerly a convent, and still retains that name. There are a great number of Jews here, who seem to me to be used chiefly as luggage porters, for you will see three or four of these circumcised gentlemen with a great chest or bale hanging by the middle on a long pole, which they carry across their shoulders, and so trudge along with it at a surprising rate. Their usual dress is a little short black cassock, bound round their middle with a piece of blue or other coloured linen, and falling down, in a kind of close drawers, as low as their knees. They always go barefoot through choice, by reason of the heat of the climate, and partly through poverty. Gibraltar is a place of very great trade for cloths, silk, &c., and contains upwards of 4,000 inhabitants, exclusive of a garrison of 3,000 always kept here. From the town we got out by the Landiport gate into the lines, which run and meet those of the Spaniards upon the little neck of land or marsh which joins Gibraltar to the Spanish main. This gate is about a mile distant from the South-port gate, being the length of the garrison. Near it is the Waterport, or Old Mole, formerly the place for careening ships, but since the building of the new by the English, it only serves as a kind of haven for market-boats, xebeques, &c. There is a very handsome parade for the troops, about half the bigness of that at Whitehall. Opposite to this hill lies the town of Old Gibraltar, in the possession of the Spaniards, who are frequently spectators of their own ships made prizes, and brought in by us under their inspection.

> "I have the honour to be, &c.,
>
> "THOMAS DUNCKERLEY."

"The Earl of Chesterfield, London."

The Freemasons' Magazine, August, 1794.

A DESCRIPTION OF LEGHORN.

"From Vado we were dispatched by the admiral to Leghorn, where we arrived the 27th of June.

"Leghorn is a sea-port town of vast trade and commerce in Tuscany, belonging to the Emperor as Grand Duke. o has a deputy or vice-duke at Florence, the capital of this dutchy, distant hence about four leagues. Leghorn stands in a plain on the sea-side, and is very well fortified with fossées and half-moons about it; there are several other fortifications near it. Before the great town, to the westward, there are two large basons or moles for galleys, and even ships, which are shut up with a great chain; you pass into it through a very narrow channel between two forts. Without these basons there is a spacious mole; as you approach the town you see two small towers surrounded by the sea, one of which is white, and called Marseca; abreast of the mole upon a rock is a watch-house. At the head of the mole there are two very considerable batteries, one above another. Ships water without the town, near a convent of Capuchins. You pass in boats along the mole through the ditches under a bridge.

"Without the mole there is a tower standing upon a rock, with the sea all round it; on the top of this tower there is a lanthorn which is lighted every night for a mark.

"The Legonese are a people greatly given to traffick; the city is very beautiful both in its situation and buildings; the houses are very high and uniform, of a white stone or marble, and over the doors of the best part of them are beautifully painted in large oval shields the arms of the Grand Duke, the streets are very beautiful, well paved, and wide; the Exchange, or place where the merchants meet, is a large spacious square, not unlike Covent-Garden, the houses being all raised on piazzas. Straw hats, silks, velvets, embroideries, gold and silver lace, &c., are very cheap & good here. The two chief things that attract the eye of a stranger at his landing are, the Brazen Men, as they are called, and the Courtezanes Galley. The former is a piece of statuary, universally allowed to be the most finished work of its kind; it is erected in the market-place. On a large square black marble pedestal stands the figure of a man, larger than the life, habited like a Roman, with a truncheon in his hand; the statue is of white marble, about the size of that of King James in the college-garden of Chelsea. Round the pedestal are the figures of four men chained, three times as large as the life, the eldest of these is represented with his back bowed and broke, and surely nothing but the view of these admirable pieces can give an adequate idea of their beauties. Sorrow, distress, age, and misery, are lively represented in the old man. In the three young ones appear a mixture of manly courage and filial tenderness contending for the superiority; two of them have their looks turned toward their suffering father, and seem to tell him with their eyes the share they bear in his misfortune; the other looks up to Heaven as imploring assistance in their behalf; not a muscle nor vein but what are as justly expressed here as in the most correct anatomical print. The occasion of erecting this statue is said to be as follows :—

" One of the Dukes of Tuscany, in his excursions on the Barbarians, having taken prisoner an old man and his three sons of a more than common and gigantic stature and strength (and who had frequently made great depredations on the Legonese in their small feluccas, or row-boats, and bearing all before them by their sole strength and powers), was particularly pleased with this his conquest, and reserved them for an appointed day to satisfy his people's desire in putting them to death. One night, however, having by some means or other escaped from their guard, they seized on a small boat lying in the harbour, and rowed off till they came to the great chain which goes across the entrance of the mole, which they with prodigious strength of rowing burst open, unperceived by the guard that were asleep, and passed out, but the centinel being awaked by the noise alarmed the town; it was, however, day before it was known that it was the Moors who had made their escape. The

duke was greatly troubled at their flight, which the young
prince his son perceiving, offered himself, on the forfeiture
of his head, to fetch these fugitives back; upon which his
father gave him several small vessels, and a sufficient number of armed men, with which he immediately set out, and
overtook these poor wretches just as they were on the point
of landing on the Barbary coast, which is a considerable
distance from Leghorn. In the despair of being overtaken
they exerted their utmost strength; the old man, who till
now had been indulged in sitting still, took an oar, but upon
the first effort broke his back; here their distresses were
redoubled, and in this crisis we have them represented.
The prince came up with them, and after a bloody resist-
ance on their sides, unequal as they were in force, took and
carried them into Leghorn. Nothing was heard but shouts
of joy at their approach, the Duke himself, attended by all
his court, came to receive and welcome his victorious son.
The youth, impatient to embrace his father, leaps on the
shore, and in that leap to death. As soon as it was known
that he had been on the Barbarian coast the whole assembly
was struck with grief, a law then being in force by which
whosoever should on any pretence offer to set foot on the
shore after having been on the coast of Barbary, without
first receiving pratique or performing quarantine, was to
forfeit his life. Justice, then, doomed this unhappy prince
to death in the midst of his triumph. The wretched father,
overwhelmed with grief, was obliged to pronounce his son's
sentence; and, in order to make some retaliation for the
cruelty of his fate, sacrificed the four slaves on his tomb,
and afterwards caused this statue to be erected in commem-
oration of the fact.

"The Grand Duke's state-galley (better known by the
name of the Courtezanes, from the money arising from the
licences granted these women to follow their miserable occu-
pation, being appropriated to the maintenance and repairs of

it) is a vessel the most magnificent that can be imagined; it is very long with a sharp prow, much after the manner of the vessels we see delineated on antient medals; it is most beautifully carved and gilt to the water's edge; at the entrance into the great cabin there are two figures, as large as the life, of angels, who hold a very beautiful canopy over the door, on which are painted the arms of the Duke and Dutchess, the present Emperor and Empress Queen of Hungary, on each of which are their heads in profile; the whole richly gilt and painted. This vessel lies in the mole, and is free to any person that has an inclination to visit it. There are fifty benches of oars on a side, each bench has three or four miserable tenants chained by the legs together, but having their hands at liberty they are continually employed in some business, so that on entering you think yourself in a fair; some are knitting gloves, stockings, &c., others making fine basket-work, hats, &c., in short, every one of these poor wretches are employed in something to procure them a small pittance from those whom charity or curiosity excite on board. But, surely, never were creatures more dextrous at filching, for if your eye or hand is an instant off your pockets, they find a way to lighten them of their contents, and they will often rise eight or ten at a time, and make such a horrid rattling with their chains as surprise a stranger, and leave him wholly open and unguarded to their mercy. Near the head of the vessel they open up one of the planks of the deck, and show you a great Couchee piece, called the Grand Duke's piece; it is of brass, very curiously wrought, with the arms of Tuscany on it: the weight of the ball is 42lb.

"At Leghorn we received orders from the admiral to proceed immediately for the Gulph of St. Florenzo, or St. Florence, there to relieve the Nassau, a 70 gun ship, commanded by Captain Halcombe, who was stationed there to protect the malcontent Corsicans, in conjunction with the troops of the King of Sardinia and Empress Queen of Hungary, against the Genoese and their allies the French, who were then in possession of Bastia, the metropolis of the island, Calvi, Ajaccia, and several other strong places in the country.

"Accordingly we set sail from Leghorn, the 27th of July, and anchored in the said gulph the 30th following.

"I have the honour to be, &c.,

"THOMAS DUNCKERLEY."

The Freemasons' Magazine, October, 1794.

THE EARL OF CHESTERFIELD.

Philip, Earl of Chesterfield, the celebrated statesman, courtier, ambassador and author, is said, by our historian, Dr. Anderson, to have been made a Mason in Grand Lodge on the 24th of June, 1721, and we learn from the same authority that in 1731, when he was "Lord Ambassador" at the Hague, he assisted at the making of His Royal Highness, Francis Duke of Lorrain, both of which statements were published in the Earl's lifetime.* I can find no evidence that his lordship ever took much interest in Masonry, yet he seems to have attracted the notice of the "Ancients" or Anglo-Irish Masons in London when they were on the look-out for a Noble Grand Master to preside over them.

At a "Grand Committee November 3rd, 1752," it was "Ordered, that the Grand Secretary shall draw up a proper petition to the Rt. Honourable Philip Earl of Chesterfield, an Ancient Mason, begging his Lordship's sanction as Grand Master."

The Grand Secretary, with the Masters of five lodges, were ordered to present the said petition, but the Grand

---

* *Constitutions* 1738, pp. 112 and 129. H. S.

Secretary begged the Committee to postpone the business until they had made choice of a more suitable place in which to receive and instal his Lordship. As the subject is not again mentioned in the records it is probable that no further steps were taken with regard to the petition. It will be observed that the noble Lord is referred to by the petitioners as an "Ancient Mason" or one of themselves; meaning, I assume, that he had entered the Society at a time when English and Irish Masonry were one and the same. Their selection may have been also influenced by the fact that some few years earlier the Earl had been exceedingly popular in Ireland when filling the post of Lord Lieutenant of that kingdom. It is somewhat difficult to account for the apparent intimacy between the "British Cicero," as his lordship was called, and the comparatively unknown gunner of the Crown, who was then only about twenty-four years of age, and the greater portion of whose life had been spent in the sea-service.

A plausible explanation would be that the Earl might have been a passenger in one of Dunckerley's ships and so have become acquainted with him; it being usual in those days for representatives of the Government, and other great personages to make their voyages under the protection of the guns of a Man-of-War. Or, is it possible that the noble lord, who was thoroughly well versed in the Court intrigues and gossip of the period, could have been then in possession of the secret of Dunckerley's parentage, and was prompted by curiosity or some other motive, to make his acquaintance? That some kind of intimacy existed between them for a considerable period is evinced by the fact of Dunckerley having mentioned his lordship in his biography as one of the noblemen who had befriended him in the year 1767, when the story of his birth was brought to the knowledge of the King.

MISCELLANEOUS LETTERS, &c.

"Hampton Court Palace, Nov. 22nd, 1785.

"Dear Brother,

"I transmit to you the produce of my labours during the last summer, with an account of £201. 10s. 0d., which you will do me the favour to lay before the Grand Lodge. The flourishing state of Masonry at Pool in Dorsetshire; and in the Counties of Essex, Gloucester, and Somerset; is flattering to me; and I hope and trust that the success I have acquir'd, will be equally pleasing to the Society.

"Success has follow'd me to the gates of this Palace; where, I have (in the space of three months) establish'd a very respectable Lodge.

"The Lodges I have constituted at Bath, Bristol, Gloucester & Wells, are daily increasing, and the greatest harmony prevails in those Cities. My Endeavours to promote the Dignity & Credit of the Royal Craft, have Cross'd the Atlantic, and I have had the pleasure to obtain Constitutions for two Lodges in Newfoundland.

"It was with much regret that I found myself necessitated to eraze from my list, the Lodges, Nos. 339, & 399; which I hope the Grand Lodge will confirm, for the reasons I have given on the other side. The Loans to the Hall Fund, which you will also read to the Grand Officers & Brethren, are expressive of the very great regard those Brethren and the three infant Lodges have for that excellent Institution.

"Present my most respectful Regard to the Grand Officers & Brethren & believe me Yours &c.

"THOS. DUNCKERLEY."

The "other side," contains Dunckerley's annual report of the lodges under his care with their contributions, &c.; by which it appears that No. 399, at Weymouth, was erazed because the lodge was dissolved and the furniture sold; and No. 339, at Malden, for not having met for several years.

No. 472, at Bristol, was forfeited by Thos. Tomes who had partly " paid for the Warrant, but did not pay the remainder ; tho' he made several Masons." There is also a balance sheet as follows :—

"Debt^{r.}	£	s.	d.
To Contributions, &c., ye Charity Fund .	26	5	0
Regist'ring Fees, &c., to the Hall Fund .	43	9	0
Fees for Constitutions, & Removals . .	6	16	0
Henry Sperling, Esq., Dennis Hall, Essex	25	0	0
Samuel Tyssen, Esq., Felix Hall, Essex .	25	0	0
458 Royal Cumberland Lodge , Bath .	25	0	0
462 Royal Gloucester Lodge ; Gloucester	25	0	0
474 Lodge of Harmony ; Toy, Hampton Court	25	0	0
	201	10	0

"Cred^r				£	s.	d.
1785.	June 3rd.	By paid Bro. Berkley		50	0	0
	Oct. 28th.	By paid Bro. White .		50	0	0
	Nov. 16th.	By	Do.	61	17	0
	„ 18th	By	Do. .	25	0	0
	„ 22nd.	By Ballance . . .		14	12	6
				201	10	0 "

It is highly probable that each of these loans of £25 to the Hall Fund was the result of Dunckerley's " Endeavours to promote the Dignity & Credit of the Royal Craft."

" Bro Lewis of Bristol Debtr to Bro. White.

Two Constitution Books . . .	£1	4	0
Three Certificates	0	19	6
	2	3	6 "

"Hampton Court Palace, Nov. 15, 1786.

" Dear Brother,

"As Bro. Lewis is about to leave England he has desir'd me to pay the above to you for which you will please make me your Debtor. I am also to desire you will send six Grand Lodge Certificates to Bro. Palmer, at the George Inn, High Street, Portsmouth, Master of the *Phœnix* Lodge, No. 485, who will pay me for them, and I shall take care to return you the names when they are fill'd up; they are also indebted Nine Shillings to you, which they will pay to me for you.

"I do myself the pleasure to enclose a Bank Post Bill for Sixty Pounds which Bro. Heseltine will place to my Credit on Account of Contributions to the Charity and Registring Fees to the Hall Fund. Let me have a line by to-morrow night's post to certify the receipt. The state of the whole Account, with the several Lists from the Lodges, I will send (by the Coach) address'd to you at the Hall next Monday. I keep it back as I expect remittances from Bristol & Southampton.

"I spent near £30, last Summer, holding Grand Lodges in Dorset, Essex, Glo'ster & Somerset; in journeys of five hundred miles—Blue & Red Aprons have excited Great Emulation in these Counties : all the Fraternity *under my care* do me great honour, and are careful not to give offence by irregularity; being sensible it would endanger the stability of their Lodges.

"Entre nous—I am not only *lov'd* but *fear'd*—I hope you will not accuse me of Vanity or Arrogance (as this is a private letter) I wrote the above to shew you that ye preferments on one hand and discipline on the other has produced the money I *now* send and hope to send.

"Bro. Heseltine will see this letter—assure him of my most sincere regard—Accept the same from your Affect. & Zealous Brother and faithful Servant (to ye Society),

"William White, Esq."   "THOS. DUNCKERLEY.

Grand Lodge Minutes, November 22nd, 1786.

"It was Resolved unanimously,

"That the Rank of past Senior Grand Warden (with the right of taking place immediately next to the present Senior Grand Warden) be granted to Thomas Dunckerley, Esq., Provincial Grand Master for Dorset, Essex, Gloucester, Somerset, and Southampton, with the City and County of Bristol, and the Isle of Wight, in grateful Testimony of the high sense the Grand Lodge entertains of his zealous and indefatigable Exertions for many years to promote the honour and interest of the Society."

"Hampton Court Palace, Nov. 24th, 1786.

"Dear Sir,

"I am this morning favoured with your very obliging letter to inform me of the high honour I have received from the Grand Lodge; for which I shall endeavour to return every grateful service in my power. I have served the Society *twenty-one* years as a Grand Officer; and am now amply rewarded.

"A *truly* masonic Friendship has subsisted between Bro. Heseltine and myself, for the same number of years; to him, and you I return my warmest thanks for the active part you have taken.

"The Hampton Court Lodge does not meet before February perhaps several Members may buy Calendars in town, if you send ten (with my Patent) I will try to dispose of them; if any are left I will deliver them to you in person.

"Sister D—— unites in sincere regard and am,

"Your much obliged Bro. & Servant,

"Thos. Dunckerley.

"William White, Esq."

It will be noticed that in the foregoing letter the writer states that he has been a Grand Officer twenty-one years, or from the year 1765; but the Grand Lodge Records contain no mention of him previous to his appointment as

Provincial Grand Master in February 1767. It seems therefore probable that, as already suggested, he had held some informal office, which would not appear in the records, such as Superintendent of a County, before he was regularly appointed by Patent.

"Nov. 3rd, 1795.   38 Bishop Street,
"Sir,   "Common, Portsmouth.
"Mr. Dunckerley being so very ill as not to be able *himself* to write, has commissioned me to say that by this day's post he has transmitted you in two packets (marked 1 and 2) the sum of £9. 4s. 6d.—viz from the Lodges at Southampton (323 & 503) £4. 2s. 0d. from that at Frome (469) £3. 12s. 0d. and £1. 10s. 6d. from the Lodge at Shaston (396) the receipt of which he begs you to acknowledge as early as possible.

"I have the honour to be Sir,
"Your very humble Servant,
"Jas. Heseltine, Esq."   "ED. ROBINSON.

This was probably the last communication received from Dunckerley on Masonic business, and it goes far towards disproving the assertion made by Recorder Cooper as to his receiving monies and not accounting for them. The lodges mentioned are duly credited with the amounts remitted, in the Treasurer's printed list of receipts for November 25th, 1795.

It is not unlikely that this letter was dictated by Dunckerley, and from the fact of certain additions having been made after it was written I am inclined to think that he was then residing at the address given ; and that he probably died there. A brief personal inspection of the premises, and the result of enquiries made by a friend many years a resident in the neighbourhood has led to the conclusion that the present No 38, Bishop Street is the identical house referred to.

The Register preserved among the archives of St. Mary's Church, Kingston—the parish church for Portsea—contains a bare record of the interment of Thomas Dunckerley on the 27th of November, 1795. This edifice has recently been rebuilt, consequently many of the old tomb-stones have been disturbed, and are not now accessible; it is therefore impossible to ascertain whether anything of the kind ever marked the place of his burial. The kind friend recently referred to, who is himself a warm admirer of Dunckerley, has assisted me in several careful examinations of the stones and monuments still standing, but up to now with a negative result, although it seems most improbable that a person who had done so much for Masonry—who passed away while in the discharge of his official duties to that Society and whose influence and popularity in the Order were without a parallel—should have been allowed to rest in a nameless grave.

ODE.

For an Exaltation of Royal Arch Masons.

BY BROTHER DUNCKERLEY.

Almighty sire! our heavenly king,
  Before whose sacred name we bend,
Accept the praises which we sing,
  And to our humble prayer attend.
    All hail, great Architect divine!
    This universal frame is thine.

Thou who did'st Persia's King command,
  A proclamation to extend,
That Israel's sons might quit his land,
  Their holy temple to attend.
    All hail, &c.

That sacred place, where three in one
  Compris'd thy comprehensive name,
And where the bright meridian sun,
  Was soon thy glory to proclaim

Thy *watchful eye*, a length of time
  The wondrous *circle* did attend :
The glory and the power be thine,
    Which shall from age to age descend.
      All hail, &c.

On thy omnipotence we rest ;
    Secure of thy protection here ;
And hope hereafter to be blest,
    When we have left this world of care.
      All hail, &c.

Grant us, great God, thy powerful aid,
    To guide us through this vale of tears ;
For where thy goodness is display'd,
    Peace soothes the mind, and pleasure chears.
      All hail, &c.

Inspire us with thy grace divine,
    Thy sacred law our guide shall be :
To ev'ry good our hearts incline,
    From ev'ry evil keep us free.
      All hail &c.*

ANOTHER.

By the same AUTHOR.

Hail, Universal Lord !
    By heav'n and earth ador'd ;
    All hail! Great God !
Before thy name we bend,
To us thy grace extend,
And to our prayer attend,
      All hail! great God !

The foregoing effusions were considered worthy of a place in the " Constitutions of the Antient Fraternity of Free And Accepted Masons," London, 1784.

COPY OF DUNCKERLEY'S WILL.

IN THE NAME OF GOD AMEN. I Thomas Dunckerley of
Hampton Court Palace in the County of Middlesex
Barrister-at-Law do this eleventh day of March in the year
of our Lord one thousand seven hundred ninety-four make
and publish this my last Will and testament in manner
following First I desire to be decently buried in the Temple
Church near the Knights Templars if I should die in London
or at Hampton Court or within twenty miles of London but
if at a further distance from London then it is my desire to
be buried at the place or in that Parish Church or Church
Yard where I may happen to depart this life as the carriage
of my corpse to London might be attended with too great
an expence I give and bequeath unto my much valued
and esteemed friends Arthur Robinson Esq. and James
Rowley Esquire the former of Pall Mall London and the
latter of Reigate in the County of Surrey all my plate
pictures and household goods bedsteads bedding and other
furniture In trust for the sole use and behoof of my wife
during her natural life* and after her decease I give and
bequeath to my aforesaid much esteemed friends Arthur
Robinson Esquire and James Rowley Esquire the plate of
which I am possessed In trust for the sole use and behoof
of my much loved friend Ann Siddall of Hampton Court in
the County of Middlesex Spinster in grateful testimony for
her affectionate regard and attention to my wife and self I
also give and bequeath to the aforesaid Ann Siddall and her
sister Susannah Siddall of Plymouth Dock in the County of
Devon Spinster all my pictures household goods bedsteads
bedding and other furniture to be divided between them
share and share alike I hereby request of my aforesaid

friends Arthur Robinson and James Rowley Esquires who I hereby appoint Executors of this my last Will and testament that they will cause this to be executed according to the true intent and meaning thereof. It is my desire that my Post Chaise and Law books may be sold for the payment of my debts and funeral expenses if it should be found necessary. THOMAS DUNCKERLEY.

Signed declared and published as and for his last Will and testament in the presence of us—Thomas Macklin, William Steele.*

Proved at London 19th Dec.r 1795, before the Worshipful John Fisher Dr. of Laws and Surrogate by the oaths of Arthur Robinson and James Rowley Esquires the Executors to whom administration was granted, having been first sworn duly to administer.

Arthur Robinson was initiated in the Prince of Wales's Lodge (now No. 259) on the 17th of March, 1788. James Rowley was initiated in the London Lodge (now No. 108) in 1771, of which lodge he was many years Treasurer. He joined the Prince of Wales's Lodge in 1790.

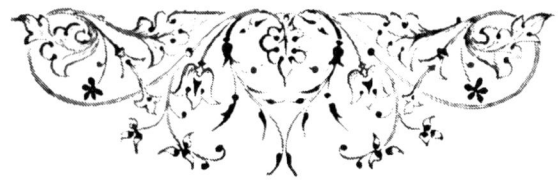

---

* Members of the Royal Gloucester Lodge, Southampton. H. S.

CONCLUDING REMARKS.

Those who have read the preceding pages have doubtless formed an opinion as to the disposition and Masonic qualifications of Dunckerley and as this volume has already exceeded its intended limits, little more need be said on that subject.

The series of letters written in confidence to his most intimate friends are probably sufficient to indicate the character of their writer, although they only represent a portion of the correspondence which, had space allowed, I should have been to glad to have offered for the information of the Craft. *Excelsior* might well have been added to the motto on his Coat of Arms,* since every branch of Masonry, as well as each province and lodge with which he identified himself seems to have had an upward tendency from the moment of his taking an active part in its affairs. It will have been observed that prior to Dunckerley's coming to the front, the Grand Lodge itself had neither Habitation, Furniture, Jewels, Register, nor a regular system of communication with the Provincial Lodges; and within a few years of his advent these wants and omissions were supplied. Although I have no desire to claim for him exclusive credit for these and many other improvements, I am fully satisfied that if they were not actually the outcome of his suggestions, by his earnest enthusiasm, methodical habits, energy, and example, he did far more than anyone else towards bringing them about and establishing them as essentials in the Masonic system. His earliest Address, of which we have any knowledge,—and in all probability it was his first effort in that direction—was delivered on the occasion of the dedication of a room to the purposes of Masonry, at Plymouth, in the year 1757.†

---

* "*Fato non merito.* By fate not desert. FITZ GEORGE." ' Elvin's Handbook of Mottoes."

† See page 280.

x

If this was not really the first event of the kind, I am inclined to think that very few earlier instances are on record. It however, shows the bent of his mind and in some measure explains the active part which he afterwards took in the erection of the Freemasons' Hall in London, towards the cost of which he not only personally contributed to the utmost extent of his limited income, but also induced many others in better circumstances to give liberally for the same worthy object, and in this he had no equal. His services in the Royal Arch seem to require no comment whatever, for there can scarcely be a doubt that the Grand Chapter of that Order was the creation of Dunckerley and some of his friends, and that for a considerable period he was its principal supporter. In all probability the first application for a Charter for a private Chapter was made through him and at his suggestion.

With reference to the Order of Masonic Knights Templar, it is perfectly clear that, however it may have come into existence, Dunckerley was its first recognized head. When and where he became a member of this body will perhaps never be known; yet bearing in mind that we were in darkness as to the time and place of his entry into the Craft and the Royal Arch until quite recently, we need not give up all hope on this point. However that may be, the correspondence on this subject, which I have fortunately been able to publish, clearly proves that it was mainly owing to his influence and exertions that a few scattered enthusiasts were formed into an organization which has since become exceedingly popular in all parts of the world.

During the preparation of these memoirs I have frequently been asked; Did Dunckerley leave any relatives? A question I cannot answer with certainty, as the only relative named in his Will was his wife, who outlived him about five years. He certainly had a son and a daughter, the latter being mentioned in the narrative of his troubles on page 30, but whether it was this lady or another daughter who became the wife of a Mr. Edgar at Salisbury and died there in 1783, I am unable to determine.

His son is not mentioned in any of his letters that have come under my notice, but this is not to be wondered at, as for the most part they relate to Masonic matters only, his wife and daughter being occasionally mentioned.

A Thomas Dunckerley, aged seventeen, was on board the Guadaloupe during a portion of the time that Dunckerley himself was in that ship, and this was probably the son referred to. "The Freemasons' Quarterly Review, 1842," contains a biographical sketch of Dunckerley, which is merely an abridged version of that which commences on page 17 of the present volume, to which, however, is added the following : —

"Brother Dunckerley's Masonic example was lost on his son, whose follies embittered the last years of his existence. Extravagance straitened the means, disorderly conduct afflicted the mind of the fond, unhappy parent Every means were tried, ineffectually, to reclaim the wretched son. At his father's death, there being no provision left, he became a wanderer and an outcast. Being a Mason, he was ever besieging Lodges and individuals. At last he became a bricklayer's labourer, and was seen, carrying a hod on his shoulder, ascending a ladder! This poor fellow's misfortunes and misconduct at length terminated, and *the Grand-son of a king died in a cellar in St. Giles's.*"

I have no means of testing the accuracy of this story, it is, however, to some extent, corroborated by an item in the Treasurer's book of the Sarum Lodge, under date "1779, Oct. 6.—To Brother Dunckerley's son in distress 10s. 6d."*

The enquiry just referred to is invariably made by the few, who, having already some knowledge of Dunckerley's

career, are desirous of "more light," but there is another
question put to me occasionally by some of my friends who
cannot properly be described as "Masonic Students." It
is usually something after this style : "What do you want
to go digging up this old man for, after he has been dead
and buried such a long time—Who cares about *him now ?* "
In answering questions of this kind I fear I am sometimes
a little too scrupulous in my observance of a certain ancient
mandate which begins with "Answer" and ends with
"folly" and is easily found in an old volume of frequent
use in our lodges. Although I do not myself consider that
anything in the shape of an apology is either needed or
expected—and will certainly not be offered—yet in order
to meet the wishes of those who may still feel a little par-
donable curiosity on the subject, I will now state that I had
various reasons for entering upon my present undertaking,
a few of which will doubtless suffice for present purposes.

Somehow I seem to have a natural liking for this kind
of "digging." Probably the feeling is inherited, although
I have only heard of one ancestor who did anything in that
line, but he was not in the habit of waiting until *his*
"subjects" had been buried for any great length of time;
indeed, the fresher they were, the higher were they valued.
He was such an enthusiast in the cause of Science and
became so expert in the business, that ultimately he attracted
the notice of the Government and so obtained a Colonial
appointment in which he continued during the rest of his
"natural life."

Many years ago it occurred to me that out of the mate-
rials at hand relating to Dunckerley it might be possible to
produce a book, which, while throwing new light on the
"ways and means" of our Masonic ancestors, would prove
more entertaining and therefore more acceptable to the
general reader than those works devoted exclusively to
Freemasonry, with which the literature of the Craft abounds.

Time will show whether I was right or wrong. A disposition (not an extensive one I must admit) having been evinced—probably owing to the absence of reliable information—to depreciate Dunckerley's Masonic services, and being myself well aware of their importance and value, I had no doubt whatever that if those services were more generally known, they would be properly appreciated, at all events there would be no excuse for ignoring them in the future. For my own part I have no hesitation in saying that I consider Dunckerley was by far the most pains-taking, unselfish, zealous, and practical enthusiast we ever had in our ranks—that his merits were by no means over-estimated by his contemporaries, and that since his decease our historians have not adequately acknowledged them. Some few there are who seem disposed to find fault with him for not having been the son of his mother's husband; as however, it is most unlikely that he was allowed a voice in this matter, common fairness demands that he should be absolved from all responsibility therein. Hitherto, I have said but little on this subject, the peculiar circumstances of the case rendering it extremely difficult, at this distance of time, to obtain reliable information bearing upon it; I am, moreover, of opinion that his work as a Mason will have a much greater attraction for my readers than anything in the nature of a discussion on the subject of his parentage. Personally I do not care the value of a straw who his father was; neverthless, I have perfect confidence in the truth of his story, as had doubtless his Royal relatives or they would not have given him their countenance and support. Although I will not go so far as to assert that Dunckerley's reputed father actually knew of his existence, I am inclined to think that some of his courtiers did, and that it was from this source that George III. obtained the information which induced him to acknowledge Dunckerley's claims and to extend to him his

Neither George II. nor George III. were members of the Craft, but we learn from G. W. Speth's interesting little brochure "Royal Freemasons," that the two sons of the former who attained maturity are said to have enrolled themselves under our ancient banner. With regard to his first-born, Frederick Lewis, the records leave no room for doubt, but in the case of that much abused though unquestionably brave soldier, William, Duke of Cumberland (his third son), who fought under his father at Dettingen and was wounded in the battle, the evidence is not so conclusive. Taking, however, the attendant circumstances into consideration, it seems highly probably that he entered the Order about the time stated in "Multa Paucis" (1743), but doubtless his military avocations precluded his taking an active part in its affairs. Three out of the five brothers of George III. were members of the Order as were also six out of the seven of his sons who arrived at man's estate, the exception being Adolphus, the late Duke of Cambridge.

I find I have omitted to mention that Dunckerley's last attendance at Grand Lodge was on May the 7th, 1794.

In bringing my labours to a conclusion I beg to acknowledge, with the warmest feelings of gratitude, the kindly assistance freely rendered by numerous friends; some in furnishing material for this volume, and others in extending its sale. My thanks are especially due to William Harry Rylands, Esq., F.S.A., for his most valuable aid during the preparation and progress of the work, the fact of the Seals and Book-plate contained herein having been furnished by him will doubtless be a sufficient guarantee of their accuracy.

INDEX.

In Demy 8vo., Cloth Boards. Red edges. Price 2s. 6d.

NOTES ON THE

Ceremony of Installation,

BY

HENRY SADLER

(Author of "Masonic Facts and Fictions")

Opinions of the Masonic Press.

" We consider Bro SADLER has fully made out his case, and that he merits the thanks of the brethren generally for the important service he has thus rendered * * * * * * * * * * These anecdotes are very interesting, and will greatly edify the Craft, but they would have been better in a more subordinate position Except as regards this trifling blemish, Bro SADLER has succeeded admirably, and the book has the further merit of being clearly printed, neatly bound, and embellished with a portrait and short biographical notice of Bro SIR ALBERT WOODS, to whom, indeed, it is dedicated "—*The Freemason*, London

" The book throughout is of an interesting character, showing a part of the work done by the Craft in days gone by, and introducing the reader to most of those who took a prominent share in its affairs."—*The Freemasons' Chronicle*, London

" It is an interesting little volume, showing that there is an authorised Ceremony of Installation dating back to 1723, how it was sanctioned, and what, in outline, it is "—*The Keystone*, Philadelphia

" The book is one of the most valuable Masonic monographs that we have yet read, and we advise every thinking and reading Brother (alas how few of them ') to get a copy and read it from cover to cover " —*The South African Freemason.*

GEORGE KENNING,

16 & 16a, Great Queen Street, London, W.C.

Lightning Source UK Ltd.
Milton Keynes UK
20 October 2010

161606UK00005B/47/P